What to Do
WITH THE KID
Who...

Third Edition

*I dedicate this book to my husband, Frank Burke;
my mother, Lois Brown; the memory of my father, Bob Brown;
and all the members of the Brown and Burke families.*

*My family taught me the importance of cooperation, self-discipline,
and responsibility long before I tried to instill these traits in my
own students or write about them in this book.*

What to Do
WITH THE KID
Who...

Third Edition

Developing Cooperation, Self-Discipline, and Responsibility in the Classroom

KAY BURKE

CORWIN PRESS
A SAGE Company
Thousand Oaks, CA 91320

For information:

Corwin Press
A SAGE Company
2455 Teller Road
Thousand Oaks, California 91320
www.corwinpress.com

SAGE Ltd.
1 Oliver's Yard
55 City Road
London EC1Y 1SP
United Kingdom

SAGE India Pvt. Ltd.
B 1/I 1 Mohan Cooperative
    Industrial Area
Mathura Road, New Delhi 110 044
India

SAGE Asia-Pacific Pte. Ltd.
33 Pekin Street #02-01
Far East Square
Singapore 048763

Printed in the United States of America.

Library of Congress Cataloging-in-Publication Data

Burke, Kay.
What to do with the kid who . . . : developing cooperation, self-discipline, and responsibility in the classroom / Kay Burke. — 3rd ed.
    p. cm.
Includes bibliographical references and index.
ISBN 978-1-4129-3700-9 (cloth)
ISBN 978-1-4129-3701-6 (pbk.)

1. Classroom management—United States—Handbooks, manuals, etc. 2. School discipline—United States—Handbooks, manuals, etc. I. Title.

LB3013.B88 2008
371.102′40973—dc22   2007031985

This book is printed on acid-free paper.

08   09   10   11   12   10   9   8   7   6   5   4   3   2   1

Acquisitions Editor:	Hudson Perigo
Editorial Assistants:	Cassandra Harris, Lesley Blake
Production Editor:	Eric Garner
Copy Editor:	Paula L. Fleming
Typesetter:	C&M Digitals (P) Ltd.
Proofreader:	Charlotte J. Waisner
Indexer:	Molly Hall
Cover Designer:	Michael Dubowe
Graphic Designer:	Lisa Riley

Contents

Acknowledgments   **vii**

About the Author   **ix**

Introduction   **1**

1. Meeting the Educational Challenges of the Twenty-First Century   5
2. Reviewing Current Teaching and Learning Theories   31
3. Setting a Positive Classroom Climate for Learning   61
4. Teaching Students How to Use Appropriate Social Skills   91
5. Helping Students Who Won't Accept Responsibility   147
6. Helping Students Who Lack Effective Interpersonal Skills   171
7. Addressing Students Who Cause Class Disruptions   193
8. Working With Students Who Have Special Needs   227

Epilogue   **267**

Final Thoughts   **277**

References   **279**

Index   **287**

Acknowledgments

I am a part of all that I have met.

—From the poem "Ulysses"
by Alfred Lord Tennyson

This quotation by Tennyson describes how I feel about all the mentors who have had a profound influence on my life and the thousands of professionals with whom I have had the privilege to work throughout my 38 years in education.

A cooperative environment where people feel free to share ideas is important for the classroom and for the creative process. I would like to thank my mentors Jim Bellanca and Robin Fogarty from the early days of SkyLight Training and Publishing for encouraging me to write this book in 1992. It was my first book, and their critiques helped me integrate current research and concrete examples to help teachers meet the challenges of creating a caring classroom community.

Many outstanding instructors have taught university courses using this book. The instructors in the Effective Teaching Program of the New York System of United Teachers (NYSUT), the Field-Based Masters Program of Saint Xavier University in Illinois, and many other traditional and distance learning programs have helped teachers develop problem-solving strategies to manage their own classrooms effectively.

I would also like to thank my own community of learners who have been a part of my professional journey working with classroom management strategies: Patsy Clark, Miriam Cotton, Hope Jordan, Ron Nash, Lorrie King, Sharon Kimmel, Kevin McIntyre, Steve Peist, Roz Brown, Susan Belgrad, Hillyn Sennholtz, Bob Basofin, Yvonne Stroud, and Patricia Jackson are just a few of the many people who inspire me every day with their commitment to helping teachers succeed in the cooperative classroom.

Finally, I would like to thank Hudson Perigo, executive editor, and the team of Cassandra Harris, Lesley Blake, Eric Garner, Paula Fleming, and many others at Corwin Press as well as my personal team of Donna Ramirez and Susan Gray for their assistance and patience throughout this extensive and *extended* revision process.

Hopefully, the theories, philosophies, and strategies included in this book will help educators and students develop a spirit of cooperation, respect, and responsibility that transcends the classroom and becomes an integral part of their daily lives.

—Kay Burke
November 2007

The contributions of the following reviewers are gratefully acknowledged:

Katy Olweiler, MA, MPA, NCC
Counselor
Lakeside School
Seattle, WA

Barbara R. Dowling, MAT, MS, MA
Educator SD Teacher of
    the Year 2006
Early Childhood Education
Sioux Falls, SD

Dr. Cheryl Fields-Smith
Assistant Professor of Elementary
    Education
University of Georgia
Athens, GA

Jennifer W. Ramamoorthi
Professional Development School
    Coordinator
CCSD 21/ Illinois State University
Wheeling, IL

Marjorie Bleiweis
Conflict Resolution Specialist
Fairfax County Public Schools
Fairfax, VA

Marguerite Lawler-Rohner
Art Teacher
2004 Maine Teacher of the Year
Cape Elizabeth Middle School
Cape Elizabeth, ME

About the Author

Kay Burke, PhD, is an award-winning teacher and author who taught at the middle school, high school, and university levels and served as a department chairperson, dean of students, mentor, and administrator. She was also the Director of the Field-Based Master's Program sponsored by SkyLight Professional Development and Saint Xavier University in Illinois. In 1992, she wrote the first edition of the book *What to Do With the Kid Who. . .* for the Positive Discipline Course in the Field-Based Master's Program. Since then she has trained teachers, coaches, mentors, and staff developers to facilitate classroom management courses for onsite university programs, online distance learning programs, and professional development workshops.

Dr. Burke works with her colleagues at Kay Burke & Associates, LLC, to design and present professional development training to teachers and administrators in classroom management, mentoring, performance assessment, standards-based teaching, and portfolio development. She has presented at district, state, and national conferences such as ASCD, NSDC, NMSA, IRA, NAESP, NASSP, and IRA, as well as international conferences in Canada and Australia.

Kay Burke is the coauthor of *Foundations of Educational Assessment* (in press for 2008) and coauthor of *The Portfolio Connection: Student Work Linked to Standards*, third edition published by Corwin Press. Other books written by Kay and published by Corwin Press include *How to Assess Authentic Learning*, fourth edition; *Designing Professional Portfolios for Change*; *Mentoring Guidebook, Level 1: Starting the Journey*, second edition; *Mentoring Guidebook, Level 2: Exploring Teaching Strategies*, and *Tips for Managing Your Classroom*.

One of Kay's latest best-selling books, *From Standards to Rubrics in Six Steps: Tools for Assessing Authentic Learning, K–8*, was a 2007 Finalist for the Distinguished Achievement Award for Excellence in Educational Publishing presented by the Association of Educational Publishers.

Introduction

In describing the climate of a classroom, we are often guided by a certain set of values, a vision of what school ought to be like. We might begin with the premise, for example, that an ideal climate is one that promotes deep understanding, excitement about learning, and social as well as intellectual growth. (Kohn, 1996, p. 54)

Every educator works toward establishing and maintaining an improved school climate to enrich school conditions so that teachers can teach better and students can learn more (Hansen & Childs, 1998). This goal is challenging because students in the twenty-first century live in an age of information overload and high-stakes testing; Internet access and text messages; personal insecurity and drug use; and sometimes violence in their homes, schools, and society. Thus, it is difficult for students to walk through the doors of a school and leave all their distractions and problems behind them.

In the students' search for their own identities and, sometimes, their search for an escape from family and societal problems, they look to the schools for the constant that is often missing in their home lives. Educators today need to do more than help students meet standards, score high on standardized tests, master the curriculum, secure jobs, or get accepted into college. Educators are also responsible for teaching students how to interact in socially acceptable ways and how to develop the interpersonal skills necessary to be successful in life. We need to focus on the "whole child."

The obedience model of discipline used by many educators in the past is no longer effective in today's world. Glasser (as cited in Gough, 1987) states that no amount of coercion in the schools is going to make students learn. "The old theory, 'we can make 'em work; all we have to do is get tougher,' has never produced intellectual effort in the history of the world, and it certainly won't work in this situation" (p. 657). Glasser (1997) advocates "choice theory" to help students. Choice theory shows people that behavior can only be controlled by themselves. If people are not personally satisfied with what they are doing, no amount of punishment or number of rules and restrictions will force them to comply with ideas or systems they do not believe in. "Individuals need to belong, to have power, to have freedom, and to have fun" (Glasser as cited in Hansen & Childs, 1998, p. 16).

Making students work and learn by "getting tough" is not the answer. Moreover, the "pour and store" philosophy of filling students' heads with knowledge has been dispelled by brain research that shows students need time to make connections and process information. New strategies for instruction, assessment, curriculum, and classroom management that reflect students' learning needs are beginning to be implemented by schools throughout the world to meet the needs of all learners.

ABOUT THIS BOOK

The purpose of this book is to help beginning teachers and veteran teachers alike establish a climate in their classrooms and schools that fosters a spirit of cooperation, a sense of responsibility, and a love of learning. Educators need to make the environment conducive for learning before they can address standards, curriculum, or assessment. The atmosphere of the classroom and the respect and courtesy students show to themselves, their peers, and their teachers form the essential foundation for engaged learning and increased student achievement.

This book is divided into eight chapters and an epilogue that can be summarized as follows:

Chapter 1 addresses current issues in education such as Response to Interventions (RTI), attention deficit disorder (ADD), and violence in schools.

Chapter 2 discusses the theories of brain-based learning, multiple intelligences, differentiated learning, authentic assessment, standards, the emotional intelligence, and cooperative learning.

Chapter 3 introduces specific strategies to establish a positive classroom climate where students create rules and consequences to guide their conduct.

Chapter 4 integrates the explicit teaching of social skills into the curriculum so that students are taught how to interact with peers, work in cooperative groups, and resolve conflicts.

Chapter 5 explores strategies to deal with students who have trouble accepting responsibility for their behavior and learning.

Chapter 6 introduces methods to help students who have weak interpersonal skills that hurt their relationships with peers and teachers.

Chapter 7 offers problem-solving strategies to prevent and handle more serious discipline problems caused by aggressive, attention-seeking, or power-seeking students.

Chapter 8 reviews Response to Interventions (RTI) and ways to help students with special needs deal with their learning challenges, behavior problems, and language and physical challenges.

The *Epilogue* provides an example of a class meeting where teachers and students meet to discuss problems and solutions to situations.

While Chapters 1 and 2 provide a review of issues, theories, and research related to classroom management, Chapters 3–8 contain scenarios that outline a specific social skill problem as well as activities, assignments, possible solutions, and specific strategies to address not only the problems outlined in the book, but also the real problems teachers experience in the classroom every day.

There are no "right" answers for the daily problems teachers face. Hopefully, however, educators can use or adapt some of the techniques presented in this book to achieve success preventing or solving problems they face in their own classrooms. To some, the words *discipline* and *management* sound somewhat coercive—almost conveying the idea that teachers are trying to "control" students. The techniques presented in this book, however, are problem-solving ideas that may be an alternative to traditional discipline or classroom management techniques. These techniques can help prevent, reduce, or resolve the disruptions that detract from a positive learning environment. Teachers can facilitate their students in developing their own sense of cooperation, self-discipline, and responsibility by establishing a caring classroom climate and providing a safe environment in which students can interact with others and learn.

What's New in This Third Edition

In this new third edition, the research has been updated and integrated into each chapter rather than concentrated in a single chapter. Additional topics and/or current statistics address the following: the "silent epidemic" of high school dropouts, problems with General Educational Development (GED) options, No Child Left Behind (NCLB) regulations, the Reauthorization of the Individuals with Disabilities Education Act (IDEA 2004), Response to Interventions (RTI) approaches to helping all students learn, demographics about English Language Learners (ELL), grading issues related to classroom management, bullying and cyber-bullying, and children of poverty.

New activities and templates focus on how teachers

1. establish appropriate procedures and behavior expectations for the K–2, elementary, middle school, and high school classrooms;

2. differentiate learning to meet the needs of all students;

3. manage the standards-based classroom;

4. include more performance-based learning to motivate students;

5. develop formative assessments to provide constructive feedback to students; and

6. utilize effective brain-compatible instructional strategies to promote positive classroom interaction.

In addition, 10 new performance tasks, checklists, and rubrics have been added, including three checklists designed to help students self-assess their social skills, cooperative learning skills, and ability to accept responsibility for their own attitudes, behaviors, and learning goals.

Meeting the Educational Challenges of the Twenty-First Century 1

Figure 1.0 Agree/Disagree Chart

Check if you agree or disagree with these statements *before* you read the chapter and again after you read it.	Before		After	
	Agree	*Disagree*	*Agree*	*Disagree*
1. The No Child Left Behind law has improved education in the United States.				
2. The term *learning disabled* (LD) is used to label more than half the students in special education programs.				
3. The number of non-English speaking students enrolled in U.S. schools will be 40% by 2030.				
4. Almost one-half of all public high school students in America fail to graduate.				
5. Among U.S. youth ages 15 to 19, suicide is responsible for more deaths than any disease.				
6. Attention Deficit Disorder (ADD) is just a myth.				

Teachers in the twenty-first century are faced with a variety of issues and challenges that go beyond day-to-day classroom instruction. Many teachers are unsure how to address these challenges and how to best meet the needs of specific learners in the context of larger issues. The sections of the book address each of these issues through the use of scenarios and problem-solving activities that are designed to help teachers select appropriate methods to address problems with specific students. It is important, however, that educators first review the background of the issues that form the context for problems. Educators need to know the "big picture" and the legal and historical frames of reference for the challenges that affect them and their students.

NO CHILD LEFT BEHIND

The No Child Left Behind (NCLB) law is the newest version of the Elementary and Secondary Education Act (ESEA). The original law provided funding to school districts to help low-income students. The law proposes to close achievement gaps and aims for 100 percent student proficiency by the year 2014. Today, NCLB holds Title I schools that receive federal money accountable by requiring them to meet proficiency targets on standardized assessments. The number of tests that states administer annually is expected to rise to 68 million. Guilfoyle (2006) states,

> These tests carry consequences for the schools and districts that administer them. Schools that fail to bring enough of their students to proficiency face escalating requirements, such as having to offer public school choice or provide supplemental education services. If the school is considered "in need of improvement" for five consecutive years, it risks being restructured or taken over by the state. (p. 8)

The NCLB law is complex because it regulates 14,000 school districts in 50 states through 588 regulations. Standardized testing is the linchpin of the law, and the task of assessing each student's reading and math skills requires 45 million students be tested annually, with another 11 million tests being introduced to meet the new science testing requirements (Scherer, 2006, p. 7).

The tremendous pressure to raise test scores has caused controversy among educators. Many feel multiple measures are needed to assess students' deep understanding of curriculum and ability to use higher-order problem-solving skills and thinking skills. Critics feel the curriculum has been narrowed and teachers tend to "teach to the tests" at the expense of teaching a rich curriculum to meet the differentiated needs of the students.

Scherer (2006) states,

> Despite the fact that different states use different tests and thus determine proficiency differently, despite the fact that the testing industry is scrambling to produce valid tests, and despite the fact that designing learning around test taking is no one's vision of best practice, testing has become a way of life in classrooms. (p. 7)

CHILDREN OF POVERTY

Poverty-level students often come from diverse backgrounds where English is not spoken in the family and the culture is dramatically different from that of American public education.

According to Barr and Parrett (2003), many children from these homes suffer from inadequate nutrition and the compromised mental and physical health that is associated with the complex problems of poverty. In addition, poverty-level children often grow up with significant deficiencies in communication skills, which impair their ability to read, write, and spell. Bracey found that parents employed in professional occupations talked to their children using almost 2,200 words an hour; blue-collar parents spoke about 1,300 words per hour; and parents on welfare spoke only 600 words to their children per hour. The children who lack exposure to communication skills arrive at school less prepared than their more advantaged peers (Bracey as cited in Barr and Parrett, 2003, p. 96).

In addition, children living in poverty do not have the rich experiences, such as books in their homes, private lessons, opportunities to travel, and organized sports activities, that enrich the lives of middle-class children. Moreover, these children often are assigned to the most ineffective teachers in the schools. Research by Sanders and Rivers as cited in Barr and Parrott (2003) reported that if a student has an ineffective teacher during the elementary years, it will take that student two years to recover academically. However, if a student has *two* ineffective teachers during the elementary years, the student may never catch up (p. 99).

Strategies to Help Students of Poverty

Many schools are helping children of poverty achieve academic success. The Education Trust has identified more than 4,500 high-poverty and/or high-minority schools throughout the United States where students are scoring in the upper 30 percent of their respective states in reading, math, or both. This evidence suggests that students from distressed communities can achieve high levels of academic performance (Jerald as cited in Barr & Parrett, 2003, p. 29). Schools that establish before- and afterschool programs; provide intensive instruction to poor students; develop summer programs and year-round schools; provide nutritional meals, books, and educational stimuli on a year-round basis; and offer preschool programs and full-day kindergarten are making a difference. "Schools and teachers can make the difference for poverty-level children. Understanding these students and their lives must become a priority of every public school in America" (Barr & Parrett, p. 101).

INCLUSION

For many years, students with behavior, learning, and physical disabilities have been classified as special education students and placed in separate classrooms or schools. A report of the National Academy of Sciences in 1982, however, found the classification and placement of children in special education to be ineffective and discriminatory. The panel recommended that children be given noninclusive or extra-class placement for special services "only if (a) they can be accurately classified, and only if (b) noninclusion demonstrates superior results" (as cited in Baker, Wang, & Walberg, 1994/1995, p. 33).

Labeling Learners

The report by the National Academy of Sciences in 1982 prompted the early research on the inclusion, or integration, of children with disabilities into regular classrooms.

Many categories of children are in need of special education. One problem some researchers, teachers, and parents have is that they feel these programs contribute to severe disconnection and disjointedness in schools. Usually eight or nine varieties of special-needs programs are offered in a school or district, and children in the programs are labeled according to the special places they go and the so-called disabilities they possess. Wang, Reynolds, and Walberg (1994/1995) describe the two largest categories of children in special education as those who are learning disabled (LD) and those who are mentally retarded (MR). The MR category is for students who score low on IQ tests and, therefore, are not expected to do well in school. The LD category is for the surprises—those students who have high enough IQs to do well but are not achieving in basic subjects such as reading. Many specialists think that children with learning disabilities have underlying perceptual or neurological problems, even though these problems have not been diagnosed as such. Students are labeled E/BD or ED if they are emotionally/behaviorally disordered and emotionally disordered, respectively; DCD if they are developmentally/cognitively disordered; OHI if they have other health impairments; and ODD if they have an oppositional defiant disorder (Wang, et al., 1994/1995).

Several major studies in the 1980s, however, showed that classifying children accurately is difficult and that classification systems for placing students in special programs are seriously flawed. Although the term *learning disabled* was relatively new in 1975, by the year 2000 it was used to label more than half of the students in special education programs. Two or three times as many African American students as White students are labeled retarded or behaviorally disturbed. Research by Spear-Swerling and Sternberg (1998) suggested that one system of identifying learning disabled students was flawed. The IQ/Achievement Discrepancy Operation shows that students with learning disabilities are seen as having low achievement relative to what would be expected based on their IQ scores. "Children with learning disabilities in reading unquestionably need instructional help—but they do not appear to need qualitatively different kind of remedial program than do other poor readers" (p. 398). Spear-Swerling and Sternberg believe that just because students need additional help in special learning areas doesn't always mean they need to be labeled with a learning disability.

Least Restrictive Environment (LRE)

Since the Least Restrictive Environment (LRE) was introduced in 1975 in Public Law 94–142, supporters have been trying to help educators implement the concepts of LRE into classrooms. The work of Falvey (1995); Stainback and

Stainback (1992); Thousand, Villa, and Nevin (1994); and others has helped the least restrictive environment mandate become a leading force in the development of "mainstreaming" or "integration" of students with disabilities into part-time or full-time enrollment in general education settings. Current programs of mainstreaming and integration have "rejected the segregation and isolation of people with disabilities" (Villa & Thousand, 1995, p. 5). In the past, mainstreaming often required students with disabilities to achieve a predetermined criteria (readiness model) before they could participate in general education. According to Villa and Thousand (1995); McIntosh, Vaughn, Schumm, Haager, and Lee (1993); and Baker and Zigmond (1990), mainstreaming and integration became a disaster in need of a major overhaul. These researchers and others felt that mainstreaming failed an enormous number of students because the students were provided inadequate support when they entered general education classrooms. In addition, many regular education teachers were not prepared to vary their instructional and assessment practices to meet the diverse needs of students with disabilities. As a result, students with special needs suffered, while teachers became increasingly frustrated by the demands placed upon them. Regular education teachers were often left without the training they needed or the teacher aides promised to help implement the program.

Regular Education Initiative (REI)

The U.S. Department of Education issued the Regular Education Initiative (REI) in 1986 to eliminate many "pull out" programs. The REI encourages special educators to work in close partnerships with general educators to develop strategies to educate special education students in general education classrooms. Often, special education teachers partner with regular education teachers to present lessons to the whole class. These co-teachers share their strategies for educating all students in understanding the content lessons. Inclusion is a commitment by educators and staff members to ensure that all students receive the quality education to which they are entitled and the belief that in most cases, quality education can be obtained in the regular education classroom with support from special education teachers (Baker, Wang, & Walberg, 1994/1995). In addition, the Individual Education Plan (IEP) is no longer the sole responsibility of special education teachers. According to Sigford (2006), each student who has an IEP will have a case manager who has the responsibility of writing the IEP with the help of a team which consists of administrators, regular education teachers, and parents who review the assessment data. Even though special education teachers help design the program and monitor its implementation, they are not the only ones responsible for its delivery. Others may be involved in delivering the program, depending on the disability and its severity.

The research that examined the effects of inclusive versus noninclusive educational practices demonstrated a small to moderate beneficial effect of inclusive education on the academic and social outcomes of students with special needs. According to Baker, Wang, and Walberg (1994/1995), "*academic outcomes* are learning measures generated by standardized achievement tests, whereas *social outcomes* are obtained by self, peer, teacher, and observer ratings of special needs students' success in relating with others in the classroom" (p. 34). Students with special needs need to attain both academic and social success in the school setting. As schools are challenged with the need to serve an increasingly diverse student population, educators must decide how to implement inclusive education to benefit all children, especially those with special needs. Moreover, they need to measure the effectiveness of their efforts by authentic assessments to evaluate improvement in socialization skills—not just by standardized tests to measure academic growth.

Response to Intervention (RTI)

The No Child Left Behind (NCLB) legislation and the 2004 Reauthorization of Individuals with Disabilities Education Act (IDEA) prompted Response to Intervention (RTI) that was introduced in 2006. RTI is a new feature for IDEA that is a multi-step approach to providing instructions and interventions to struggling students. Teachers monitor the progress students make at each intervention level and use the assessment results to decide whether or not students need additional instruction or intervention in the general education classes or if they need referral to special education services (Council for Exceptional Children Web site). In RTI all educators will become involved in implementing programs to demonstrate how students respond on an individual basis to various behavioral and academic interventions based on monitoring and frequent assessments. Both general educators and special educators are required to apply research-proven educational interventions, monitor student progress daily or weekly, and plan tiers of additional interventions for students who are not progressing adequately.

Bender and Shores (2007) strongly support this renewed emphasis on monitoring students' response to educational interventions. They say,

> Within the next two or three years, education will change rather dramatically, because of the implementation of Response to Intervention (RTI) procedures across the nation. Teachers in both general and special education classes will find their jobs transformed as we move into a research-proven instructional method that will benefit many children who are challenged by the academic content. In fact, all students will benefit from implementation of this procedure, as teachers become more fluent in truly individualized progress monitoring and instruction (p. vii).

One of the reasons RTI has gained momentum as an approach to LD eligibility determination over the past decade is because of the dissatisfaction with the discrepancy procedure that documents a disability by demonstrating a large difference between a child's cognitive level (using IQ scores) and his or her achievement. Since the late 1990s, many policymakers and researchers such as Spear-Swerling and Sternberg (1998) cited previously have indicated the discrepancy procedures result in over-identification of students with learning disabilities, and thus, that the procedure seemed to be somewhat inexact in documenting exactly who manifested a learning disability and who did not (Bender and Shores, 2007).

From the original studies, two distinct RTI models emerged: the problem-solving model and the standard protocol model. The problem-solving approach involves the implementation of interventions designed for individual student needs. The problem-solving model has been replicated and refined in several school systems, including Minneapolis Public Schools and the Heartland Area Educational Agency in Iowa. The Minneapolis Public Schools began their formal implementation of the problem-solving model in 1992 (Marston, Muyskens, Lau, & Canter) as cited in Bender and Shores (2007).

Problem-Solving RTI Model

The problem-solving model is a sequential pattern of steps divided into three tiers or stages. According to Bender and Shores (2007), they are as follows:

Stage 1. Classroom Interventions: This stage is implemented by classroom teachers in the general education classrooms. Teachers identify students who are experiencing difficulties, implement instructional strategies or modifications based on individual students' needs and begin to monitor the student's progress. Teachers gather information regarding strengths and specific weaknesses, previous strategies attempted and outcomes, any available screening data, student health, and other information from parents. If the teacher determines the intervention is not successful, the student is referred to Stage 2.

Stage 2. Problem-Solving Team Interventions: Student information is reviewed by a multidisciplinary team, which may include school psychologists, general education and special education teachers, reading specialists, and school administrators. The team considers whether other risk factors (language, poverty, cultural factors) are attributing to or causing the student's lack of progress. Interventions are reviewed and adjusted to more specifically address students' needs. Teachers continue to monitor progress and adjust instruction. If teachers determine the student is not sufficiently responding to instruction, the student is referred to Stage 3.

Stage 3. Special Education Referral and Initiation of Due Process Procedures: The school district obtains parental consent and begins evaluation procedures for the student. The evaluation consists of a review of all information available on the student from Stages 1 and 2, including data on the student's response to interventions, direct observation, and the formulation of a means of obtaining cognitive, achievement, and adaptive behavior functioning. The team utilizes all available information to determine eligibility while considering the possible impact of risk factors such as culture, language, and socioeconomic status (Marston, et al., 2003 as cited in Bender and Shores, 2007, p. 9).

Bender, W. N., & Shores, C. (2007). *Response to intervention: A practical guide for every teacher.* Thousand Oaks, CA: A Joint Publication from the Council for Exceptional Children and Corwin Press. Used with permission.

Standard Protocol Model

The Standard Protocol RTI Model "utilizes a set of standard research-based interventions usually implemented in two, three, or four tiers or levels. In contrast to the problem-solving model, the interventions occur in a natural progression from tier to tier, and are similar for all students experiencing the same learning problems rather than being specifically designed for each individual student" (Bender and Shores, 2007, p. 12). The standard treatment protocol involves exposing a child to a variety of research-based educational interventions and using data points to monitor progress to see how she responds. After well-documented instructional interventions, the student would be expected to achieve academic growth. In the absence of academic growth in the new RTI procedures, it could be assumed that the student has a learning disability (Fuchs & Fuchs, and Marston as cited in Bender and Shores (2007).

The final IDEA regulations were released in August 2006 and it is expected that many states will incorporate some form of RTI into their policies and procedures. The emphasis on monitoring students' response to educational interventions has been proven to be among the best instructional practices available to reform education and to impact all teachers and all students.

> Although RTI has received recent interest as one way to document eligibility for students suspected of having a learning disability, there are many other applications of RTI including using the RTI process to curb inappropriate behavior. . . . As we move into this new emphasis, we should focus on the benefits of RTI for all children in our classes. RTI is, in effect, one of the best instructional practices we can implement for our students. Implementation of RTI will enhance learning across the board in our classes, and ultimately benefit all of the students whom we serve. (Bender & Shores, 2007, p. viii)

Classroom Management

Despite the controversy over diagnosing and labeling students, most teachers agree that they are challenged by disruptions caused by any students. They also agree that classroom disruptions often increase when students with special needs are integrated into their classrooms—sometimes without the support systems or assistants required. According to Rivera and Smith (1997), "Students with special needs are often more disruptive than students with no special needs. Students who have special needs may disturb the learning environment for themselves and their peers. They follow the classroom and school rules less frequently" (p. 9). It is evident that disruptive students spend a great deal of time not learning. Research in the 1970s concentrated on reducing disruptive classroom behaviors to improve students' academic achievement. Even when disruptions declined, however, achievement did *not* improve. Disruptive students, therefore, often have requirements beyond behavioral needs that must be met for them to achieve academically.

Current research focuses on discovering if students who improve their learning and achieve academic success also improve their behavior, rather than the other way around. The link between meaningful and motivating instruction and classroom management has never been stronger. If students are either bored or frustrated with the academic materials presented to them, they act out. One important study by Center, Deitz, and Kaufman, as cited in Rivera and Smith (1997), found a dramatic correlation between task difficulty and inappropriate behavior. When teachers simply adjusted curricular demands to make sure the material was neither too difficult nor too easy, most student disruptions were eliminated. It is important, therefore, for teachers to achieve a sense of flow (Csikzentmihalyi, 1990) in their classrooms so students feel challenged in their work as opposed to feeling either overwhelmed or bored. If teachers know what causes behavior problems, they can work to reduce them in their classrooms. Rivera and Smith (1997) cite six reasons why behavior problems sometimes occur:

1. Students are either bored or frustrated with academic materials.

2. Students see no relevance for tasks or activities and are not motivated.

3. Students may not understand when certain behaviors are permissible and when they are not.

4. Teachers may send inconsistent messages about their expectations or consequences for not meeting the expectations.

5. Students are experiencing family problems and suffer emotionally from their dysfunctional family.

6. Teachers lack awareness of what is happening in the classroom at all times.

Adapted with permission from Rivera, D. P., and Smith, D. D. (1997). *Teaching students with learning and behavior problems*, 3rd ed., pp. 191–192. Needham Heights, MA: Allyn & Bacon.

The challenge for teachers is to develop proactive strategies to adjust or revise their curriculum, instruction, and assessment practices to motivate all students to learn. In addition, it is crucial for teachers to develop appropriate interventions to prevent or at least manage disruptions so improved learning can occur for all students, regardless of their classifications or labels. Teachers also must make sure that the disruptions of a few do not ruin the learning environment for all.

ATTENTION DEFICIT DISORDERS

Attention deficit disorder (ADD) constitutes a chronic neurobiological condition characterized by developmentally inappropriate attention skills and impulsivity. Attention deficit hyperactivity disorder (ADHD) is also characterized by inappropriate attention skills and impulsivity as well as symptoms of hyperactivity. At home, children with these disorders may not be able to accommodate routines and manifest this by breaking toys during play and resisting going to bed. At school, such children may be extremely restless and easily distracted. They often have trouble completing work in class because they miss valuable information due to their underdeveloped attention capacity. "They speak aloud, out of turn, and find themselves in trouble for their behavior. Their inattention, impulsivity, and hyperactivity can also be detrimental to their social lives, hampering their ability to make and keep friends" (Lerner, Lowenthal, & Lerner, 1995, p. 5).

According to Thompson (1996), ADHD has been described as the display of inattention, impulsivity, and overactivity with developmentally inappropriate frequency. To be considered symptoms of ADHD, these behaviors must initially have been exhibited in early childhood (prior to age seven) and displayed across a variety of settings. (See Figure 1.1, which summarizes the characteristics of these disorders.)

Figure 1.1   Characteristics of ADD and ADHD

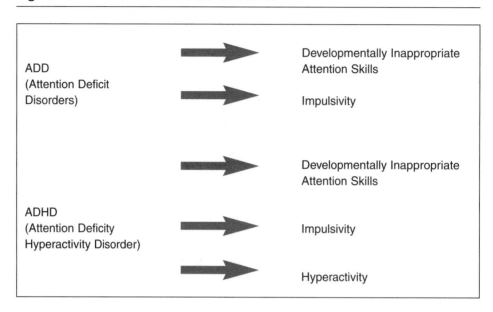

Marzano, Marzano, and Pickering (2003) described ADHD as one of the severe problems facing students. They noted that 3 to 7 percent of school-age children, mostly males, experience ADHD disorder (American Psychiatric Association as cited in Marzano et al., p. 46) and approximately 50 percent of the 1.6 million elementary school-aged children with ADHD also have learning disorders (National Centers for Disease Control as cited in Marzano et al., p. 46). To meet the diagnostic criteria of the American Psychiatric Association, the child must have been creating disturbances for at least six months, during which time at least eight of the behaviors in Figure 1.2 must have been exhibited.

In addition, many students who do not have the clinical diagnosis of ADD/ADHD exhibit many of its behavioral symptoms. Healy, as cited in Cummings (2000), has evidence that kids' brains really have changed because they have been exposed to flickering electronic fields during their formative years instead of the three-dimensional experiences necessary for normal wiring. "Their learning habits have been shaped by fast-paced media that reduce attention, listening, and problem-solving skills as they habituate the brain to rapid-fire visual input" (p. 40). Shapiro, as cited in Cummings (2000), says that most five-year-olds have watched between 4,000 and 5,000 hours of TV by the time they reach first grade—the equivalent of four years of college (p. 124). That's valuable time wasted that should be spent socializing with other children and exploring an enriched environment. Shapiro believes that "television may be the single greatest deterrent to developing social and emotional skills" (as cited in Cummings, p. 124).

In addition to medications, multiple strategies and interventions are needed to help students with both ADD and ADHD. Recently the American Medical Association expressed concern about the increasing number of preschool students who are on medications. The members of this organization question

Figure 1.2 Diagnostic Criteria for ADHD

The student

1. often fidgets with hands or squirms in seat (though in adolescents, this symptom may be limited to subjective feelings of restlessness);

2. has difficulty remaining seated when required to do so;

3. is easily distracted by extraneous stimuli;

4. has difficulty waiting for turns in games or group situations;

5. often blurts out answers to questions before the questions have been completed;

6. has difficulty (not due to oppositional behavior or failure of comprehension) following through on instructions from others;

7. has difficulty sustaining attention in tasks or play activities;

8. often shifts from one uncompleted activity to another;

9. has difficulty playing quietly;

10. often talks excessively;

11. often interrupts or intrudes on others (e.g., butts into other children's games);

12. often does not seem to listen to what is being said to him or her;

13. often loses things necessary for tasks or activities at school or at home (e.g., toys, pencils, books, assignments); or

14. often engages in physically dangerous activities without considering possible consequences (e.g., runs into the street without looking) but not for the purpose of thrill seeking.

Reprinted with permission of *Phi Delta Kappan,* from "Attention Deficit Hyperactivity Disorder: A Parent's Perspective," by Anna M. Thompson, February 1996. *Phi Delta Kappan,* p. 434.

the use of drugs to medicate the behavior of young children. Parents and teachers need to explore behavior management, time management, and organizational training techniques to help students follow classroom rules, stay on task, and practice appropriate social skills with other students rather than relying on medications. The simplest instructions and rules may require practice, repetition, and reinforcement to make them part of a student's routine. In addition to establishing organizational techniques and routines, teachers also need to provide motivational instruction and interactive learning strategies to keep the attention of all their students.

The Case Against Attention Deficit Disorders

A section on Attention Deficit Disorders would not be complete without a discussion of the controversy over the disorders. Thomas Armstrong, among others, is troubled by the speed at which both the public and the professional community have embraced this disorder over the past 20 years, thanks in part to best-selling books, the support of mainstream psychiatry, general medicine, and government approval. He says that the paradigm suggests that ADD and ADHD are "disorders that are said to be biological in origin, affecting from 3 to 5 percent of all children in North America" (1999, p. vi). Armstrong, however, has questioned whether ADD and ADHD are biological disorders, how the symptoms are assessed, the effectiveness of treating the disorders with medications and behavior modifications, and whether or not children will continue to have ADD/ADHD throughout their lives. Armstrong agrees that school children manifest symptoms of hyperactivity, distractibility, and impulsivity. But he disagrees with the claim that these kinds of behaviors represent the chief manifestations of something called ADD/ADHD because he believes these behaviors are among the most global and widespread types of behaviors seen in childhood and adolescence.

> One can observe them in virtually all children during certain parts of their lives [especially in the early years and during adolescence], and under certain types of conditions at other stages of life that involve stress, boredom, excitement, and the like. A child can be hyperactive, distractible, or impulsive because she is depressed, anxious, allergic to milk, highly creative, bored with schoolwork, unable to read, or temperamentally difficult, among a host of other factors. (pp. 8–9)

Armstrong wonders how society can label children as ADD or ADHD based upon the combination of three kinds of behavior—hyperactivity, distractibility, and impulsivity.

Cummings (2000) believes that teachers need to change their approach by changing the environment because some of today's students cannot fit into the traditional classroom structure. If ADD/ADHD students are not allowed out of their seats without asking permission, cannot speak without being called upon, and are expected to follow complex directions the first time they are given, they are set up for failure.

> When the ADD/ADHD child doesn't comply with these demands, he's broken the classic rules and is often given the negative consequences. As a result, too high a proportion of these children fail or become underachievers. Frankly, the modifications that help special-needs children create a better learning community for all children. (p. 125)

According to Smelter, Rasch, Fleming, Nazos, and Baranowski (1996), parents often feel relieved when their children are diagnosed with ADD or ADHD because it absolves them of guilt associated with not being able to "control" the behavior of their children. They can then use Ritalin or some other drug to cure the dysfunction without carefully examining other family, medical, or sociological issues that could be affecting the child. The reality could be that the student hates school; therefore, the student's attention wanders. The student's different behavior could be that child's own choice. As Smelter et al. conclude, "We must, therefore, be somewhat skeptical about ADD-classified children, who, when removed from the classroom setting, magically lose their ADD symptoms" (p. 432).

Teaching Strategies

Despite the medical controversy surrounding diagnosis and treatment of Attention Deficit Disorders, the challenge for teachers "is to implement and adopt methods that will help students meet their potential. Teachers must understand the learning characteristics of all their students and possess knowledge about both curricular content and instructional methodology" (Rivera & Smith, 1997, p. 1). Teachers must be familiar with best practices in teaching and learning and be aware of methods and strategies that help all students learn, no matter what their needs are.

According to Collier (1995), some strategies teachers can use to set up the classroom include creating a positive classroom climate, engaging students in bonding activities to help them become more comfortable with each other, establishing rules and expectations, practicing routines, and developing logical consequences if students don't follow rules. In addition, Collier suggests that teachers can teach social skills by modeling appropriate social interactions, giving students time to develop and practice group and social skills, and demonstrating self-control and stress management techniques. Finally, she proposes that teachers plan instruction to meet both standards and the needs of students, use appropriate instructional materials, set the right pace for the class, and challenge and motivate all students.

Teachers can also improve the learning of students with special needs by implementing some of the same strategies they use with regular education students. All students can benefit from a variety of teaching strategies. For example, the strategies in Figure 1.3 could be used with ADD/ADHD students.

Figure 1.3 Strategies to Use With ADD/ADHD Students

- Provide both oral and written instructions.
- Encourage students to use highlighters, sticky notes, and colored pens for note taking.
- Modify assignments by changing their quantity—but not their quality.
- Allow students to stand over their desks, spread out on the floor, and go to stations.
- Allow students to use headphones to block out extraneous noises.
- Provide time cues about when the current activity will end and the next activity will begin.
- Provide agendas with schedules of the day so they know what to expect.
- Provide checklists for assignments that break down skills into manageable chunks.
- Provide opportunities for some choice in assignments or presentation methods.
- Shift activities to allow for movement.

In addition to the strategies mentioned above, teachers also need to use language—the correct rate of speech, appropriate vocabulary, and simple syntax—so that students can understand directions and comprehend concepts. Equally important, teachers should develop a comfortable style of working with and respecting their students. In turn, students should respect and enjoy their teachers.

> Learning does not have to be dull and routine. . . . Teachers need to diversify educational experiences and add occasional elements of fun into the learning environment. This can be accomplished by allowing students to work on interesting topics, solve problems, or use technology as an enhancement to instruction. (Rivera & Smith, 1997, p. 14)

ADD and ADHD students, like all students and adults, want to engage in meaningful activities with their peers and achieve successful academic results. Students also want some choice in what, when, and how they accomplish their goals, and they want to know that what they are doing will be relevant in their lives. Thus, the use of effective instructional strategies and classroom management techniques can help these learners meet their goals and succeed, regardless of the labels attached to them.

ENGLISH LANGUAGE LEARNERS (ELL)

The population of the United States has always been multiracial. After analyzing demographic data from the 2000 census, demographer Harold Hodgkinson, as cited in Hill and Flynn (2006), found that almost 9 million U.S. children between the ages of 5 and 17 speak a language other than English at home, and a full 2.6 million of them do not speak English well. If these students do not get special help in preschool and kindergarten, elementary school teachers will be expected to teach proficiency in English along with academic context. Most teachers have not been trained to help students master content standards at the same time as language-speaking standards. Moreover,

> English Language Learners (ELLs) may once have been viewed as "belonging" to English as a second language (ESL) staff, but now, due to changing laws and policies, the students are in every classroom in the school, making the job of teaching that much more challenging. (Hill & Flynn, p. xii)

In 2003, according to the National Center for Education Statistics, 19 percent of all school-age children were English language learners. Census projections show that the number of non–English speakers enrolling in U.S. schools will be 40 percent by the year 2030 (Pardini, 2006, p. 20). One challenge concerns the quality of education these immigrant students have had in their native countries. Immigrant groups from Africa and Asia continue to grow, and Sigford (2006) describes how

> some have been forced to live in refugee camps, and others are from nomadic cultures where education is about daily survival not about reading and writing. It is one thing to teach literacy skills to someone who is literate in one culture and quite another to teach literacy to someone who is preliterate in their native language. (p. 134)

Limited English Proficient (LEP)

One of the groups targeted by NCLB is the limited English proficient subgroup. The LEP subgroup is expected to make adequate yearly progress (AYP) toward proficiency. According to NCLB, all English language learners in the subgroup must pass their state's accountability tests by 2014, or the school will be designated as failing and may be subjected to sanctions. Some critics of NCLB believe that if states administer a test to students in a language they don't understand, they probably won't do well on it.

> NCLB contradicts itself on this very point. The law describes a limited proficient student as one "whose difficulties in speaking, reading or understanding the English language may be sufficient to deny the individual the ability to meet the State's proficient level of achievement on State assessments." Nevertheless, NCLB mandates that English language learners do just that, and schools are punished if they don't. (Wright, 2006, p. 22)

Recent discussions about the reauthorization of the law have focused on changing some of the regulations pertaining to LEP students.

Strategies to Use With LEP Students

The research on LEP students has some implications for regular education teachers who work with students with limited English proficiency. For example, regular education teachers could use the strategies in Figure 1.4 with LEP students.

Figure 1.4   Strategies to Use With LEP Students

- Pause frequently to check for understanding.
- Use short and simple sentences and speak slowly.
- Learn some key phrases in the student's language.
- Utilize an active, hands-on teaching style rather than a lecture style.
- Repeat key concepts and content pieces in different ways.
- Structure the class to include social and cultural bridges between the non-English-speaking student's home life and school life.
- Utilize cooperative groups for instruction and include a bilingual student who speaks the same language as a partner for non-English-speaking group members.
- Write things down so students can get help with translations.
- Design interactive lessons that target multiple intelligences.
- Assess students' progress using a repertoire of evaluation strategies, such as checklists and rubrics to provide expectations, portfolios to show growth and development, and performances and projects to demonstrate application and transfer. (See Chapter 2.)
- Integrate the minority students into the social structure of the classroom and the school by building a community of learners that will produce positive results for all the students and, ultimately, society.

The school environment is critical in helping immigrant students succeed. Their initial experiences can be rewarding and positive or traumatic and negative. Pipher, as cited in Sigford (2006), says,

> Schools are often where kids experience their first racism and learn about the socioeconomic split in our country. There is the America of children with violin lessons, hockey tickets, skiing trips, and zoo passes, and there is the America of children in small apartments whose parents work double shifts. (p. 114)

Teaching a diverse population can be a unique, enriching, educational, social, and cultural experience. Educators who are sensitive to the needs of all students, including students with limited English proficiency, provide a nurturing climate where students learn language skills, academic content, and social skills necessary for school and life.

HIGH SCHOOL DROPOUTS

Researchers working for the Bill and Melinda Gates Foundation released a report in March of 2006 entitled *The Silent Epidemic: Perspectives of High School Dropouts*. The report describes how the dropout epidemic in the United States disproportionately affects high school students who come from low-income, minority, urban, single-parent families and attend large public high schools in the inner city.

Nationally, research puts the graduation rate between 68 and 71 percent, which means that almost one-third of all public high school students in America fail to graduate. For minority students (black, Hispanic, or Native American), the rate at which they finish public high school with a regular diploma declines to approximately 50 percent. (Bridgeland, Dilulio, & Morison, 2006, p. 1)

Olson (2006) showed that among 2002–2003 graduates nationally, 69.6 of all students in the nation graduated with a regular diploma. According to gender, 65.2 percent of males and 72.7 percent of females graduated with a regular diploma. The rates according to ethnic groups were as follows (Olson, p. 7):

American Indian: 47.4%

Black: 51.6%

Hispanic: 55.6%

White: 76.2%

Asian: 77%

Consequences of Low Graduation Rates

The Silent Epidemic Report states that in today's technological age, when workers need at least a high school diploma to compete in the workforce, the decision to drop out of school is disastrous. "Dropouts are much more likely than their peers who graduate to be unemployed, living in poverty, receiving public assistance, in prison, on death row, unhealthy, divorced, and ultimately single parents with children who drop out from high school themselves" (Bridgeland et al., 2006, p. 2).

In addition, the prevalence of the high school dropout rates impacts communities because of the loss of the earnings and revenues that productive workers would generate. Four out of every 10 young adults (ages 16–24) lacking a high school diploma received some type of government assistance in 2001. Moreover, a dropout is more than eight times as likely to be in jail or prison as a person with at least a high school diploma. Studies show that the lifetime cost of the nation for each youth who drops out of school and later moves into a life of crime and drugs ranges from $1.7 to 2.3 million (Bridgeland et al., 2006, p. 2). When researchers interviewed students for the report, respondents gave several reasons for dropping out of school. The following are the top five reasons dropouts identify as major factors for leaving school:

1. Classes were not interesting. (47%)

2. Missed too much school and could not catch up. (43%)

3. Spent time with people who were not interested in school. (42%)

4. Had too much freedom and not enough rules in my life. (38%)

5. Was failing in school. (35%) (Bridgeland et al., 2006, p. 3)

Barr and Parrett (2003) report that retention in schools is also one of the primary causes of dropping out. In too many schools, students who do not master basic skills quickly or pass the standardized tests required by NCLB are retained and are required simply to repeat everything again, or they are "tracked" into basic classes with low expectations. "Students who are retained and tracked almost never catch up to their age-group peers, and many fail to advance from the slow-learning track" (p. 19).

General Educational Development Certificate (GED)

The General Educational Development Certificate (GED) is not a diploma, nor, some research suggests, is it equivalent to one. The GED is a battery of five tests taken over the course of 7.5 hours, covering mathematics, science, reading, writing, and social studies, which is designed to certify the mastery of high school level knowledge and skills. According to Miller (2006), the GED is available in all 50 states, and test takers must score at least 410 out of a possible 800 on each of the five subject tests, with an overall average of 450 across all subject areas. The GED is designed for adults who did not receive a diploma because they dropped out of school or failed to meet a state's graduation requirements. In 2004, 662,000 people nationwide took the GED tests; the average age of GED candidates was 25, though a full 30 percent of candidates were ages 16 to 18 (American Council on Education as cited in Miller, p. 8).

The American Council on Education (ACE), a Washington-based umbrella group for higher education, coordinates the GED. According to ACE, 62 percent of those who passed the GED in 2004 reported that they took the tests to be able to enroll in two-year and four-year colleges. However, an April 2006 study by Boston-based Jobs for the Future, a nonprofit research and advocacy group, found that "44 percent of dropouts who received a GED later enroll in two- or four-year colleges, but only 10 percent succeed in earning a degree" (Miller, 2006, p. 8). In addition, studies by University of Chicago economist James J. Heckman and colleague Stephen Cameron, as cited in Miller, found in 1993 that GED holders were not significantly more likely than high school dropouts to land a job or earn high wages. In 2005, Heckman and Paul A. LaFontaine, as cited in Miller, re-examined the earlier research and found that GED recipients who did not continue on to college earned the same wages as uncertified high school dropouts, thereby leaving many no better off than they were before taking the tests.

Because 30 percent of GED test takers in 2004 were ages 16 to 18, it is evident that many young people are looking for an alternative to graduating from high school. Even though dropouts may think they can substitute the GED for an official high school diploma and still succeed in careers and college, recent research is not very encouraging. The GED certificate does not provide the same pathways to earnings or schooling as high school graduation.

> While it [the GED] can provide a valuable second chance for those without a high school diploma who desire to continue their education, research suggests it should not be seen as equivalent to a high school diploma, or as an easy alternative to finishing high school by those considering dropping out. (Miller, 2006, p. 8)

VIOLENCE IN SCHOOLS

The haunting images of school violence at Columbine High School in Littleton, Colorado; at public schools in Jonesboro in Arkansas, Paducah in Kentucky, and Pearl in Mississippi; and universities such as Virginia Tech, among many, have moved the issue of school safety to the forefront of education. Federal legislation—such as the Gun-Free Schools Act in 1994, which required states to expel weapon-toting students for at least a year, and the Goals 2000: Educate America Act, which stipulated that by 2000, every school "will offer a disciplined environment conducive to learning"—emphasizes a safe school environment. Despite legislation, sniper attacks, bombs, revenge killings, Internet conspiracies, murders and suicides, and violence against students and educators continue to traumatize people in their schools and communities.

Barr and Parrett (2003) believe that high-visibility school violence is only the tip of the iceberg. They note that for every dramatic school shooting, there are thousands of other teenager murders or negligent homicides. Each year, between 2,500 and 3,000 teenagers are arrested and charged in the deaths of other teenagers and adults. Between 1985 and 1994, the arrests of 10- to 17-year-old children and youth for homicide, rape, robbery, and assault increased by 70 percent. During the next decade, the number of teenagers in the United States will increase by more than 20 percent, and the majority of them will be poor, minority, and residents of impoverished inner-city neighborhoods (Walsh; Burke; as cited in Barr & Parrett).

Public Response to Violence

The immediate response to the increase in acts of school violence is to call for more police protection for schools. Students and teachers have to feel safe; therefore, society's first reaction is to install metal detectors, hire hall monitors, initiate security measures, enforce dress codes, and suspend or expel any student who even jokes about getting revenge, bringing a weapon to school, or hating a teacher.

Research by Elias, Lantieri, Patti, Walberg, and Zins (1999) and others, however, indicates that society is only "responding to the fires instead of building the safety nets over time" (p. 45). One of the reasons people give to explain the violence in schools is the prevalence of violence in society at large. Society bombards young children with images of violence. Many feel the media suggests that violence is an acceptable way to resolve conflicts and that treating others with disrespect and sarcasm is funny. "The American Psychological Association reports that by the age of 18, the typical child will have seen 16,000 simulated murders and 200,000 acts of violence. Moreover, in most cases, the perpetrators were not punished" (Elias et al., p. 45). The issue of guns and gun control continues to be a concern in society and cannot be separated from the issue of weapons in schools.

Statistics

One of the most recent studies, the 2000 U.S. Department of Education, National Center for Statistics, *School Survey on Crime and Safety*, reveals some important facts about violence and crime in schools. The survey is a nationally representative sample of 2,270 regular public elementary, middle, secondary, and combined schools in the United States.

The survey reports the following statistics:

- In 1999–2000, 71 percent of public and elementary and secondary schools experienced at least one violent incident.
- Approximately 1.5 million incidents of theft and violence occurred in about 59,000 public schools that year.
- Schools reported bullying (29 percent) as the serious discipline problem that occurred most frequently, and student acts of disrespect toward teachers were reported as the second most frequent serious discipline problem by 19 percent of schools. (Rosen, 2005, p. 77)

In another study during the 1997–1998 school year, middle schools experienced more problem behavior than other schools. Twenty-one percent of middle schools had one or more incidents of a physical attack or a fight with a weapon, compared to 2 percent of elementary schools and 11 percent of high schools; moreover, 19 percent of middle school students were physically attacked in schools, compared with 10 percent of high school students (Crosse, Burr, Cantor, Hagen, & Hantman as cited in Rosen, 2005, p. 78).

According to a 1999 report by the Office of Juvenile Justice and Delinquency Prevention (as cited in Rosen, 2005, p. 78), the number of street gangs in the United States has doubled since 1995. Also, an estimated 42 percent of youth groups were involved in the street sale of drugs between 1996 and 1997. Unfortunately, schools reflect the communities in which they are located, and the availability of 200 million guns in the United States remains a serious threat to children and youth (Rosen). The executive director of the National School Safety Center noted that an estimated 5,000 teachers are assaulted each month, and one-fifth of them are injured seriously enough to require medical attention (Ward as cited in Marzano et al., 2003).

With all the emphasis on curriculum improvement and the pressure from the NCLB Legislation to raise student achievement, it is imperative for principals and teachers to pay attention to improving school discipline procedures and practices. Data from research conducted by the Educational Testing Service (Barton & Wenglinsky, 1998) show that school discipline is everybody's problem.

> Schools from east to west; north to south; schools in cities, suburbs, and rural areas; and schools serving students from all racial/ethnic background—all experience problems with student behavior. Moreover, these problems are more than a security and safety problem—they are critical factors in student academic achievement. Without order in our classrooms, teachers can't teach and students can't learn. (p. 5)

Profile of Violence-Prone Youth

At-risk youth often feel that they are outsiders because no one cares for them or cares about them. Often schools don't help students feel as though they belong to a caring community, and at-risk students become isolated or turn to the Internet for their social interaction. They may also turn to causing school disruptions, violence, or suicide, as they feel increasingly alone and alienated and unable to connect with their parents, teachers, or classmates. According to Barr and Parrett (2003),

> these teenagers seem desperate for guidance, and when they do not find it at home or at school, they cling to cliques of other isolated outsiders and, of course, immerse themselves in the brutal world of television, movies, and computer games. Too often, the feelings of being slighted, ignored, bullied, and victimized lead to a growing internal rage. (p. 227)

In the current climate of standardized testing, it is apparent that teachers feel pressured to focus on academics—often at the expense of communication skills and social skills some students desperately need. A national study of youth violence conducted by Washington State Attorney General in 2000, as cited in Barr and Parrett (2003), identifies home life and peer harassment as two major causes of youth violence. Educators may not always be able to control their students' home lives, but administrators can control the school environment and teachers can control the classroom climate. Hopefully their efforts will help reduce the feelings of isolation, hopelessness, and disengagement felt by most violent youth.

A policy information report titled *Order in the Classroom: Violence, Discipline, and Student Achievement* (Barton & Wenglinksy, 1998) confirms the link between order in the classroom and academic achievement. The report shows that the frequency of serious and nonserious offenses is negatively related to academic achievement in all four subject areas studied—mathematics, reading, science, and social studies. The report begins with a warning:

> Recent tragic events have riveted public attention to the behavior of students in the nation's schools. As the nation focuses on improving the academic achievement of its students, we need to remember the caution given by the late Al Shanker, former president of the American Federation of Teachers, Unless you have order and civility, not much learning will go on. (p. 3)

TODAY'S YOUTH

Adolescent Angst

> Jocks, Preps, Punks, Goths, Geeks. They may sit at separate tables in the cafeteria, but they all belong to the same generation. There are now 31 million kids in the 12 to 19 age group, 35 million teens by 2010, a population bulge bigger than even the baby boom at its peak. (Kantrowitz & Wingert, 1999, p. 36)

These numbers show that the teenage population is exploding. In addition, the structure of the family is changing. Kids have less access to parents and more access to potentially damaging information from their home computers. The Internet, movies, and television are desensitizing students to violence and catering to children's fantasies about violence. Etzioni (1999) describes three Canadian villages that were prevented from receiving TV signals because of their location. Shortly after these communities started watching TV as a result of cable, crime rose significantly—more than in other Canadian towns. Etzioni states, "To the social scientist, this natural experiment shows that television added something to the causes of crime" (p. 57). The Internet also gives children access to violence—if children are predisposed to violence and aggression, the Internet helps connect them with other people who share their thoughts.

Many teenagers report that they feel overwhelmed by pressures and responsibilities. Many juggle part-time jobs, homework, and social pressures. Half have lived through their parents' divorce. Sixty-three percent are in households where both parents work outside the home, and many babysit younger siblings when they get home from school (Kantrowitz & Wingert, 1999, p. 36). Today's teenagers are experiencing more pressures at earlier ages, and often their fears, anger, and frustrations do not disappear when they walk through the doors to school. Students must learn how to handle these pressures without resorting to harming themselves. Federal studies indicate that 1 in 5 high school students have considered suicide and 1 in 10 have actually attempted it (Goldberg as cited in Duke, 2002, p. 30). "At other times, the harm young people bring on themselves is inadvertent, the result of poor judgment or ignorance. Examples of such behavior include experimentation with drugs and risky activities such as driving at high speeds" (Duke, p. 30).

Loneliness and Depression

University of Chicago sociologist Barbara Schneider studied 7,000 teenagers for five years in the 1990s and found that the issue that troubles adolescents more than anything else is loneliness. She found that the teenagers in her study spent an average of 3.5 hours alone every day. "Teenagers may claim they want privacy, but they also crave and need attention—and they're not getting it" (Schneider as cited in Kantrowitz & Wingert, 1999, p. 38).

Loneliness creates an emotional vacuum that is often filled by peers. When teens are isolated from parents and teachers, they become more vulnerable to emotional problems. They also become more easily influenced by a peer group because they want desperately to "fit in." Sometimes, teachers contribute to the students' feelings of loneliness and isolation by belittling students or even worse, ignoring them altogether.

Tony Wagner (1999) describes how many high school teachers, in particular, use sarcasm and ridicule to show how clever they are and to keep students submissive and compliant. He suggests that a solution might be to move to smaller school units and have the same teacher stay with students for several years in an attempt to overcome the problem of disconnection. When students feel disconnected from their family, teachers, or peers, they sometimes resort to "fight" by disrupting their class or school or "flight" by withdrawing mentally, emotionally, and sometimes physically from school and daily life.

Rejection and Alienation

Feeling rejected by peer groups and ignored by parents can cause confusion and hurt in teenagers, which in turn can develop into hate and violence. Reports alleging that Columbine High School gunmen Eric Harris and Dylan Klebold hated jocks, because jocks taunted them and called them "rejects" and "inbreds" and pushed them up against lockers in the halls, demonstrate how strong revenge can become in a desperate attempt to get attention and respect. Students who feel alienated and disconnected from peer groups either withdraw in "flight" or retaliate in "fight."

A 17-year-old Columbine High School junior framed the problem clearly: "I mean, it was just like it must be at every other high school in America. You know, kids can be really mean to each other, really cruel" (Wagner, 1999, p. 48). The mass killings at Virginia Tech by a student who rarely talked or socialized with other students indicate how desperate young people can become when they feel they do not get the attention and respect they so desperately seek.

The gulf between young people and adults has reached alarming proportions, causing teenagers to become alienated from their families and teachers as well as peers. The same students who resent parents as authority figures can transfer that dislike to teachers and principals, bosses at work, and fellow students whom they perceive as the "goodie-goodie" kids trying to please and impress adults. At the center of this gulf is the family under pressure. Parents are too stressed, schools are too impersonal, and the community is too disorganized to fulfill that most basic human need of children—to belong. Estranged from family, friends, school, or productive work, children are sown with the seeds of discouragement.

Alienated young people are assigned a multitude of labels, most of them unfriendly. They are described as aggressive or anxious, as attention disordered or affectionless, as unmotivated or unteachable, as drug abusers or dropouts. Most terms label and sort students or follow the pattern of blaming the victim. The catch phrase *zero tolerance* is popular because expulsion is felt to be the best punishment for offenders. Violence needs to be addressed to ensure school safety, but as Goodlad (as cited in Brendtro & Long, 1995) states:

> If we cease trying to teach difficult students, we shift the responsibility for their enculturation elsewhere—and there is no elsewhere. Excluding violent students from an education is no more moral than forcing the most critical patients from an emergency room. These students need to belong *somewhere.* (p. 112)

Brain Dysfunction

The importance of the early development of the brain has been a subject of intense interest because of the series of students involved in school shootings around the country. The debate over nature versus nurture has surfaced as researchers search for the biological roots of violence. Begley (1999) states that a child's brain is more malleable than an adult's. She believes that the young brain is extra vulnerable to hurt in the first years of life.

> A child who suffers repeated 'hits' of stress—abuse, neglect, terror— experiences physical changes in his brain. . . . The incessant flood of stress chemicals tends to reset the brain's system of fight or flight hormones, putting them on hair-trigger alert. (p. 32)

Begley believes that as a result of these early traumatic experiences, kids may show impulsive aggression to anyone who "disses" them, gets up at a cafeteria table when they sit down, or embarrasses or humiliates them in front of peers.

One early warning sign of potential violent behavior is the infliction of extreme cruelty upon animals. Kip Kinkel, the 15-year-old who killed his parents and then shot 24 schoolmates in Springfield, Oregon, in 1998, had a history of abuse to animals. Luke Woodham, who killed three schoolmates and wounded seven at his high school in Pearl, Mississippi, in 1997, "had previously beaten his dog with a club, wrapped it in a bag and set it on fire" (Begley, 1999, p. 33).

Scans of the brain of one 16-year-old assailant who assaulted another student showed several abnormalities. They reflected some combination of early childhood head injuries, depression, and exposure to violence. Lesions in the frontal lobe can induce apathy and distort both judgment and emotion. Such abnormalities and factors are often found in violent students.

Risky Student Behavior

Educators have always realized that students' behavior is affected by emotional events such as the death of a parent, family divorce, the breakup of a teen romance, or the taunts of a bully. These traumatic events may cause many students to be at risk of failing in school, dropping out, or turning violent (Barr & Parrett, 2003). The Centers for Disease Control and Prevention has coordinated surveys to monitor the risky behaviors among the young that cause the most significant health risks. Results of the 2000 survey related to alcohol, drugs, sexual activity, tobacco, safety, and nutrition dramatized the many risky behaviors of teenagers today and the alarming percentage of youth involved in these behaviors. For example, 47 percent of students surveyed drank alcohol on one or more days during the preceding month; 13 percent drove a vehicle after drinking alcohol; and 31 percent rode with a driver who had been drinking (Kann et al., National Center for Disease Control Surveillance Summaries, as cited in Barr & Parrott, 2003).

Growing up is a "risky business" in the United States, and at-risk youth are present in all socioeconomic groupings of adolescents. But as Barr and Parrett (2003) note,

> Schools need to establish expectations that all students will become connected to a caring adult at school. When schools place a priority on educators and staff developing positive relationships with all students, negative behavior, and dropout rates can rapidly diminish. (p. 41)

SUMMARY

This chapter highlights some of the issues facing educators today, but it cannot possibly address all of the problems and concerns. It is evident that teachers in the twenty-first century must know more than their subject area content to meet the needs of the diverse students they teach. It is also evident that classroom management problems cannot be attributed to "students' just not behaving" after examining all the potential reasons why children might feel and act the way they do. The challenges presented by students require a repertoire of problem-solving strategies to address multiple causes.

Reviewing Current Teaching and Learning Theories

2

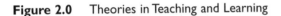

Figure 2.0 Theories in Teaching and Learning

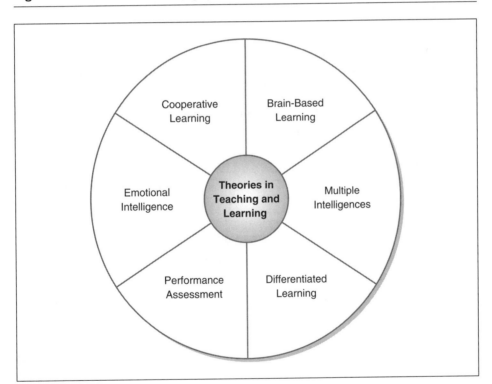

Theory and theoretical frameworks play important roles in the teaching and learning process. Eisner (1985) feels that educational theories help teachers focus on aspects of classroom life that might otherwise be neglected. Psychological theory might address questions of self-esteem, forms of reinforcement, or the need to provide students with guided practice. However, these issues might be neglected if educational theories did not remind teachers of them. Glatthorn (1996) agrees, saying, "The professional who knows the theory and research on student motivation will be better able to develop the skills to motivate students than those who operate without that knowledge base" (p. 46).

There are many theories regarding students' abilities to learn and what can be done to help foster a better learning environment in schools. Some of these theories are outlined in this chapter and are applied in the activities in this book. The Industrial Revolution introduced society to a standardized "conveyor belt" curriculum, often called the "factory model," that "emphasized useful skills like obedience, orderliness, unity and respect for authority" (Jensen, 1998b, p. 2). In the 1950s and 1960s, psychologists John Watson and B. F. Skinner introduced behaviorist theories that attempted to modify human behavior with reinforcers. These theories advocated rewarding good behavior (gold stars, bonus points, food, and recess) and punishing bad behavior (name on the board, removal of privileges, detentions, time-out, and low grades). Behaviorism became an accepted form of educational practice during those decades and is still used in some classrooms. Some teachers still subscribe to discipline programs that advocate public embarrassment, removal of privileges such as field trips or recess, and a top-down approach to establishing rules and consequences.

Recent research and theories, however, indicate that this traditional model is not effective for all youth today. Several new theories, which support the use of block scheduling, brain-compatible learning techniques, and emotional intelligence, support the idea that educators need to look beyond controlling students' behavior and redefine their management and teaching approaches to best meet students' needs instead. Despite the comment "It worked for us, why won't it work for kids today?" research indicates that the ways that teachers taught students 50 years ago are not necessarily the best ways to teach the new generation.

As Jensen (1998b) notes, "We are on the verge of a revolution: the application of important new brain research to teaching and learning. This revolution will change school start times, discipline policies, assessment methods, teaching strategies, budget priorities, classroom environments . . ." (p. 1).

Emerging scientific research is providing educators everywhere with new directions for teaching and learning. Research on brain-based learning, the multiple intelligences, differentiated learning, authentic assessment, standards-based teaching, the emotional intelligence, and cooperative learning has important implications for establishing effective classroom management.

BRAIN-BASED LEARNING

Effective teachers have always been aware of how students learn best, but they knew it either innately or from experience—not necessarily from scientific evidence. Now scientists studying the brain have substantiated effective teaching practice with evidence that supports the importance of establishing a brain-compatible classroom.

A brief synthesis of the experts' views on how brain-compatible classrooms affect learning and behavior includes the following:

- Brain structures are modified by the environment. An enriched environment stimulates growing dendrites or the creating of connections between brain cells (Diamond & Hopson, 1998).
- The brain needs to connect the new to the old. Students need to relate what they are learning—new knowledge—to what they already know—prior knowledge (Wolfe & Brandt, 1998).
- The brain is innately social and collaborative. Students' learning is enhanced when they discuss their learning out loud, share ideas with peers, and produce collaborative work (Wolfe & Brandt).
- Learning is strongly influenced by emotion because the stronger the emotion connected with an experience, the stronger the memory. Also, when emotions are involved with an experience, chemicals in the brain send a message to remember information, thereby increasing retention (Wolfe & Brandt).
- Learning occurs more easily in environments that are free from threat or intimidation (Sousa, 2001).
- When you're experiencing stress, the brain is more likely to recall stressful memories from your past than to recall upbeat ones (Johnson, 2004).
- Chronic negative feelings, limited academic engagement, and frequent disruptive behavior may have their roots in childhood traumas (Given, 2002).

Teachers who display students' work, take time to check for prior knowledge, allow students to talk about their learnings, and relate new ideas to prior learnings or experiences are establishing a climate conducive for learning. They are also engaging students in meaningful learning that has value to them.

School Readiness

The first critical step in preparing students for learning occurs in the womb. If a pregnant mother takes drugs, smokes, drinks alcohol, has poor nutrition, or is under stress, problems result for the developing fetus. Also, the first few years of a baby's life and its relationship with its primary caretaker often determine whether or not the child develops learning problems. A troubled relationship in the child's early years causes the child's brain to consume glucose in dealing with stress—glucose that instead could be used to develop early cognitive functions. Therefore, if a baby or small child is dealing with an unpleasant environment, poor nutrition, parental apathy, or dangerous conditions, the brain consumes the glucose that should be used to develop patterns, recognize sounds and pictures, and form connections in response to mental stimulation (Kotulak, 1996).

Kotulak (1996) discusses how a child's early exposure to stress or violence causes the brain to reorganize itself, increasing reactivity to people, actions, or comments, and raising blood pressure, which causes the child to be more impulsive and aggressive later on in school. Brain growth and development are also affected by the presence or absence of opportunities for mental stimulation. Parents who talk to their children and offer a rich sensory environment by providing mobiles, sounds, pictures, and music help them form connections in their brains by actually growing dendrites. Dendrites are branchlike extensions that grow outward from a nerve cell's body when the environment is enriched (Jensen, 1998b). Providing children with an enriched environment early in life provides them with the stimulation they need to grow emotionally and intellectually. A dangerous, apathetic, or stressful environment, on the other hand, causes children to react impulsively and sometimes aggressively—a pattern that continues into school and sometimes throughout life.

The Importance of Sleep

In addition to aggressive and impulsive behavior, some of the biggest management problems facing teachers today are students' lack of motivation, inattention to schoolwork, and apathy as evidenced by coming late to class or falling asleep in class. Biologists have learned that puberty could be the cause of preteen and teenage students' listlessness. Sleep is regulated by many chemicals, one of which is oleamide, a drowsiness-inducing substance. The hormonal changes of puberty cause a delayed accumulation of oleamide, which results in a teen's natural sleep clock generating a bedtime closer to midnight and a wake-up time closer to 8 AM. If students wake up early (6:00 AM to catch the bus to high school, 6:30 AM for middle school), they will naturally be tired in school because of a lack of sleep. They may also miss out on the dream state or rapid-eye movement (REM) time, the type of sleep thought to be critical to maintaining memories. Therefore, they will not only be sleepy and inattentive in classes, but they also may have forgotten everything they learned the day before because they missed the REM time that is necessary for "rehearsing" the learning (Jensen, 1998b).

Carskadon (1999) discusses why teenagers may need more sleep as they get older as well as extra help (e.g., parents, alarm clocks) to get up in the morning. Other factors contributing to changing sleep patterns include an active social life, increased academic demands, and employment. One survey of young people in New England in the late 1980s reveals that two-thirds of the high school students had jobs and "nearly 30 percent worked 20 or more hours in a typical school week" (p. 349). Those kids reported later bedtimes, more frequent oversleeping resulting in tardiness to school, and more frequent episodes of falling asleep in class.

Because of the research, many middle schools and high schools across the country are starting school at 9:00 or 9:30 A.M. Schools that have established the later start time are reporting better learning, fewer teens sleeping in schools, and fewer discipline problems. If kids are going to learn, they need to stay awake in school and get enough sleep to reinforce their learning at night— especially during REM time. The REM time also helps them process intense emotions from the previous day that may "spill over" into the next day and give them a rough start in the morning. Therefore, a lack of quality sleep might also explain the grumpiness of many teens in the morning and how minor negative exchanges at the bus stop or in the hallways early in the day can sometimes escalate into more serious problems later in the day.

Other factors that impact student learning and behavior in middle schools and high schools are short class periods (42–50 minutes) and short intervals (3–5 minutes) between classes. Short class periods don't allow students enough time to engage in interactive activities and process or reflect on the information they learn. They have to rush to their next class, where they must adjust to another teacher's rules and procedures and are once again inundated with new information before rushing to the next class. This scenario is often intensified on Fridays, when students may be taking a test in every class period. Many schools are moving to block scheduling or extended-time formats to allow students more time to learn and process information. They also have more time between classes to visit the crowded restrooms, go to their lockers, or relax and socialize. Having appropriate downtime helps students cope with the intense academic and social pressures of school.

Chunking Direct Instruction

Because so many students come to school stressed and tired, teachers are challenged to motivate them to learn. Even though educators may feel that students will learn more if a teacher lectures for the full class period, current research suggests that teachers should subscribe to the "less is more" philosophy of information input. By reducing "teacher talk," students have more time to apply their knowledge in authentic ways and to reflect on their learning. Requiring students to maintain their undivided attention on the teacher for extended periods of time often creates resentful and disruptive learners and, ironically, an environment not conducive to learning.

Many teachers have had good results through a practice referred to as "chunking" the lesson. When a teacher "chunks" a lesson, she may give a brief lecturette for 10 to 15 minutes, depending on the ages and attention spans of her students. She then stops the direct instruction and allows students some time to reflect on the information and connect it to prior knowledge. When students process information, they achieve deeper understanding (Jensen, 1998a).

The remaining time in the class could be used for students to discuss new ideas, work in groups, engage in partner work, self-assess their work, write in journals, or discuss key concepts or new insights with peers or teachers. It is also important for teachers to schedule practice time after each introduction of new material. The guided practice time allows students to make choices, make mistakes through problem-based learning, build teams to solve problems, and create projects that allow opportunities for self-correction and independent learning.

Working memory in the brain is limited, but if information is chunked into meaningful units, students can increase the amount of information that can be stored in each chunk (Wolfe, 2001).

The following is an example of chunking:

Lesson: Greek Mythology

Direct Instruction: Teacher introduces how the Greeks explained things in nature. She tells the story of Narcissus who was cursed by the gods to fall in love with his own image when he gazed into a pond in the forest. Because of his curse, the narcissus flower is usually found near water.

Group Interaction: Teacher asks groups of three to spend five minutes thinking about other Greek myths that helped explain elements in nature.

Group Sharing: Each group reports on a nature myth, such as why sunflowers always face the sun.

Group Application: Teacher asks each group to write an original myth explaining something scientific. Why do lightning bugs glow in the dark? Why does the zebra have stripes?

Group Sharing: A member of each group reads the original myth to the class.

Direct Instruction: Teacher introduces the characteristics of the Greek hero by showing a short video on Hercules.

Group Interaction: Students brainstorm a list of characteristics of a hero.

Group Sharing: Teacher compiles a list that includes the characteristics from each group.

Individual Application: Each student is assigned to write an original story about a modern-day hero. The twenty-first-century hero needs to possess the characteristics compiled in class. The teacher gives specific criteria for the story.

Basically, *chunking* means varying the activities and changing the pace of a lesson so students do not get bored. Listening to someone else talk is not as effective as actually doing something that requires thinking, collaboration, critical and creative problem solving, and the application of knowledge.

Metacognition

Allowing students time to apply their learning is important. Research by Vygotsky, Feuerstein, Perkins, Costa, and Gardner, as cited in Fogarty (2002), stress the importance of metacognition or "thinking about thinking" as essential to the learning process. In the processing time, students reflect on the lesson and plan, monitor, and evaluate their own thinking and learning.

Teachers can put metacognitive stems on the board to help students reflect on their learning. Sample stems include the following:

- One thing I learned I'll never forget is . . .
- The thing that surprised me the most was . . .
- One thing I am confused about is . . .
- This reminds me of . . .
- I want to learn more about . . .

Many middle schools have gone to integrated teaming—where students can work on one unit that incorporates different subject areas—and high schools have adopted block scheduling models that may have 70- to 90-minute classes. Traditional time structures in schools do not always foster a reflective learning environment. Fogarty (2002) states, "The reflection is the pause in the act of learning that deepens understanding and gives meaning to the learning" (p. 211). If students cannot cope with the fast-paced school schedule, they may become frustrated, anxious, angry, and even violent. By establishing schools that build in time for learning and reflection, educators foster a brain-compatible learning environment as well as prevent many discipline problems.

Positive Feedback

Effective teachers have long known about the benefits of positive feedback on students' self-esteem and self-concepts. Research on the effects of serotonin suggests that social feedback creates fluctuations from the basal serotonin levels, and these fluctuations help determine a person's current level of self-esteem. Social success elevates self-esteem (and serotonin levels) and further raises students' social expectations, perhaps allowing them to try out for a team or pursue a leadership role they never thought of pursuing when they had lower levels of serotonin (Wright as cited in Sylwester, 1998).

Sylwester (1998) says,

> If positive social feedback is nature's way of regulating the serotonin system so that both an inexperienced substitute football player and the team's star can work together comfortably and effectively, then positive feedback in the classroom is a powerful social device for helping us to assess and define ourselves (self-concept) and to value ourselves (self-esteem). (pp. 47–48)

Positive reinforcement and social acceptance can help students achieve a sense of belonging and community.

Feedback is important not only socially but also academically. Students need to receive specific feedback on their work. The feedback needs to relate to the goals or standards, it must provide specific suggestions on how to reach the target, and it must be immediate (Ainsworth & Viegut, 2006). Hattie reviewed almost 8,000 classroom studies focused on determining the impact of feedback on student improvement. Hattie's 1992 study led him to conclude that "The most powerful single modification that enhances achievement is feedback. The simplest prescription for improving education must be 'dollops of feedback'" (as cited in Ainsworth & Viegut, p. 89).

Implications for Classroom Management

Cognitive scientific research is proving a biological foundation for practices many educators have always known were right. Now educators have the support of the science community in creating a learning environment that enhances learning and helps students feel that they belong and are important. Research on the brain has tremendous implications for curriculum, instruction, and classroom management. It is the umbrella field of knowledge that affects everything educators do. Educators can utilize the research on brain-compatible learning by implementing some of the following strategies to establish a positive climate for learning:

- Provide an enriched environment for students (stimulation).
- Limit direct instruction to one minute per the age of the students (chunking).
- Help students apply what they learn (practice).
- Allow students time to process and reflect on their learnings (metacognition).
- Reduce tensions in the class that cause students stress (positive climate).
- Provide positive social feedback and encouragement (self-esteem).
- Provide specific feedback on student work to improve academic achievement (standards-based teaching).

By implementing brain-based instructional strategies, teachers establish a climate that nurtures both the socialization skills and academic skills students need to survive and thrive in both school and life. Just as a home environment is critical for a child's health and happiness, so too is the classroom environment critical for a child's academic growth and sense of well-being.

MULTIPLE INTELLIGENCES

By now, educators are accustomed to seeing chapters dealing with Howard Gardner's 1983 theory of multiple intelligences in curricula and instruction books, but they may be surprised to see it mentioned in a book on classroom management. Yet the link connecting quality curriculum, engaging instruction, and effective classroom management is critical.

A teacher can initiate an effective classroom management system, but it will not last more than a few weeks if students do not see the value of the curriculum being taught or experience enjoyment in learning; moreover, they must also feel that the assessments are fair (reliable) and measure what was taught (valid). The components necessary for effective classroom management are shown in Figure 2.1.

In 1979, a Dutch philanthropic group asked Harvard researcher Howard Gardner to investigate human potential. This invitation led Gardner to establish

Figure 2.1 Effective Classroom Management

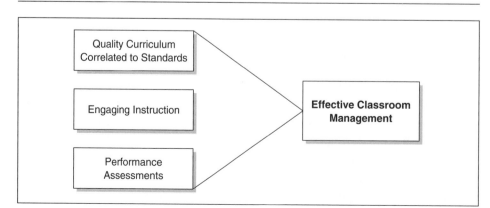

Harvard's Project Zero, which served as the "institutional midwife" for the theory of multiple intelligences (MI) (Armstrong, 1994). The 1983 publication of Gardner's book *Frames of Mind* marked the effective birth date of MI theory.

Gardner argued that traditional ideas about intelligence required reform. He felt that the concept of an intelligence that can be measured by standardized verbal instruments like a single IQ score was flawed and that intelligence is not a singular phenomenon but a plurality of capacities. He concluded that there were at least seven types of intelligences (he added the naturalist in 1993), which people possessed in different degrees. Armstrong (2003) says that "each intelligence represents a set of capacities that are brought to bear upon two major focuses: the solving of problems and the fashioning of significant cultural products" (p. 13).

In *Frames of Mind*, Gardner (1983/1993) writes,

> In my view, if we are to encompass adequately the realm of human cognition, it is necessary to include a far wider and more universal set of competences than we have ordinarily considered. And it is necessary to remain open to the possibility that many—if not most—of these competences do not lend themselves to measurements by standard verbal methods, which rely heavily on a blend of logical and linguistic abilities. (p. x)

According to the theory of multiple intelligences, the mind's problem-solving capacities are multifaceted, exceeding the traditional view of intelligence as being only verbal or mathematic. In 1983, Gardner identified seven forms of intelligence:

1. Verbal/linguistic—the capacity to use words effectively, whether orally or in writing

2. Logical/mathematical—the capacity to use numbers effectively and to reason well

3. Visual/spatial—the capacity to perceive the visual-spatial world accurately and to perform transformation upon these perceptions

4. Bodily/kinesthetic—expertise in using one's whole body to express ideas and feelings or the ability to use one's hands to produce or transform things

5. Musical/rhythmic—the capacity to perceive, discriminate, transform, and express musical forms

6. Interpersonal/social—the ability to understand and work with other people

7. Intrapersonal/introspective—the ability to perceive and make distinctions in the moods, intentions, motivations, and feelings of other people (Armstrong, 1994, pp. 2–3)

In 1993, he added an eighth intelligence:

8. Naturalist—one who specializes in recognizing and classifying natural and human-made phenomena (Campbell & Campbell, 1999, p. 5)

Fogarty and Stoehr (1995) recommend teachers use a chart that describes the types of skills, products, or verbs that can be associated with each of Gardner's eight intelligences to plan their lessons and assessments (see Figure 2.2).

Figure 2.2 Performances Classified According to Gardner's Eight Intelligences

Visual/Spatial

Images, graphics, drawings, sketches, maps, charts, doodles, pictures, spatial orientation, puzzles, designs, looks, appeal, mind's eye, imagination, visualization, dreams, nightmares, films, and videos.

Logical/Mathematical

Reasoning, deductive and inductive logic, facts, data, information, spreadsheets, databases, sequencing, ranking, organizing, analyzing, proofs, conclusions, judging, evaluations, and assessments.

Verbal/Linguistic

Words, wordsmiths, speaking, writing, listening, reading, papers, essays, poems, plays, narratives, lyrics, spelling, grammar, foreign languages, memos, bulletins, newsletters, newspapers, e-mail, faxes, speeches, talks, dialogues, and debates.

Musical/Rhythmic

Music, rhythm, beat, melody, tunes, allegro, pacing, timbre, tenor, soprano, opera, baritone, symphony, choir, chorus, madrigals, rap, rock, rhythm and blues, jazz, classical, folk, ads, and jingles.

Bodily/Kinesthetic

Art, activity, action, experiential, hands-on experiments, try, do, perform, play, drama, sports, throw, toss, catch, jump, twist, twirl, assemble, disassemble, form, re-form, manipulate, touch, feel, immerse, and participate.

Interpersonal/Social

Interact, communicate, converse, share, understand, empathize, sympathize, reach out, care, talk, whisper, laugh, cry, shudder, socialize, meet, greet, lead, follow, gangs, clubs, charisma, crowds, gatherings, and twosomes.

Intrapersonal/Introspective

Self, solitude, meditate, think, create, brood, reflect, envision, journal, self-assess, set goals, plot, plan, dream, write, fiction, nonfiction, poetry, affirmations, lyrics, songs, screenplays, commentaries, introspection, and inspection.

Naturalist

Nature, natural, environment, listen, watch, observe, classify, categorize, discern patterns, appreciate, hike, climb, fish, hunt, snorkle, dive, photograph, trees, leaves, animals, living things, flora, fauna, ecosystem, sky, grass, mountains, lakes, and rivers.

From Howard Gardner, *Multiple Intelligences*. New Horizons, 2006.

The theory of multiple intelligences provides a more holistic and natural profile of human potential than an IQ test, and it offers teachers a repertoire of activities and assessments to meet the needs of diverse students.

Multiple Intelligences Grid

To meet the needs of all students, teachers can construct lessons and assessments that allow students some choice as to how they demonstrate their understanding of key concepts or content. By including a number of activities from the eight intelligences, teachers allow students to demonstrate their strengths and enjoy their interests. The Multiple Intelligences Learning Experiences Grid (see Figure 2.3) classifies activities and assessments that allow students some choice in demonstrating their understanding. It is evident that most experiences touch upon several intelligences, but the grid helps teachers provide a variety of opportunities to help students become more interested in their learning and more empowered to make choices about how they learn.

Multiple Intelligences Unit

Teachers create units that address goals or standards and still allow students some choice in selecting group projects or specific items to include in their portfolios. The Greek Mythology Unit (see Figure 2.4) integrates several subject areas so that students make connections among social studies, science, language arts, physical education, art, and music. It also allows students to study mythology in depth and demonstrate they have met learning standards or goals. The assessments include traditional evaluations, such as teacher-made tests and literary papers, as well as authentic tasks, such as group projects and portfolios that require a rubric to address specific criteria. The culminating event pulls all the learning together and serves as a celebration to showcase the students' learning.

Implications for Classroom Management

The age-old question of "What came first, the chicken or the egg?" also applies to effective classroom management.

What comes first? An organized classroom where all students know the expectations, procedures, and rules and have respect for themselves, fellow students, and the teacher? Or an enriched learning environment where students are engaged in meaningful learning experiences that address learning standards and goals by allowing students to demonstrate their talents?

The answer to this question is simple. The truly effective teacher knows he must enact both areas *simultaneously*. Teachers know they must teach classroom rules and procedures the same day they introduce the rules and procedures. If teachers lecture and give completed handouts of the rules without allowing for student input or interaction, they won't get the students' buy-in.

Moreover, effective management can never be maintained—even by the most authoritative teacher with the most cooperative students—without also implementing a quality curriculum and effective instructional strategies.

Figure 2.3   Multiple Intelligence Learning Experiences Grid

Verbal/ Linguistic

Speeches
Debates
Storytelling
Reports
Crosswords
Newspapers
Internet

Logical/ Mathematical

Puzzles
Outlines
Timelines
Analogies
Patterns
Problem solving
Lab experiments
Formulas

Visual/Spatial

Artwork
Photographs
Math manipulatives
Graphic organizers
Posters, charts
Illustrations
Cartoons
Props for plays
Use of overhead

Bodily/ Kinesthetic

Field trips
Role playing
Learning centers
Labs
Sports/games
Cooperative learning
Body language
Experiments

Musical/Rhythmic

Background music
Songs about
   books, people,
   countries,
   historic events
Raps
Jingles
Choral readings

Interpersonal

Group video, film,
   slides
Team computer
   programs
Think-pair-share
Cooperative tasks
Jigsaws
Conferences

Intrapersonal

Reflective journals
Learning logs
Goal-setting journals
Metacognitive
   reflections
Independent reading
Silent reflection
Diaries

Naturalist

Outdoor education
Environmental studies
Field trips (farm, zoo)
Bird watching
Nature walk
Weather forecasting
Stargazing
Exploring nature
Ecology studies
Identifying leaves

Figure 2.4   Greek Mythology Unit

Subject Area: _____ *Integrated Unit—Middle School* _____   Timeline: _____ *4–6 weeks* _____

Standards:
1. *Communicate ideas in writing to describe, inform, persuade, and entertain.*
2. *Demonstrate comprehension of a broad range of reading materials.*
3. *Use reading, writing, listening, and speaking skills to research and apply information for specific purposes.*

List at least three learning experiences/assessments under each intelligence.

Verbal/Linguistic	Logical/Mathematical	Visual/Spatial	Bodily/Kinesthetic
• Read *The Iliad*. • Read *The Odyssey*. • Read Edith Hamilton's *Mythology*. • Write an original myth to explain a scientific mystery. • Write poems about mythology. • Write a eulogy for a fallen Greek or Trojan warrior.	• Use a Venn diagram to compare the Greeks and the Trojans. • Create original story problems that can incorporate the Pythagorean theorem. • Draw a family tree of the 12 Olympians and their children. • Complete a time line of Odysseus's trip home from Troy.	• Draw the battle plan for the Greeks' attack on Troy. • Draw Mt. Olympus. • Sketch the Greek gods and goddesses. • Create a video of the Olympic games. • Draw items that relate to mythology.	• Act out a Greek tragedy. • Re-create some of the Olympic events. • Act out a myth. • Create a dance for the forest nymphs. • Re-enact the battle scene between Hector and Achilles.

Musical/Rhythmic	Interpersonal	Intrapersonal	Naturalist
• Write a song for a lyre. • Pretend you are Apollo, god of music, and CEO of Motown. • Select music that correlates with each god or goddess.	• Interview Helen about her role in the Trojan War. • Work in a group to create a computer crossword puzzle about mythology. • Find an Internet pen pal in Greece.	• Pretend you are a Greek soldier away from home for 10 years. Keep a diary of your thoughts. • Write a journal about how you would feel if you were Prometheus chained to a rock. • Reflect on the effects of war on civilians.	• Using scientific data, predict how long it will take before anything grows after the Greeks destroy Troy and sow the fields with salt. • Describe the animals and plants on Mt. Olympus. • Describe a centaur in the forest.

1. Whole-class learning experiences	Read Hamilton's *Mythology*	Read excerpts from *The Iliad* and *The Odyssey*	Select a group project or performance	Portfolio that contains 7–10 items
	↕	↕	↕	↕
2. Whole-class assessments for learning experiences	Teacher-made test	Write a paper comparing the Greeks to the Trojans	Rubric to assess each one	Rubric created by class
3. Culminating event for unit	Exhibition in the school gym—students and teachers dress up as favorite mythological characters. Invited guests view videos, portfolios, artifacts, and an original skit.			

Differentiated Learning

No Child Left Behind legislation and the standards movement mandate that *all* students are expected to achieve at a higher level. In the past, many classes were tracked, and students were grouped homogeneously by ability levels. In today's inclusive classrooms, however, students are grouped heterogeneously, but they *all* are expected to improve their academic achievement and meet and exceed state standards.

Benjamin (2002) says, "Differentiated instruction is a broad term that refers to a variety of classroom practices that accommodate differences in students' learning styles, interests, prior knowledge, socialization needs and comfort zones" (p. 1). Standards may tell teachers *what* the students need to know and be able to do, but differentiated instruction practices help show students *how* to get there. Teachers need to vary instructional strategies to allow students to construct some knowledge for themselves.

Gregory and Chapman (2002) discuss how teachers need to create a climate for learning, get to know the learner, and assess the learner; then adjust, compact, and group as needed to meet the learner's goals. They developed a planning model called "Tools and Strategies for Designing Inclusive Classrooms for Diverse Learners" (Figure 2.5) that shows ways to target specific components of differentiated learning.

Tomlinson and Eidson (2003) define *differentiated instruction* as a "systematic approach to planning curriculum and instruction for academically diverse learners. It is a way of thinking about the classroom with the dual goals of honoring each student's learning needs and maximizing each student's learning capacity" (p. 3).

Teachers who create meaningful curriculum units that interest students and then employ a range of instructional strategies will most likely reduce their classroom management problems. Intellectually engaged as well as emotionally involved with their fellow students and their own learning, students will be too busy to be disruptive.

PERFORMANCE ASSESSMENT

> *The widespread use of paper-and-pencil testing in schools was due, at least in part, to the efficiency with which they could measure a large number of learning outcomes and the ease of scoring and recording the results.* (Gronlund, 1998, pp. 1–2)

Because of the increased emphasis on standardized tests, many educators believe there has been a reaction to the heavy emphasis on paper-and-pencil testing and a shift to authentic assessments that involve "real-life" tasks, such as solving problems that exist in the world. A commonly used term is *performance assessments*, which Gronlund (1998) defines as "assessments requiring students to demonstrate their achievement of understanding and skills by actually performing a task or set of tasks (e.g., writing a story, giving a speech, conducting an experiment, operating a machine)" (p. 2).

Figure 2.5 Tools and Strategies for Designing Inclusive Classrooms for Diverse Learners

Climate	Knowing the Learner	Assessing the Learner	Adjustable Assignments	Instructional Strategies	Curriculum Approaches
• Safe • Nurturing • Encouraging risk tasking • Inclusive • Multisensory • Stimulating • Complex • Challenging • Collaborative • Questioning • Cubing • Team- and class-building norms	• **Learning Styles** Dunn & Dunn Gregoric 4Mat Silver/Strong/Hanson • **Multiple Intelligences** Using observation checklists, inventories, logs, and journals to become more aware of how one learns	• **Before:** **Formal** Written pretest Journaling Surveys/inventories **Informal** Squaring off Boxing Graffiti facts • **During:** **Formal** Journaling/portfolios Teacher-made tests Checklists/rubrics **Informal** Thumb it Fist to five Face the fact • **After:** **Formal** Posttest Portfolio/conferences Reflections **Informal** Talking topics Conversation Circles Donut	• **Compacting** T.A.P.S. **Total Group:** Lecturette Presentation Demonstration Jigsaw Video Field trip Guest speaker Text • **Alone:** Interest Personalized Multiple intelligences • **Paired:** Random Interest Task • **Small Groups:** Heterogeneous Homogeneous Task-oriented Constructed Random Interest	• **Brain-Research Based** Memory model Elaborative rehearsal • **Focus activities** • **Graphic organizers** Compare and contrast webbing • **Metaphors** • **Cooperative group learning** • **Jigsaw** • **Role play**	**Centers** **Projects** **Problem-Based** **Inquiry** **Contracts**

NCLB legislation has focused attention on standardized tests, college admissions tests, and national norm-referenced and criterion-referenced tests as yardsticks to measure success in education. These external examinations have been referred to as "assessments *of* learning" because they happen *after* learning is supposed to have occurred to determine if, in fact, it did.

Stiggins, Arter, Chappuis, and Chappuis (2004) believe assessments *for* learning happen while learning is still underway. These are the assessments that are conducted throughout teaching and learning "to diagnose student needs, plan our next steps in instruction, provide students with feedback they can use to improve the quality of their work, and help students see and feel in control of their journey to success" (p. 31).

Figure 2.6 Balanced Assessment

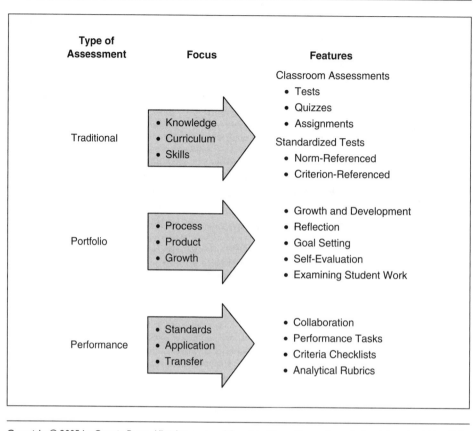

Type of Assessment	Focus	Features
Traditional	• Knowledge • Curriculum • Skills	Classroom Assessments • Tests • Quizzes • Assignments Standardized Tests • Norm-Referenced • Criterion-Referenced
Portfolio	• Process • Product • Growth	• Growth and Development • Reflection • Goal Setting • Self-Evaluation • Examining Student Work
Performance	• Standards • Application • Transfer	• Collaboration • Performance Tasks • Criteria Checklists • Analytical Rubrics

Burke (2005) adapts Fogarty and Stoehr's "Tri-Assessment Model" and labels it "Balanced Assessment." In this model, three methods—traditional, portfolio, and performance assessments—are used in combination to focus on knowledge, curriculum, skills, process, product, growth, standards, application, and transfer (see Figure 2.6). Each of the three methods by itself is insufficient to provide a portrait of the student as a learner. Teachers need all three in combination to allow students a repertoire of opportunities to demonstrate their learning.

A portfolio is one form of authentic assessment that provides students a chance to collect evidence of their work. Students collect, select, and reflect on their work in a portfolio that showcases their learning over time. Portfolios show a student's growth and development and allow for student reflection. By the same token, performances demonstrate a student's ability to use the attained knowledge and skills. These applications become the performances or the projects that mirror the skills needed in life. To arrive at an accurate portrait of the student as a learner and to set new goals to reach the standards, educators need to integrate the three types of assessments appropriately.

Standards

Standards provide educators with guidelines for curriculum and teaching that ensure that students have access to the knowledge believed to be necessary for success later in life. Standards help educators focus on clear expectations for all students to achieve (Darling-Hammond & Falk, 1997). One of the most important results of the standards movement is the emphasis on establishing specific criteria for all student work. By determining the criteria for quality work, students know the expectations and the specific steps they need to take to meet those expectations.

Almost every state has implemented standards as a framework for teaching and learning. Most states have also developed mandatory high-stakes standardized tests (assessments *of* learning), which students take to determine if they have met the standards. Reeves (2004) contrasts the traditional, norm-referenced evaluation based on the bell curve with a model in which students compete against other students for their scores. In standards-based evaluation, the standards are fixed, but the norms move. Reeves describes the norm-based system as one in which students don't know how they did in a performance until it has been compared to the work of others (similar to a speech contest where you judge all contestants before announcing a winner). In a standards-based environment, on the other hand, students, teachers, and parents know immediately when success has been achieved.

> If success has not been achieved, then we need not wait for an external judgment to be rendered, but can immediately determine the difference between the student's performance and the expected standard, provide timely feedback, and within minutes give students additional opportunities to achieve success. (Reeves, pp. 110–111)

Checklists

When students demonstrate what they know through authentic performance, they create projects or perform tasks that correlate to life. Because feedback is essential, teachers provide criterion-based checklists to guide students through each step of the process. Nitko (2004) discusses the importance of *scaffolding*, or the degree of support, guidance, and direction teachers provide to students as they set out to complete a task. The amount of scaffolding determines how structured the task is. Less scaffolding means less structured; more scaffolding means more structured.

Checklists provide specific feedback to students to help them know the clear expectations for their assignment. Scaffolding is very important for group work so that students know their specific assignment. For example, fourth-grade teachers presenting a science unit on weather assigned four group projects to their classes. Group one had to create a commercial; group two had to present a skit; group three presented a song; and group four built a weather station. The vocabulary and content related to weather types, symbols, instruments, maps, and cycles were similar, but the method of presentation required different criteria.

Notice how the content standards could be different depending upon the assignment. All groups would also have different guidelines for organization or presentation. The commercial and skit would address criteria such as:

Presentation

- Did you present your ideas in a logical sequence?
- Did you have a clear focus?
- Did you use appropriate visuals like charts, diagrams, and illustrations?

Figure 2.7   Group Checklists for Weather Projects

Group 1: Commercial on Weather Symbols on Maps	Group 2: Skit on Water Cycle
Weather Symbols—Did you show symbols for . . . • high and low (barometric pressure)? • cold and warm fronts? • precipitation? • temperatures? • cloud cover?	Water Cycle—Does your skit include . . . • how water changes from one state to another? • how water freezes? • how ice melts? • the cycle of evaporation, condensation, and precipitation?
Group 3: Song About Types of Clouds	Group 4: Weather Station With Instruments
Types of Clouds—Did your song mention weather that comes from . . . • cumulus clouds? • cumulonimbus clouds? • cirrus clouds? • stratus clouds?	Weather Instruments—Does your weather station include a/an . . . • thermometer? • anemometer? • weather vane? • rain gauge? • barometer? • a method to measure snow? • a method to measure hail?

Created by Kristine Klein and Jenny Wenner, Westerville City Schools, Westerville, Ohio.

Communication

- Did you use appropriate language for your purpose?
- Did you speak clearly?
- Did you speak loudly enough for your audience to hear you?

All groups could have the same criteria for appropriate social skills in their group checklist.

Social Skills

- Did you perform your assigned roles?
- Did you stay on task?
- Did you encourage each other?
- Did you complete your part within the timeframe?
- Did you contribute to the group?
- Did you respect the opinions of others?

Figure 2.8 shows the checklist that each individual student will use when completing the coloring book for the weather unit. Each student knows the expectations for the project in advance, before attempting to demonstrate an understanding of the major objectives, standards, and indicators of the science unit.

Figure 2.8   Individual Student Checklist: Coloring Book

Standard: <u>Earth and Space Science/Weather</u>

Checklist: Individual Student Checklist: Coloring Book

Assessment: Create a Coloring Book about weather that includes the criteria in this checklist.

Criteria/Performance Indicators	Not Yet 0	Some Evidence 1
Research		
• Did you use at least three resources to gather your information?		
• Is your information accurate?		
• Is your information current?		
Content		
• Did you include information about five weather instruments and how they are used?		
• Did you include information about the water cycle, including evaporation, condensation, and precipitation?		
• Did you include information about weather map symbols and the weather they represent?		
• Did you include information about how water exists in air in different forms (clouds, fog, rain, snow, hail, etc.)?		
• Did you include information about the four types of cloud formations and when they develop?		
Organization/Style		
• Does your book have a title?		
• Does your book contain all six topics we have covered with our group work?		
• Is your book interesting to look at?		
• Is your book written in kid-friendly language?		
• Have you used graphs and illustrations to explain your information?		
Writing		
• Do you have a variety of sentence lengths?		
• Do your paragraphs have topic sentences and supporting sentences?		
• Have you reread your writing to be sure that it is clear?		
• Have you used descriptive words and details?		
• Have you proofread and made revisions to your work?		

(Continued)

Figure 2.8 (Continued)

Criteria/Performance Indicators	Not Yet 0	Some Evidence 1
Writing Mechanics		
• Did you spell your words correctly?		
• Did you capitalize words correctly?		
• Did you punctuate sentences correctly?		

Total Points

(21)

Student Comment:

> **Scale:**
>
> 19–21 (90%) = A
> 17–18 (80%) = B
> 15–16 (70%) = C
> _____
> 14 or below = Not Yet

Teacher Comment:

New Goal: **Final Grade:** _____

Student Signature: _____

Teacher Signature: _____

Parent Signature: _____

Created by Kristine Klein and Jenny Wenner, Westerville City Schools, Westerville, Ohio.

Rubrics

Even though checklists provide students with specific feedback on their task, they do not describe the level of quality expected. Rubrics are scoring guides that describe the performed behaviors that mark the comparative characteristics between different levels.

Teachers can develop the checklist into a more specific rubric or scoring guide that describes levels of quality with specific descriptors as to what constitutes a "1" in each criterion along a continuum to what constitutes a "4."

> Descriptions can be defined as a set of guidelines for distinguishing between performance or products of different quality. Rubrics should be composed of scaled descriptive levels of progress towards an end result, which is based on the stated content standards. (Solomon, 2002, p. 59)

Rubrics that contain the criteria for a performance or product and descriptors of what constitute quality or a grade help students perform better. Students who know what is required, who see the consistency of the grading system, and who perceive grading is objective feel better about their learning environment. One of the underlying causes of discipline problems involves students' feeling upset about grading procedures. When students say, "I didn't know what you wanted," "I didn't understand the assignment," or "You gave me a bad grade because you hate me!" the teacher likely was not clear about how assignments would be graded.

Rubrics should be correlated to performance tasks, standards, benchmarks, or goals, and they should be constructed so that students can self-evaluate and revise their work before the teacher evaluates the work. Students can assess their efforts and see what grade they will receive. Teachers should distribute the rubric prior to the assignment, so students know the expectations and requirements for each score.

The scoring rubric for a letter to the editor is more complex (see Figure 2.9). The criteria contain subheadings, and the scoring system is developed to show students and parents how the rubric scoring system translates to a traditional number or letter grade.

Implications for Classroom Management

Educators teaching in the classrooms of the twenty-first century need to address the areas in Figure 2.10 if they are to become successful classroom managers.

Classroom management does not exist in a vacuum. It is dependent upon many variables. The variables include the teacher's love of children and love of the profession, the climate of the school, the quality of the curriculum, the effectiveness of the instruction, and the performance-based assessments used to evaluate students' academic ability. If students perceive the standards as fair and consistent, if they feel that the teacher treats students fairly, and if they feel

Figure 2.9   Rubric for a Letter to the Editor

Task: Write a letter to the editor of your local paper persuading readers to take a stand on a controversial issue.

Goal/Standard: Compose well-organized and coherent writing for specific purposes and audiences.

Scoring / Criteria	1 *Rejected by Church Bulletin Committee*	2 *Published in High School Newspaper*	3 *Published in Local Newspaper*	4 *Published in The New York Times*	*Score*
Accuracy of Information	3 or more factual errors	2 factual errors	1 factual error	All information is accurate	___ × 5 ___ (20)
Persuasiveness • Arguments • Examples	• No logic • No examples	• Faulty logic • 1 example	• Logical arguments • 2 examples	• Logical and convincing arguments • 3 examples	___ × 5 ___ (20)
Organization • Topic Sentence • Support Sentences • Concluding Sentence	Missing 2 elements— fragmented	Missing 1 element— lacks coherence	Includes all organizational elements	Elements provide coherence and clarity	___ × 5 ___ (20)
Style • Grammar • Sentence Structure • Transitions	4 or more errors— (distracts from arguments)	2–3 errors— choppy style	1 error— style reinforces arguments	Fluid style that informs and convinces	___ × 5 ___ (20)
Mechanics • Capitalization • Punctuation • Spelling	4 or more errors	2–3 errors	1 error	100% accuracy	___ × 5 ___ (20)

Note: To change a rubric to a traditional grade that students can understand, use a scale to convert the points to a percentage or, as in this example, multiply each score to arrive at a percentage that can be converted to a letter or number grade.

Scale
A =
B =
C =
D =

Final Score: _____ (100)

Final Grade: _____

Figure 2.10 Effective Classroom Managment

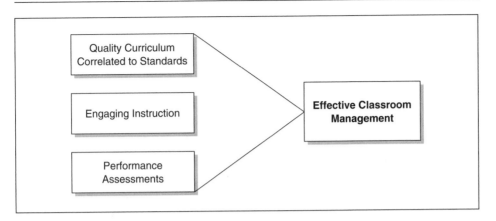

they know in advance what is required and how it will be scored, they are more likely to follow classroom procedures and less likely to "act out" to protest their frustrations about grading issues. Unfair or inconsistent grading practices hurt a student's self-esteem and self-concept and undermines the foundation of an effective classroom management system.

THE EMOTIONAL INTELLIGENCE

People with well-developed emotional skills are also more likely to be content and effective in their lives, mastering the habits of mind that foster their own productivity; people who cannot marshal some control over their emotional life fight inner battles that sabotage their ability for focused work and clear thought. (Goleman, 1995, p. 36)

The sheer volume of information related to the study of emotional intelligence provides the first clue to how important emotions are in the study of the brain. It is well documented that "emotions are the gatekeeper to the intellect" (Fogarty, 2002, p. 30).

Fogarty and Stoehr (1995) discuss five major components of the emotional intelligence. They include the following:

1. Self-awareness: Understanding one's own feelings, self-confidence, ability to put feelings into words

2. Self-regulation: Controlling impulsivity and emotions to enhance living, the ability to control or redirect disruptive impulses

3. Motivation: The ability to delay gratification and set goals and pursue them with zeal

4. Empathy: Reading others' feelings, caring, interacting with others and responding to their emotions

5. Social Skills: Influence, leadership, teamwork, interpersonal skills, the ability to read other peoples' verbal or nonverbal cues and respond appropriately (Fogarty & Stoehr, p. 49)

These components represent aspects of the positive emotional climate that teachers must foster in classrooms to unlock the gates of learning. Goleman's investigation of the emotional intelligence shows that IQ contributes, at best, about 20 percent to the factors that determine life success; 80 percent is left to everything else. He contends that a person's destiny in life depends on having the skills that make up emotional intelligence: self-awareness, self-regulation, motivation, empathy, and social skills (Robbins & Alvy, 2004).

For example, Goleman (as cited in O'Neil, 1996) explains that boys who are very impulsive and are always getting in trouble in second grade are six to eight times more likely than other kids to commit crimes and be violent in their teens. By the same token, sixth-grade girls who confuse their feelings of anxiety, anger, boredom, and hunger are the ones most likely to develop anorexia nervosa and bulimia when they become teenagers. These students' lack of awareness and sense of confusion about their feelings are skill deficits that cause trouble for them as they grow into adulthood. Teachers must address students' self-awareness and ability to self-regulate their emotions through a classroom management plan that teaches these life skills and helps students clarify and deal with their behavioral feelings.

The Marshmallow Test

The relationship between emotional intelligence and success is demonstrated by a study that involves the correlation between a person's impulsivity—inclination to act quickly or rashly—and the ability to delay gratification—sacrificing something a person wants now—in pursuit of a long-term goal. Goleman (1995) says there is perhaps no psychological skill more fundamental than resisting impulse. He describes the famous "marshmallow study" begun by psychologist Walter Mischel during the 1960s at a preschool on the Stanford University campus involving many children of the Stanford faculty, graduate students, and other employees. In the study, preschool kids were brought in one by one to a room and had a marshmallow put in front of them. The children were told they could either eat the marshmallow now, or they could have two marshmallows if they waited until the researcher returned. About one-third of them grabbed the single marshmallow within seconds of the experimenter's leaving the room on his "errand," while some waited a little longer, and about one-third were able to wait 15 or 20 minutes for the researcher to return. Goleman says that the four-year-olds who waited

> covered their eyes so they wouldn't have to stare at temptation, or rested their heads in their arms, talked to themselves, sang, played games with their hands and feet, even tried to go to sleep. These plucky preschoolers got the two-marshmallow reward. (p. 81)

The researchers tracked down the same children 14 years later and found that this test was an amazing predictor of children's success in school. The kids who had waited until the researcher returned to eat their marshmallow were more emotionally stable and better liked by their teachers and peers. Moreover, they were still able to delay immediate gratification to meet their goals. The ones who had grabbed the marshmallows immediately were emotionally unstable. These students experienced stress more often and were more irritable, more likely to pick fights, and not as well liked. The other interesting finding was that the students who had grabbed the marshmallows quickly had an average verbal score of 524 and average math score of 528 on the SAT, while the third who waited the longest had average scores of 610 and 652, respectively—a 210-point difference in total score (Goleman, 1995, p, 82).

Pool (1997) discusses some social consequences of being impulsive.

> For boys—three to six times more likely to be violent by the end of adolescence; for girls—three times more likely to get pregnant in adolescence; for kids who are chronically sad or anxious in elementary school—most likely to end up as a substance abuser in adolescence during periods of experimentation. (p. 13)

The State of Flow

After a superior performance, athletes often comment that they were in a "zone." The state they describe is called *flow*, a term coined by Mihaly Csikzentmihalyi (1990), the University of Chicago psychologist who collected such accounts of peak performance during two decades of research. Csikzentmihalyi discusses how people's perceptions about their lives are the result of many forces that shape experiences and cause people to feel good or bad. "On the rare occasions that it happens, we feel a sense of exhilaration, a deep sense of enjoyment that is long cherished and that becomes a landmark in memory for what life should be like" (p. 3). He calls this event an *optimal experience*. Flow is emotional intelligence at its best; it is the harnessing of emotions in the service of performance and learning. Students who get into a zone as they study do better—even exceeding their potential as measured by achievement tests. When they are in a "state of flow," students are absorbed in an engaging task that both challenges and exhilarates them and gives them a highly motivating feeling of pleasure (see Figure 2.11).

Figure 2.11   State of Flow

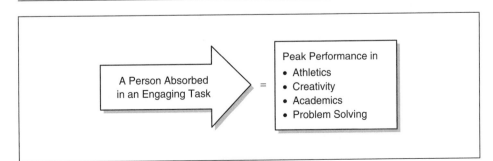

In one research study, students carried a beeper that signaled them at random times during the day to write down what they were doing and what their mood was. The study found that the low achievers spent only about 15 hours a week studying at home compared to the 27 hours a week of homework done by the high-achieving group. The low achievers spent most of their free time socializing by hanging out with family and friends (Goleman, 1995). Studying gave high achievers a pleasing, absorbing sense of flow about 40 percent of the time they spent on it. For low achievers, however, studying produced a sense of flow only about 16 percent of the time, and more often than not, studying yielded anxiety because the work was too challenging.

Students who achieve up to their level of academic potential are drawn to studying and school because studying puts them into a state of flow, and they derive true pleasure from the sense of accomplishment they get from it. Students who are underachievers, however, are often bored or frustrated with school because they do not derive pleasure or a sense of accomplishment or fulfillment from doing schoolwork. Moreover, the less fulfilling students find their schoolwork to be, the less work they do. The less work they do, the lower their grades. Thus, the cycle of not liking schoolwork, not doing schoolwork, and failing at schoolwork continues. Unfortunately, the high school dropout rate attests to the fact that as students are introduced to more content and, in most cases, more traditional lecture-type approaches to learning, many of them come to dislike schoolwork and school even more.

People experience flow when they become absorbed in doing something challenging.

> We remain aware of the goals of the task and of the feedback generated by our responses to it, but we concentrate on the task itself without thinking about successes or failure, reward or punishment, or other personal or social agendas. (Brophy, 2004, p. 11)

Students may also forget about the ultimate reward—grades. Grades will still be on their minds, but their focus becomes the learning, not the report card.

The challenge for teachers in today's diverse and inclusive classrooms is to select curriculum, assessments, and methodologies that are not so slow moving as to bore students and not so fast moving as to frustrate students. Finding the correct zone of teaching is very complicated and challenging in today's inclusive classrooms. The more diverse the students, the more difficult it is to achieve optimal learning flow for all children.

Implications for Classroom Management

Educators can implement the research on emotional intelligence by using some of the following strategies to establish a positive climate for learning:

- Help students become aware of themselves by developing positive self-concepts.
- Encourage students to self-regulate their behavior by planning, monitoring, and evaluating their own actions.

- Motivate students by challenging them with stimulating lessons that help them achieve a sense of flow, bringing satisfaction and enjoyment.
- Teach explicit social skills so students develop leadership abilities and skills in team building and conflict resolution.
- Model empathetic behavior by encouraging caring, understanding, compassion, and sympathy among students.
- Ease anxiety about tests or performances so students can use their "working brain" to retrieve information rather than to worry about failing.

The research on emotional intelligence indicates that students who are well-rounded, enjoy school and work, interact and empathize with other people, and can set and meet goals are more motivated to succeed. They also are better able to achieve personal, social, and academic success for themselves as well as contribute more to society. Many of the occurrences of school violence attest to the importance of students' achieving a sense of balance in their lives. Several of the students involved in school shootings were academically successful, but they lacked the ability to self-regulate their emotions, interact socially with their peer group, and empathize with others.

The emphasis on standards and test scores needs to be balanced by an emphasis on becoming a "whole child" and an educated citizen who respects oneself and others, who knows how to resolve conflicts through discussion rather than weapons. The social and emotional learning skills that Goleman calls the emotional intelligence help students and adults develop the necessary skills, attitudes, and values to manage life's tasks successfully. It takes an entire school to promote the social skills and values students need to acquire. The principal, teachers, custodians, bus drivers, lunchroom workers, and security personnel all must model the same courtesy, politeness, concern, and fairness expected of the students. People learn as much or more from example than from any other means, and if students' role models practice good citizenship, hopefully, students will emulate their behaviors.

COOPERATIVE LEARNING

The cooperative learning model is one of the most successful methods teachers can use to allow students to interact and learn with peers. It encompasses both brain-compatible learning theory and the emotional intelligence theory. Research shows that innovative changes in education should include the cooperative learning educational model. This model incorporates teamwork, higher-order thinking, social skills, leadership roles, and active learning in the classroom. The research of Slavin (1983), Johnson and Johnson (1986), Bellanca and Fogarty (2003), Sharon and Sharon (1996), and others has encouraged teachers to meet the challenges of teaching all students. Marzano, Marzano, and Pickering (2003) reviewed research that indicates that "cooperative learning groups have a positive impact on student achievement, interpersonal relationships, and attitudes about learning" (p. 23).

Cooperative learning helps teachers make learning more meaningful and motivating; it also encourages students to become interactive learners and to develop the social skills necessary for life. A caring and cooperative classroom, however, does not necessarily eliminate the traditional types of behavior problems.

Except for those who live in deepest poverty, the psychological needs—love, power, freedom, and fun—take precedence over the survival needs, which most people are able to satisfy. People search for ways to satisfy their needs for love, belonging, caring, sharing, and cooperation all their lives. If students feel no sense of having caring and concern expressed toward them, they will pay little attention to academic subjects. Instead, they will engage in a desperate search for friendship, for acceptance. This type of student may become a behavioral problem in the hope of attracting attention (Glasser as cited in Gough, 1987).

The importance of establishing a caring, cooperative classroom is that it provides students with the acceptance they so desperately need. Educators who have not had extensive training in cooperative learning sometimes avoid group work because they feel students are too loud and don't accomplish anything. And teachers may revert to traditional teaching methods, where students sit in rows and listen to the teacher lecture, to maintain classroom order.

Bellanca (1991) sees the establishment of a caring classroom as a significant teaching challenge because of several problems. The first problem involves the "put-down" and the competitive culture of most schools. He feels it takes time to change students' attitudes because they are immersed in the negativity they hear on television and hear from their peers. Another problem is finding the time to teach the social skills explicitly in the already overcrowded curriculum. Teachers might feel that teaching cooperation is not as important as drilling equations, but cooperation is a life skill that transcends algebra and geometry. Reider (2005) says that students who work successfully in small groups show an increase in retention of knowledge, racial tolerance, leadership skills, creativity, self-esteem, and positive peer relationships.

Group Work Versus Cooperative Learning

"Group work" is different from "cooperative learning." Group work could be as basic as assigning students randomly to a group and giving them an assignment or a task to complete. The cooperative learning model described by most researchers, however, is much more structured. It involves role assignments, timeframes, interdependency, processing, celebrating, and accountability. It also requires teachers to spend more time teaching basic social skills, communication skills, team-building skills, and conflict resolution techniques. Chapters 3 and 4 provide specific guidelines for doing this. Although cooperative learning is an effective teaching strategy that motivates students to learn and reduces overall discipline problems, it is not a panacea for classroom management. The same types of discipline problems that plague teachers in the direct instruction model will still exist—in fact, they can become more critical because one or two disruptive students cause entire groups to become dysfunctional.

Implications for Classroom Management

Educators can implement the extensive research in cooperative learning by using some of the following strategies to help students interact positively with each other:

- Teach, rehearse, and reinforce the social skills students are expected to demonstrate.
- Design cooperative tasks that require all students to participate.
- Create tasks that require all students to solve problems and integrate knowledge.
- Review and rehearse role assignments so students know how to lead, how to follow, and how to follow directions.
- Monitor interactions among group members.
- Reteach social skills as needed.
- Introduce problem-solving strategies so students can resolve their group conflicts.

Cooperative learning should not be used for all lessons. Moreover, it can be a disaster if students are not trained to handle the responsibility of taking control of their own learning. Effective teachers spend several weeks teaching and reteaching social skills and group dynamics before they assign their first cooperative task. Proactive teachers lay the groundwork for productive cooperative group work.

The educational theories discussed in this chapter as well as many additional educational theories do not work with all students in all situations. Educators need to examine the theories related to brain-compatible classrooms, the multiple intelligences, differentiated learning, performance assessment, the emotional intelligence, and cooperative learning. It is important to experiment with the different strategies to arrive at the right mix that is appropriate to challenge, motivate, and inspire all students to achieve not only academic excellence but also personal fulfillment.

Setting a Positive Classroom Climate for Learning **3**

Figure 3.0 Classroom Climate Thinking-at-Right Angles Graphic Organizer

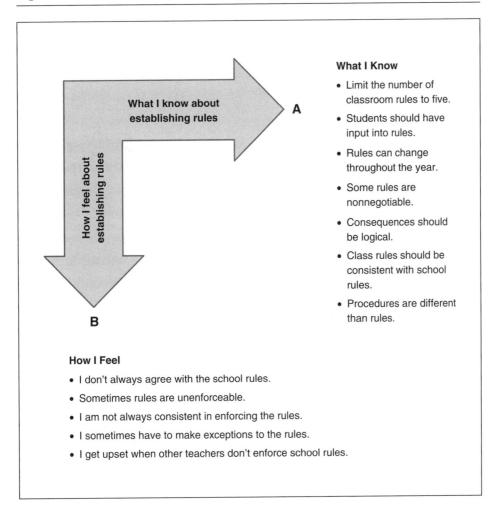

What I Know

- Limit the number of classroom rules to five.
- Students should have input into rules.
- Rules can change throughout the year.
- Some rules are nonnegotiable.
- Consequences should be logical.
- Class rules should be consistent with school rules.
- Procedures are different than rules.

How I Feel

- I don't always agree with the school rules.
- Sometimes rules are unenforceable.
- I am not always consistent in enforcing the rules.
- I sometimes have to make exceptions to the rules.
- I get upset when other teachers don't enforce school rules.

CLASSROOM CLIMATE

> *Every teacher understands the importance of promoting and maintaining a positive classroom atmosphere. Each school is a microcosm of our society with its positives and negatives, and the importance of creating cohesiveness through respect, honesty, kindness, and courtesy among our students shouldn't be minimized.* (Lindberg, Kelley, & Swick, 2005, p. 13)

A growing body of research confirms the benefits of building a sense of community in school. Schools need to cultivate respectful, supportive relationships among students, teachers, and parents. Schaps (2003) says, "Supportive relationships are the heart of community. They enable students from diverse backgrounds to bring their personal thoughts, feelings, and experiences into the classroom" (p. 32).

The climate of a classroom refers to the type of environment students are exposed to when they are learning. A person can get a "feel" for a classroom community and a school community by walking in the halls, getting a view of the surroundings, and seeing how people treat one another. The climate of a school is often difficult to define, but it has a tremendous influence on learning.

Freiberg (1998) believes that school climate is an ever-changing factor in the lives of the students and teachers and states that "much like the air we breathe, school climate is ignored until it becomes foul" (p. 22). The school climate can either enhance learning or serve as a barrier to learning. Schools that mandate attendance at all-school functions, lack choice in curriculum, emphasize high-stakes testing and evaluation, and impose a litany of "not" rules ("students shall not chew gum") created and enforced by the faculty and staff isolate and separate the faculty from the students.

An unsafe school climate that exposes students to bullying, drugs, physical violence, name calling, and psychological stress not only diminishes social and academic interactions but also exposes students to negative behavior patterns. Armstrong (2006) believes that a safe school climate is the most important factor in meeting the needs of young adolescents in a school. He reiterates Abraham Maslow's warnings that if people are struggling to meet their basic physiological and safety needs, they have "no energy left for meeting their higher needs of love, belonging, esteem, and self-actualization" (p. 122).

In describing the climate of a classroom, educators should begin with a vision of what the classroom ought to be like. Kohn (1996) talks about the idea of climate as "one that promotes deep understanding, excitement about learning, and social as well intellectual growth" (p. 54). Kohn believes students need to play an active role in the decision-making process, teachers need to work with students to structure the curriculum to meet their needs and interests, and the environment needs to support children's desires to discover new ideas and their love of learning. A classroom where the teacher depends upon compliance from the students and uses a lockstep system of rewards and punishment to ensure their compliance does not foster an environment conducive to learning. Students need to construct knowledge for themselves and feel empowered to help make some decisions about their classroom environment and their own learning.

The word *discipline* is derived from the Latin root *disciplina,* and it means learning. Therefore, discipline should be associated with positive acts of student learning rather than negative acts of punishing.

Charney (2002) says that teaching discipline requires two fundamental elements: empathy and structure.

> Empathy helps us "know" the child, to perceive his or her needs, to hear what he or she is trying to say. Structure allows us to set guidelines and provide necessary limits. Effective, caring discipline requires both empathy and structure. (p. 19)

Classroom Management

Freiberg (1999) discusses the role that behaviorist learning theory has played in classroom management. He says that the most common approach to classroom management in many schools is some form of behavior modification. The key ingredients of most teachers' discipline routines include "rules, consequences, and rewards," which have their roots in classical conditioning theory as described by Pavlov and operant conditioning as described by B. F. Skinner. Operant conditioning is the reinforcement of behavior (candy, tokens, stars) and its relationship to specific consequences. This conditioning takes place when teachers try to stop a particular response by the student with a specific action. Teachers engaging in this conditioning use a contingency plan or action that is repeated to reinforce or shape a particular response by the student. Not all psychological lessons learned from rats and pigeons in the laboratory, however, translate well to the classroom.

Freiberg (1999) says that even though cognitive learning theory, which focused on why people behave and think in certain ways, began to replace behaviorist learning theory in the 1970s, behaviorism began to flourish in the American classroom in the 1960s and 1970s. Commercial programs, such as Assertive Discipline, focused on controlling student behaviors by using punishments (name on the board, removal of privileges) and rewards (stars, tokens, extra recess). In one study, researchers Emmer and Aussiker (as cited in Freiberg, 1999) demonstrated that student attitudes toward school were *lower* in the Assertive Discipline school. Freiberg concludes that, "Discipline programs that are highly behavioristic and focus on controlling student behaviors through punishment can diminish student self-discipline" (p. 8).

On the other hand, school programs that emphasize student self-discipline (the responsibility model), rather than external controlling factors (the obedience model) (see Figure 3.1), show greater promise in improving achievement and learning environments (Gottfredson, Gottfredson, & Hybl as cited in Freiberg, 1999). Schools that improve the academic achievement of their students not only emphasize academics but also emphasize an open learning environment and a healthy school climate (Hoy, Tarter, & Kottkamp as cited in Freiberg, 1999).

Figure 3.1   Obedience Model Versus Responsibility Model

Obedience Model	Responsibility Model
• External control • Fear of getting caught • Authority figures	• Internal control • Desire to do the right thing • Self-discipline

Sources of Power

The recent shift in classroom management from a focus on the obedience model, where the teacher is the authority figure, to the responsibility model, where students take ownership of their behavior, has shifted the power base in the classroom. Larrivee (1999) discusses how traditional classroom management focuses on controlling student behavior, keeping students on task, and maintaining lesson flow. The teacher in this situation must maintain constant watch on all students and be ready to intervene at any moment to thwart the misbehaving student. Sometimes the emphasis on "vigilance" may take precedence over teaching and learning in the attempt to maintain order at all costs.

Larrivee (1999) says the students' misbehavior is deemed to be inappropriate "irrespective of consideration of individual student characteristics, performance expectations, or appropriateness of the learning task" (p. 261). She says that teachers assume the students are either unwilling or unable to solve their own problems or exercise any self-control. Therefore, teachers tend to use their power to exercise full control of the situation. Sometimes, it is easier to blame the students for "acting out" than to admit the lesson was boring, the directions were confusing, the curriculum wasn't relevant, or everyone had to do the same thing regardless of their ability levels or academic needs.

Rather than exercise authoritarian control over the classroom, teachers can foster a democratic learning community that allows both the teacher and the students to "share" the power base. When students become a part of the process of establishing classroom procedures, they feel respected and more inclined to voice their complaints by communicating with the teacher and their fellow students, rather than disrupting the class because they feel their ideas have been ignored.

Figure 3.2   Shared Classroom Power Base

Teacher	Students
• Explains the rationale for the classroom procedure. • Asks for student input about the procedure. • Shares the classroom procedures that are "nonnegotiable" because of school policies. • Allows students to vote on the "negotiable" procedures.	• Discuss the procedure and ask questions. • Provide alternative options for consideration. • Discuss the process for changing school policy through appropriate channels (e.g., the student council). • Asks about "revisiting" the vote later if the procedure does not seem fair.

Figure 3.2 shows ways that teacher and students can share the classroom power base when they work together to establish the procedures needed to operate their classroom successfully.

GETTING STARTED

Scenario

"I feel it is very important that we always walk in the halls and enter the room slowly. Why do you think that procedure is important?" asks Mrs. Saunders.

"I saw a boy get hurt once when another boy was rushing into the room and knocked him into the doorknob real hard," Mary replies.

"I don't like getting shoved by someone who is afraid of being late," adds John.

"So, you think we should all be courteous and enter the room walking rather than running or shoving?" Mrs. Saunders asks.

"Yes," says the class.

"All right, let's practice how we should all enter the room. Everyone file out quietly and stand by the drinking fountain down the hall. When I give the signal, you will all walk towards our classroom and enter the room the way we discussed."

Students rehearse entering the classroom and taking their seat.

"I really liked the way you took turns entering the room and going to your desks. Now, what do you think would be a consequence if someone forgot our procedure and ran into someone while running into the room?"

"I think that person should have to go back and practice walking into the room again just like we practiced today," says Juan.

"He should also have to apologize to whoever he ran into 'cause no one likes to be pushed," Jack adds.

"Okay," says Mrs. Saunders, "I think we all agree on the importance of this procedure. We'll add this to our list of classroom procedures and consequences."

Setting Up the Classroom

Very few students function well in a chaotic environment. Even though students may pretend to enjoy having the freedom to do whatever they want, whenever they want, most of them prefer structures or routines so they know exactly what they are supposed to do. Structure can be implemented through the arrangement of the classroom as well as through classroom procedures.

Room Arrangement

Before students walk into class on the first day of school, teachers should arrange the classroom to permit orderly movement, make efficient use of the available space, and keep potential disruptions to a minimum. This provides not only the students but also the teacher with an efficient and well-organized area for learning to take place.

Emmer, Evertson, Clements, and Worsham (1997) suggest that teachers consider the following four guidelines:

1. Keep high-traffic areas free of congestion.

2. Be sure all students can be easily seen by the teacher.

3. Keep frequently used materials and teaching supplies readily accessible.

4. Be certain students can easily see whole-class presentations and displays. (pp. 4–5)

Figure 3.3 shows one possible configuration of a room in which students sit in cooperative groups and everyone has a clear view of the teacher, blackboard, and screen.

Figure 3.3   Room Arrangement

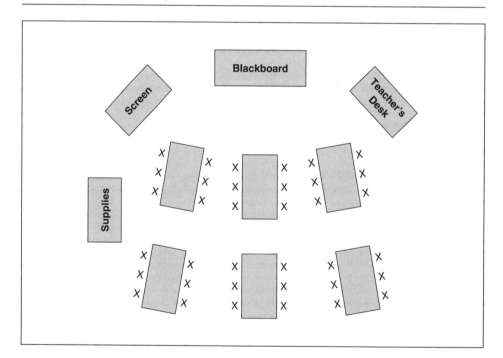

Procedures

Teachers create plans to organize open-ended cooperative activities that allow students lots of options and choices while still providing them with structure. However, students need to walk before they can run, and it is essential that they know their boundaries the first week of class. Teachers should prepare a tentative list of procedures necessary for establishing the routines essential for classroom organization; however, the entire class should discuss the rationale for the procedures and have some input into their final adoption.

The most effective way for teachers to handle discipline problems is to prevent them. The proactive teacher anticipates potential management problems and establishes a positive classroom environment, where students feel secure because they know what is expected of them. Researchers who have studied classroom management offer teachers the following tips:

- Proactive teachers help prevent discipline problems.
- Students who are actively involved in the lessons cause fewer behavior problems.
- Teachers who use instructional time efficiently have fewer management problems.

Good classroom management is primarily *prevention* (not intervention), *planning* before the year begins, *implementing* on the first day of school, and *maintaining* consistently throughout the year.

Procedures usually apply to a specific activity, and they help accomplish something. Evertson, Emmer, and Worsham (2000) believe teachers cannot communicate their expectations adequately just by telling students about the procedures. They believe they have to be taught explicitly by the following steps:

1. Describe and demonstrate the desired behavior.

2. Rehearse the desired behavior.

3. Provide feedback to individual students or the whole class.
   (pp. 56–57)

Classroom procedures will vary depending upon the age of the students and the subject area. Some classes, like art, science, music, band, physical education, and vocational education may have specific procedures related to safety and equipment. Other, more traditional classrooms may focus on supplies and textbooks. All classes, however, need to create procedures dealing with routines such as getting the teacher's attention, catching up on missed work, handing in work, and entering and leaving the classroom.

Procedures for Early Childhood. The fact that many students arrive at school with a sense of learned helplessness does not mean they can't learn to take care of themselves. Diffily and Sassman (2004) say that "when parents or caregivers attend to a child's every need, the child learns over time that adults are the ones who are supposed to solve problems. They just do not see themselves as capable" (p. 59). It is important to introduce classroom routines, teach the routines by modeling them, and practice the routines during the first few weeks of school to make sure everyone knows the expectations. Be prepared to revisit these routines throughout the year, because students need constant reinforcement. Figure 3.4 lists some typical routines necessary to help younger students learn how to function in the early grades.

Figure 3.4   Suggested K–2 Procedures

1. Use of locker during class
2. Use of backpacks and book bags
3. Daily and take-home folder
4. Going to the bathroom during class
5. Reading with a partner
6. Working in a small group
7. Putting work where it belongs
8. Eating snacks during class
9. Cleaning up after activities
10. Getting ready to go home

Procedures for Elementary Students. Beginning teachers find it overwhelming to think of all the procedures necessary to help students navigate the complexities of elementary school. Evertson et al. (2000) warn teachers about taking the time to introduce, teach, rehearse, and provide feedback on all classroom procedures. They say, "Don't hurry through it, even though some of the items may appear trivial. These bits and pieces will combine to form the mosaic of your management system" (p. 25). See Figure 3.5.

Figure 3.5   Suggested Elementary Procedures

1. Arrival in class (tardy policy)
2. Distribution of books and materials
3. Administration forms (absentee slips)
4. Getting the teacher's attention
5. Moving in and out of groups
6. Turning in homework (late work)
7. Leaving the room (restrooms, media center)
8. Use of cell phones, pagers, iPods
9. Use of supplies and equipment
10. Interruptions (intercom, fire drill)

Procedures for Secondary Students. One would think that by the time adolescents entered middle school and high school, they would have internalized all the classroom and school procedures from elementary school and would "fall into" the same routines. Unfortunately, not all teachers focus on procedures, and students may have to learn some for the first time or spend some time reviewing and revisiting others. In addition, secondary students have the additional challenge of changing classes every period, getting the appropriate books and supplies from their messy lockers, showering and getting dressed after PE class, socializing with their friends, and of course, checking their text messages—all in three minutes! Many schools now provide more time between classes and a "bell-less" school, where classes change at different times, but the pressure is on today's teenagers to maintain their "cool" and still get to class on time.

Lindberg et al. (2005) devote a chapter of *Common-sense Classroom Management for Middle and High School Teachers* to "Taking Care of Classroom Business," where they discuss developing the "meat and potatoes" of establishing a classroom management system (Figure 3.6).

Figure 3.6 Suggested Secondary Procedures

1. Seating charts and attendance (taking roll, collecting admits)
2. Dealing with tardy students
3. Handling students who are unprepared (who must return to their locker to get their work)
4. Handling students who don't have supplies (textbooks, handouts, pen, paper)
5. Dealing with homework and makeup work
6. Dealing with gum, candy, electronic devices (iPods, cell phones, pagers)
7. Procedures for leaving the classroom (counselor, restroom, office)
8. Procedures for getting into groups and working in groups
9. Interruptions (intercom, notes from the office)
10. Use of supplies, computers, lab equipment

Adapted from *Common-Sense Classroom Management for Middle and High School Teachers*, by Lindberg et al. (2005). Thousand Oaks, CA: Corwin Press, www.corwinpress.com.

Many of the procedures mentioned relate to whole-class activities. Teachers know, however, that special attention needs to be given to helping students act appropriately when they are engaged in a specific activity. Belvel and Jordan (2003) suggest some questions teachers should address when formulating procedures for students to follow when they engage in activities (Figure 3.7).

Each teacher needs to determine the procedures that will be needed to operate the classroom efficiently. Figure 3.8 asks teachers to check the procedures needed as well as list additional procedures for special events, like field trips and assemblies.

Figure 3.7 Questions to Address When Formulating Activity Procedures

1. How do you want the students to work?
    - Together?
    - Individually?
2. How do you want them to communicate?
    - Silently?
    - Using a "library voice"?
    - Using a "two-finger voice"/"2-inch voice"/"6-inch voice" (all terms to describe how far sound should travel from mouth)?
    - Should they talk one at a time?
    - Should they call out?
    - Do you want them to brainstorm?
3. How do you want them to solicit help?
    - Raise their hand?
    - Write their name on the board?
    - Use a signal card?
4. Where do you want them to sit?
    - At their desk?
    - In a particular area?
    - At a table?
    - Is moving around okay?
5. What should they do when they are finished?
    - Select an activity?
    - Begin the next task?
    - Read silently?
6. How will they be using time?
    - Will they be under time constraints?
    - How many minutes will they have?
7. What materials will they use and how?

Adapted from *Rethinking Classroom Management: Strategies for Preventive Intervention and Problem Solving* (2003) by Patricia Sequeira Belvel and Maya Marcia Jordan. Thousand Oaks, CA: Corwin Press, www.corwinpress.com.

Figure 3.8   Classroom Procedures—Do Students Know
              What Is Expected of Them for Routine Operations?

Assignment #1

Directions: Review the following procedures and check the ones your students will need to know and practice.

A. Beginning the Class?

❑ How should students enter the room?

❑ What constitutes being late (in the room, in the seat)?

❑ How and when will absentee slips be handled?

❑ What type of seating arrangements will be used (assigned seats, open seating, cooperative group seating)?

❑ How will the teacher get students' attention to start class (the tardy bell, a signal such as a raised hand or lights turned off and on)?

❑ How will students behave during public address (PA) announcements?

B. Classroom Management

❑ How and when will students leave their seats?

❑ What do students need to leave the room (individual passes, room pass, teacher's permission)?

❑ How will students get help from the teacher (raise hand, put name on board, ask other group members first)?

❑ What are acceptable noise levels for discussion, group work, seat work?

❑ How should students work with other students or move into cooperative groups (moving desks, changing seats, noise level, handling materials)?

❑ How will students get recognized to talk (raise hand, teacher calls on student, talk out)?

❑ How do students behave during presentations by other students?

❑ How do students get supplies they are missing?

❑ How and when do students sharpen pencils?

❑ How will students get materials or use special equipment?

C. Paperwork

❑ How will students turn in work (put in specific tray or box, pass to the front, one student collects)?

❑ How will students turn in makeup work if they were absent (special tray, give to teacher, put in folder, give to teacher's aide)?

❑ How will students distribute handouts (first person in row, a group member gets a copy for all group members, students pick up as they enter room)

(Continued)

Figure 3.8 (Continued)

❑ How will late work be graded (no penalty, minus points, zero, F, use lunch or recess to finish, turn in by end of day, drop so many homework grades)?

❑ How and when will students make up quizzes and tests missed (same day they return to school, within 24 hours, within the week, before school, during lunch or recess, after school)?

❑ How will late projects, such as research papers, portfolios, and artwork, be graded (no penalty, minus points, lowered letter grade, no late work accepted)?

D. Dismissal From Class or School?

❑ How are students dismissed for lunch?

❑ When do students leave class for the day (when bell rings, when teacher gives the signal)?

❑ Can students stay after class to finish assignments, projects, tests?

❑ Can the teacher keep one student or the whole class after class or school?

❑ What do students do during fire and disaster drills?

E. Syllabus or Course Outline?

❑ How are students made aware of course objectives?

❑ How are students made aware of course requirements?

❑ Are students given due dates for major assignments several weeks in advance?

❑ Are students told how they will be evaluated and given the grading scale?

F. Other Procedures

You may need to introduce procedures related to recess, assemblies, guest speakers, substitute teachers, field trips, fire drills, teacher leaving the room, etc. List other procedures that are needed.

_____

_____

_____

_____

_____

_____

_____

_____

_____

_____

WHO MAKES THE RULES?

Scenario

"Okay class," begins Mrs. Baker. *"I see that one of the rules on our web is 'Students should respect the opinions of others.' Let's talk about that rule before we vote on it."*

"I don't like that rule," Mary offers. *"What if I disagree with their opinion?"*

"Yeah," Sam agrees. *"I can't just sit here and ignore a dumb comment."*

"All right, Mary and Sam have some legitimate concerns about the rule. Let's role-play a situation and see if we can get a handle on this problem. I'll start talking about the Middle Ages, and we'll see how you express opinions."

"One of the major problems confronting the people in the Middle Ages was the bubonic plague. Researchers estimate that as many as one-third of the population of Europe died because of the plague. One interesting thing about . . . "

"Is that like AIDS today?" Jimmy interrupts.

"Didn't rats spread the plague?" wonders Susan.

"That's stupid," says John.

Mrs. Baker pauses and calmly responds, *"Yes, Jimmy, the plague compares to AIDS, and yes, Susan, the plague was spread by fleas on rats. We'll be talking about that more tomorrow."*

Mary says, *"I think I understand why we need to raise our hands to speak. When people blurt things out, we get off track. Also, it's rude to interrupt our teacher in the middle of her sentence. And it is disrespectful to say someone's idea is stupid."*

"I'm glad you can see how easy it is to get off track when somebody talks in the middle of my idea," says Mrs. Baker. *"And you see how people will get upset if we make fun of their ideas."*

"Let's take a vote. All those in favor of passing the rule to raise our hands to get recognized and respect the opinions of others? All opposed?"

"Great, 32 in favor; 3 opposed. By virtue of this class meeting, we hereby pass Rule #1. Elsa, please write 'Respect the opinions of others,' on our web of rules on the wall."

Discussing Classroom Rules

If classroom procedures form the framework for a classroom climate conducive to students' and teachers' working together cooperatively, the classroom rules form the heart and soul of caring, cooperative classrooms. If students are going to "buy into" the system, they must be part of the rule-making process. Classroom rules that are fair, reasonable, and enforceable play an important role in creating and maintaining a positive learning environment.

Terminology

Jones and Jones (1998) have some concerns about using the term *rules.* They believe the term suggests compliance to classroom management.

Therefore, they suggest instead using terms such as *behavioral standards, norms, expectations,* or *principles* to "describe the agreements teachers and students make regarding the types of behaviors that help a classroom be a safe community of support" (p. 241).

DiGiulio (2000) talks about the "limits" and "courtesies" of basic understandings, He believes that limits are boundaries that keep people from doing inappropriate things and courtesies are what we do and say. "Courtesies are how we treat others. Courtesies are how we show empathy—that we recognize that other people have feelings and sensibilities" (p. 25).

Lickona (2004) talks about teachers who propose character virtues, such as responsibility for one's own work, self-control and willpower, giving their best effort, and perseverance. Students who learn and practice these virtues can attain moral development as well as intellectual development. Regardless of the terminology used, the key to classroom management focuses on developing and adhering to classroom rules.

Guidelines

According to Kohn (1991),

an immense body of research has shown that children are more likely to follow a rule if its rationale has been explained to them. . . . Discipline based on reason is more effective than the totalitarian approach captured by the T-shirt slogan "Because I'm the Mommy, that's why." (p. 502)

Curwin and Mendler (1988) feel that effective rules describe specific behavior. They also believe that effective rules should be built on characteristics such as honesty, courtesy, helpfulness, and the like. Evertson and Harris (1991, p. 2) offer eight characteristics of classroom rules:

1. Consistent with school rules

2. Understandable

3. Doable (students able to comply)

4. Manageable

5. Always applicable (consistent)

6. Stated positively

7. Stated behaviorally

8. Consistent with teacher's own philosophy of how students learn best

Clearly stated rules that describe specific behavior enable students to understand what is expected of them. However, if rules are too specific, too many rules will be needed. Here is an example:

Too general: "Students shouldn't bother other students."

Too specific: "Students should not grab, push, shove, or trip other students."

Better rule: "It is best that students keep their hands off other people."

Other rules that could be developed include the following:

- Respect other people's property.
- Listen and be polite to other people.
- Raise your hand to be recognized.
- Obey all school rules.
- Participate in your own learning.
- Strive for excellence.
- Create quality work.
- Respect the classroom environment.
- Respect the ideas and customs of others.
- Empathize with the feelings of others.

A set of five rules should be sufficient to cover most classroom behaviors, but teachers may need to add a new rule to cover a situation not already mentioned. It is imperative that students get an opportunity to discuss the proposed classroom rules and understand the rationale behind the rules. A class meeting is the perfect opportunity to have a frank discussion of the rules, role-play situations, and come to a class consensus about the rules the students and teacher will adopt to ensure a positive and organized classroom environment. (For further discussion of an all-class meeting, see the Epilogue.)

It is important to note that some rules are nonnegotiable. Students must understand that the school district or the school sets down some rules that are not subject to a vote. Rules related to fighting, damage to property, injury to self or others, and weapons are absolute, because they set parameters for all students to ensure their health and safety. It is important that teachers review school rules and the discipline policies with all students the first day of class.

DiGiulio (2000) provides a "starter list" of four basic understandings appropriate at any level:

1. Respect is nonnegotiable.

2. Cooperation over competition

3. Achievement is valued.

4. Full inclusion is practiced.

He explains the importance of each and gives specific examples. Some guidelines are too abstract for students, so it might be necessary to list specific behaviors in a checklist so students can self-assess their own responsible behaviors. Figure 3.9 shows an example of a self-assessment checklist teachers can give students.

Figure 3.9   Students' Responsible Behavior Self-Assessment Checklist

Directions to Students: Self-assess your progress in developing these behaviors and responsibility traits in the classroom, at home, and at work.	**Not Yet** 0	**Some Evidence** 1
Quality Work		
• I always check my work before I submit it.		
• I complete several drafts of all major assignments.		
• I strive for excellence in all I do.		
Self-Discipline		
• I try to cool down *before* I speak if I am angry.		
• I finish my homework *before* I watch TV at night.		
• I study for tests *before* I go out after school.		
Flexibility		
• I adjust my social life to accommodate my schoolwork.		
• I don't get upset if my teacher changes an assignment.		
• I don't insist on getting my way in *all* our group work.		
Compassion		
• I will invite new students to eat lunch at our table.		
• I will help other students understand confusing schoolwork.		
• I will volunteer for charity events or do service learning.		
Character		
• I will state my honest opinions in class discussions.		
• I won't go along with the crowd just to be popular.		
• I will try to see both sides of an argument.		

Grading Scale:

13–15 = I am a role model.

11–12 = I am on track to be a role model.

 9–10 = I need to set some goals.

8 or Below = I need to try harder to improve.

Total Points: [   ]

(out of 15)

Consequences

Establishing rules and principles sets the stage for a classroom climate that invites the teacher and students to become a community of learners. However, even though the rules have been introduced, discussed, or voted upon doesn't mean they will be followed. If students violate the rules, they must assume responsibility and make amends for their inappropriate behavior. Gootman (2001, pp. 122–123) discusses four categories of consequences:

1. **Restoration or restitution**—Students have to fix or replace property or clean up something they did (clean off a desk, cafeteria table, etc.).

2. **Composure**—When students get out of control, they go to a time-out area to restore their composure.

3. **Restriction**—When students abuse a privilege, like time at the computer, they are not allowed to use the computer for some time.

4. **Reflection**—The student is asked to reflect on the problem and figure out how to prevent it from occurring again.

Logical Consequences. *Consequences* should relate directly to the rule violation and seem more logical and fair than *punishments*. For example, if a student draws pictures on a desk, the logical consequence would be to have the student stay in during recess or after class and clean off the desk. A punishment, on the other hand, would be to send the student to the office or forbid the student to use the computer. The desk would still be dirty, and the student would feel the punishment is unjust because of being forced to miss class time (sitting in the office) or being unable to finish the research paper without the computer.

Gootman (2001, p. 123) offers three questions that are helpful to teachers when choosing a consequence:

1. Does it make sense? Does it logically follow from what the student did? Is it related to the misbehavior?

2. Does it make the student accountable for the misbehavior? Is the student responsible for correcting any damage or harm caused by the misbehavior? Does it make the situation a learning situation?

3. Above all, does it keep the child's and my dignity intact?

Curwin and Mendler (1988) believe that consequences work best when they

- are clear and specific; and
- have a range of alternatives:
  - Reminder
  - Second reminder (kids forget)

- o Warning
- o Conference with student
- o Conference with parent
- o Conference with parent and administrator

They believe the consequences should be natural and/or logical and they should not be punishments. They feel that if students are only motivated by a reward-and-punishment system, they will only behave out of sense of social responsibility. Glasser (1990) warned that students will not be coerced into doing anything.

Figure 3.10 shows how one high school special education teacher created her classroom expectations and consequences, reviewed it with her students, and had them sign the document like a contract.

If students have some input in the establishment of consequences, they are more likely to recognize their fairness. Furthermore, teachers need to administer the consequences calmly and fairly and remind students that they still like and respect them—only their actions are unacceptable. Students who accept their consequences, realizing they have not fulfilled their responsibility or obligation, are likely to learn from their mistakes as long as they are treated with respect, confidentiality, and caring.

Assignment #2 (Figure 3.11) offers Evertson and Harris's (1991) criteria for creating effective classroom rules as well as a series of rules that may or may not meet their criteria. Assignment #3 (Figure 3.12) asks teachers to create five age-appropriate rules and the logical consequences that could be administered if students violate the rules.

Behavior Checklists

Hopefully, most students will accept the "rule and consequence" paradigm, internalize their own responsibilities, and model the positive behavior of their peers and teachers. The need still exists, however, for teachers to chronicle the behaviors of those who choose not to cooperate. It is imperative that the documentation of all violations remains private and confidential.

Teachers can use a grade book, checklists, anecdotal records, or any type of written format to monitor disruptive behavior. Writing the names of misbehaving students on the blackboard and adding checks after their names for repeat offenses is not conducive to establishing classroom trust, and it violates the confidentiality of the student.

Moreover, no teacher wants to take time away from teaching to be an accountant whose job is to debit and credit discipline violations. The checklist (see Figure 3.13) may help teachers keep track of violations without embarrassing students or losing instructional time. It is suggested that teachers record specific dates under each rule violation to determine which consequence applies and to document persistent discipline problems in case more formal referrals or follow-up actions are required later.

(*Text continues on page 83*)

Figure 3.10   Learning Center 504—Classroom Expectations

Learning Center 504

Classroom Expectations

1. Respect

Respect yourself, your peers, and all adults.

Respect the classroom environment.

Respect the meaning of the word *fair*. (Know that each person's getting what he or she needs is different from each person's being treated exactly the same.)

2. Responsibility

Take your role as a student seriously.

Be prepared and ready to work. (Remember, slacking off is neither a right nor an option!)

Be an active learner. (The one who works the hardest, learns the most.)

3. Resourcefulness

Advocate for yourself. (You are your own best spokesperson.)

Make your need known in a clear, timely, and respectful manner.

Know where and how to find the information and the help that you need.

Consequences

These consequences are intended to be used when classroom expectations are not met, even after verbal and/or nonverbal reminders have been given.

Step 1: Reminder with rationale

Teacher will remind student about the expected behavior and the reason why that behavior is needed.

Step 2: Warning with consequences

Teacher will state what will happen if behavior persists.

Step 3: Conference with student

Step 4: Conference with administrator, student, and teacher

Step 5: A call home

Step 6: Conference with parent

I have read the above expectations and consequences and agree to abide by them in the Learning Center.

Date _____   Signature _____

Created by Lorrie King, Yarmouth High School, Yarmouth, ME. Used with permission.

Figure 3.11 Creating Effective Rules

Assignment #2

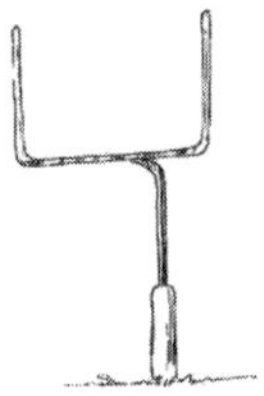

Evertson and Harris (1991, p. 2) establish some guidelines for effective rules. Effective rules are as follows:

1. Consistent with school rules
2. Understandable
3. Doable (students able to comply)
4. Manageable

5. Always applicable
6. Stated positively
7. Stated behaviorally
8. Consistent with teacher's own philosophy of how students learn best

Directions: Review the following guidelines and then check to see if the seven rules meet the above criteria for classroom rules. If so, mark the rule "Yes." If not, mark it "No" and rewrite the rule to make it a "Yes."

Rules	YES	NO
1. Don"t talk out of turn. Rewrite: _____	☐	☐
2. Be considerate of others. Rewrite: _____	☐	☐
3. Do not hit others. Rewrite: _____	☐	☐
4. Respect the property of others. Rewrite: _____	☐	☐
5. Do not use profanity. Rewrite: _____	☐	☐
6. Listen quietly while others are speaking. Rewrite: _____	☐	☐
7. Obey all school rules. Rewrite: _____	☐	☐

Figure 3.12 Classroom Rules and Consequences

<u>*Assignment #3*</u>

Directions: Develop five rules and logical consequences for violating the rules that are appropriate for your students.

Teacher: _____   Class/Grade: _____   Date: _____

Rule #1: _____

        Consequences 1. _____
                       2. _____
                       3. _____
                       4. _____
                       5. _____

Rule #2: _____

        Consequences 1. _____
                       2. _____
                       3. _____
                       4. _____
                       5. _____

Rule #3: _____

        Consequences 1. _____
                       2. _____
                       3. _____
                       4. _____
                       5. _____

Rule #4: _____

        Consequences 1. _____
                       2. _____
                       3. _____
                       4. _____
                       5. _____

Rule #5: _____

        Consequences 1. _____
                       2. _____
                       3. _____
                       4. _____
                       5. _____

Figure 3.13 Behavior Checklist

Teacher: _____   Class: _____   Date: _____

Rules:	Consequences:
Rule #1 _____	1. _____
Rule #2 _____	2. _____
Rule #3 _____	3. _____
Rule #4 _____	4. _____
Rule #5 _____	5. _____

Write the dates of all violations in boxes under rule numbers.

Class Roll	Rule					Comments
	1	2	3	4	5	
1.						
2.						
3.						
4.						
5.						
6.						
7.						
8.						
9.						
10.						
11.						
12.						
13.						
14.						
15.						
16.						
17.						
18.						
19.						
20.						

Attitude Versus Skill Issue

Regardless of the terms or methods used to handle violations of rules, teachers sometimes tend to respond to student disruptions in a punitive way rather than trying to reinforce and redirect students to the correct behavior. Jones and Jones (1998) feel that school personnel too often view inappropriate behavior as an *attitude* rather than a *skill* issue. In many cases, they assume the student's error is premeditated, deliberate, and threatening, when in fact the student could be unaware of the violation, the disruption was accidental, or the student didn't know the skill. Social skills and behavior norms need to be taught and reinforced as much as math skills. Good behavior just doesn't happen—it has to be taught and reinforced. (See Chapter 4 for a discussion on how to teach social skills.) Teachers can use Assignment #4 (Figure 3.14) as a class activity to get the class thinking about the rules needed.

ESTABLISHING A COOPERATIVE, RESPONSIBLE CLASSROOM

Scenario

"I hate doing these geometry problems," groans Chuck. *"Why do we need to know this for life? We spend half the class working on these theorems!"*

"What's the problem, Chuck?" asks Mrs. Nordstrom.

"Math is boring," Chuck explodes.

"Now, Chuck," Mrs. Nordstrom replies. *"Things are not boring—people who don't understand them just think they're boring."*

"I understand the problems," shouts Chuck. *"I just don't give a damn!"*

"If you understand so much," says Mrs. Nordstrom through gritted teeth, her voice rising, *"Why did you score a 54 percent on your last test?"*

"Because I wanted to flunk—it was my personal best."

Mrs. Nordstrom angrily shouts, *"All right, young man. You can just march yourself down to the principal's office right now."*

"Great, I'd rather sit in the office all day than sit in this stupid room!"

Creating the Climate

The climate of a classroom refers to the teacher-student and student-student relationships. A positive climate is established when a teacher not only "engages students' imaginations but also convinces them that they are people of worth who can do something in a very difficult world" (Kohl as cited in Scherer, 1998, p. 9). Kohl believes that the first big thing that makes a difference is respect. If teachers don't feel that their students have value equal to their own, then they won't teach them much. Kohl also believes that humiliation is absolutely a sin. He feels that teachers need to deal with students who

Figure 3.14   Brainstorming Web

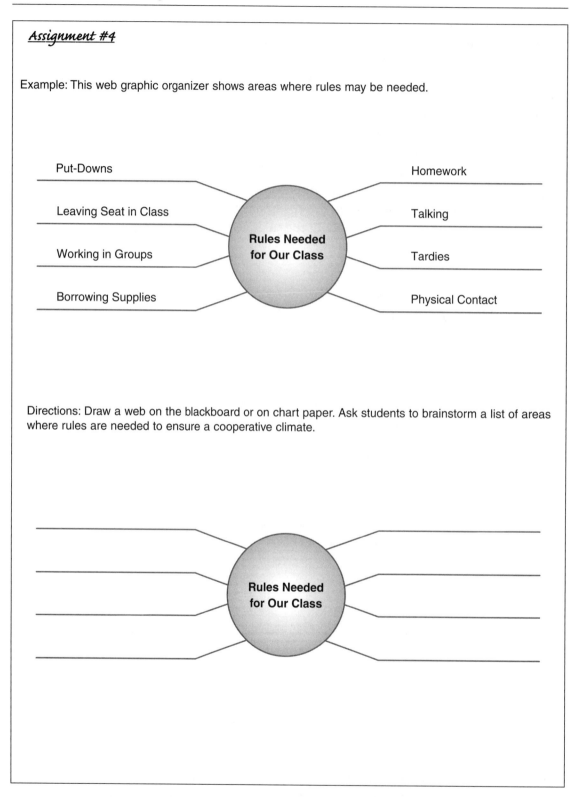

Assignment #4

Example: This web graphic organizer shows areas where rules may be needed.

Put-Downs

Leaving Seat in Class

Working in Groups

Borrowing Supplies

Homework

Talking

Tardies

Physical Contact

Rules Needed for Our Class

Directions: Draw a web on the blackboard or on chart paper. Ask students to brainstorm a list of areas where rules are needed to ensure a cooperative climate.

Rules Needed for Our Class

defy them but humiliation has to go. Lyrics from the song "The Wall" by Pink Floyd represent this point:

> *We don't need no education*
> *We don't need no thought control*
> *No dark sarcasm in the classroom*
> *Teacher leave the kids alone.*

Kohl feels students do need some education, "but dark sarcasm has to be removed from the teacher's repertoire of strategies" (Kohl as cited in Scherer, p. 9).

Publicly humiliating or embarrassing students does not help students learn from their mistakes. It could, however, make them try harder not to get caught or cause them to devise clever ways to get revenge on the person or persons who embarrassed them. Dealing with disruptive students in private and in a fair and consistent manner helps students develop an "internal locus of control" and responsibility. Students with an internal locus of control feel guilty when they misbehave, learn from their mistakes, accept the consequences for their actions, and will try to control their actions in the future. They also maintain their dignity.

Dealing with disruptive students in front of their peers in an emotional outburst of frustration and anger lowers the students' self-concepts, decreases their desire to cooperate and succeed, and prevents them from developing their own sense of responsibility. They instead learn how to become defensive and use an "external locus of control" to blame others for their problems. Consequently, these students rarely accept responsibility for their own actions. Public reprimands, moreover, eventually destroy the positive climate in any classroom. Students do not feel free to engage in interactive discussion, contribute ideas, or share experiences if they are never sure when they will incur the teacher's wrath or become the object of the teacher's sarcasm or anger. Respecting the dignity of each and every student is essential for effective classroom management.

Teacher Behaviors

If students perceive that the teacher is treating them unjustly, they may feel that the teacher is unfair" or "out to get them." The seeds of insurrection may then be planted, causing a small behavior incident to escalate later into a major discipline problem.

Teachers need to be careful in their enforcement of classroom rules and consequences. Sometimes the message can be fair, consistent, and positive, but the delivery system can be sarcastic, punitive, and negative. A 1991 study conducted by Kearney, Plax, Hays, and Ivey cited in Marzano, Marzano, and Pickering (2003) asked 254 college students to describe behaviors of their teachers they had actually witnessed that they considered inappropriate. Behaviors such as absenteeism, tardiness, keeping students after the bell, straying from the subject matter, and being unprepared or unorganized were just some of their complaints.

Figure 3.15   Inappropriate Teacher Behaviors

- Absenteeism
- Tardiness
- Keeping students over time
- Early dismissal
- Straying from the subject matter
- Being unprepared or unorganized
- Being late returning work
- Sarcasm and put-downs

- Verbal abuse
- Unreasonable and arbitrary rules
- Lack of response to student questions
- Sexual harassment
- Apathy toward students
- Unfair grading practices
- Negative personality
- Showing favoritism

Kearney, Plax, Hays, & Ivey as cited in Marzano et al., 2003.

Some of the same inappropriate behaviors cause elementary, middle, and secondary school students to voice similar concerns about how they perceive their teacher. Figure 3.16 lists the inappropriate teacher behaviors that erode a positive classroom climate and undermine any discipline program—no matter how democratic. Teachers send signals to individual students and to the whole class in both subtle and blatant ways that jeopardize the caring, cooperative classroom. It is remarkable how many people remember an incident from school in which they were treated unjustly by a teacher or administrator. Even though this incident may have occurred 30 to 40 years earlier, it became a "defining moment" they never forgot; moreover, it influenced how they treat their own students.

Assignment #5 (Figure 3.17) helps educators analyze critical incidents that they remember from their own background and reflect on how they can prevent causing their own students similar feelings.

Proactive Teachers

The effective classroom teacher engages in the "professional response" to a student's inappropriate question or comment by anticipating the types of problems that could occur and developing strategies to solve them. This type of *proactive* approach to preventing discipline problems *before* they occur is far less time consuming than the *reactive* approach, where teachers expend all their energy trying to solve problems *after* they occur.

- Anticipate potential behavior problems.
  - Prevent potential problem students from sitting together.
  - Arrange seating patterns so teacher sees all students.
  - Give both verbal and written directions to eliminate confusion and frustration, which often leads to behavior problems.
  - Create relevant, motivating, and developmentally appropriate assignments.
  - Allow enough time for students to complete assignments so they don't feel pressured.
  - Scan the class frequently to notice or respond to potential problems.
  - Make allowances for students with learning disabilities or physical handicaps, so they don't become frustrated.

Figure 3.16   Burke's "Dirty Dozen"

Teacher Behaviors That Can Erode the Classroom Climate

1. **Sarcasm**	Students' feelings can be hurt by sarcastic put-downs thinly disguised as humor.
2. **Negative tone of voice**	Students can "read between the lines" and sense a sarcastic, negative, or condescending tone of voice.
3. **Negative body language**	A teacher's clenched fists, set jaw, quizzical look, or threatening stance can speak more loudly than any words.
4. **Inconsistency**	Nothing escapes the students' attention. They are the first to realize the teacher is not enforcing the rules and consequences consistently.
5. **Favoritism**	"Brown-nosing" is an art, and any student in any class can point out the "teacher's pet" who gets special treatment.
6. **Put-downs**	Sometimes teachers are not aware they are embarrassing a student with subtle put-downs or insults.
7. **Outbursts**	Teachers are sometimes provoked by students and they "lose it." These teacher outbursts set a bad example for the students and could escalate into more serious problems.
8. **Public reprimands**	No one wants to be corrected, humiliated, or lose face in front of peers.
9. **Unfairness**	Taking away promised privileges; scheduling a surprise test; "nitpicking" while grading homework or tests; or assigning punitive homework could be construed as "unfair."
10. **Apathy**	Students do not want to be ignored. Teachers who forget students' names or appear indifferent will lose students' respect.
11. **Inflexibility**	Teachers who never adjust homework assignments or test dates to meet the needs of their students appear rigid and uncaring.
12. **Lack of humor**	Teachers who cannot laugh at themselves usually don't encourage students to take risks and make mistakes. Humorless classes lack energy.

    o   Encourage peer tutoring to help struggling students complete their work.

    o   Conference with students prone to behavior problems to find out if they have some personal or family problems that might be causing them to be uncooperative.

    o   Talk with counselors or support personnel to find out about any previous behavior problems students might have experienced and get suggestions about how to best meet the individual needs of students.

- Diffuse minor problems before they become major disturbances.
  - o   Proximity—Move close to students when you sense a problem developing.
  - o   Student-selected time-out
    - ♦   Allow students to select a time-out from the class or the group.
    - ♦   Let the agitated student go to a desk or chair in the corner of the room to collect her thoughts or calm down.
  - o   Teacher-selected time-out—Ask the student to go to the time-out area to complete work when his behavior is disrupting the group's activity.

Figure 3.17 Reflecting on the Dirty Dozen

Assignment #5

Directions: Review the Dirty Dozen list of teacher behaviors (see Figure 3.16), and select one behavior that happened to you when you were a student. Write a short description of the incident.

Behavior: _____

Description: _____

_____

_____

_____

Select *one* behavior that you may have used with your own students. Write a short description.

_____

_____

_____

_____

_____

_____

Suggest another way either one of these incidents could have been handled.

_____

_____

_____

_____

_____

_____

- Address disruptive behaviors immediately.
  - Ask to speak with the student privately in the hall, after class, or after school.
  - Ask the student to explain what she thinks the problem is.
  - Send "I-messages," telling the student how his behavior affects you. For example, "I feel upset when I see you arguing with your group members."
  - Try to identify the real problem. Use the problem-solving models in this chapter to write down steps for trying to solve the problem.
  - Remind students of the procedures or rules.
  - Address the problem quickly, calmly, and privately.
  - Avoid creating a bigger disruption when attempting to solve minor disruptions.
  - Don't "lose it" by overreacting and becoming angry.
  - Remove the offender(s) from the class so the other students are not an audience.
  - Provide students with choices, if possible. For example, "If you choose to work alone rather than with your group, you must complete the entire project by yourself."

The Last Resort: The Principal

Even if teachers are proactive, there will always be that hard-core group of students who choose to disrupt the rest of the class because the class does not satisfy their needs; moreover, some students' desire for attention, power, or recognition supersedes their need to learn or to please the teacher.

It is the teacher's responsibility to make sure these disruptive students do not destroy the positive atmosphere of the class and cooperative spirit of the learning teams. If teachers do their best to anticipate potential behavior problems, diffuse minor problems before they become major disturbances, and address disruptive behaviors immediately, they should be able to counteract most problems. However, once the teacher has done everything possible to solve the problem and to control a student's negative behavior, the teacher must resort to outside help—the administration. Sending the student to the principal is not a cop-out, unless, of course, it is done at the first sign of a problem.

Teachers should not relinquish their position of authority early on, or they will lose the respect of the student and possibly of the whole class. Once the teacher contacts the administrator, the teacher is no longer in control; the administrator is. If, however, the teacher has exhausted all available strategies, the student's behavior has not improved, and the disruptive behavior is negatively influencing the entire class, the last resort becomes the next step. The student may also have to be referred to the school counselor, psychologist, special education coordinator, or social worker. It is important that teachers have accurate documentation of the student's behavior (dates, incidents, actions taken on checklists or anecdotal records). It is also important for teachers to engage in a variety of problem-solving strategies to try to determine the underlying problem that might be causing the misbehavior.

Assignment #6 (Figure 3.18) is an agree/disagree chart; teachers read the statement about setting the classroom climate and decide whether they agree or disagree. Establishing a comfortable classroom climate is the first step toward effective classroom management.

Figure 3.18 Agree/Disagree Chart

Assignment #6

Directions: Review the following statements about classroom climate and check if you _agree_ or _disagree_ with a statement.

Setting the Classroom Climate

	Agree	_Disagree_
1. The term "_rules_" sounds too dictatorial. It should be replaced with _expectations_ or _principles._		
2. Logical consequences are the same as punishments.		
3. Writing students' names on the board improves their behavior.		
4. A "time-out" area should be designated in a classroom.		
5. Sarcasm is effective in introducing humor to the classroom.		
6. Classroom management is basically behavior problem solving.		
7. Students should be sent to the principal for violating a rule.		
8. Teachers need to create the rules.		

Select one statement and provide the rationale for either agreeing or disagreeing with it.

Statement #: _____ Rationale: _____

_____

_____

Teaching Students How to Use Appropriate Social Skills

4

Figure 4.0 Cluster of Social Skills Graphic Organizer

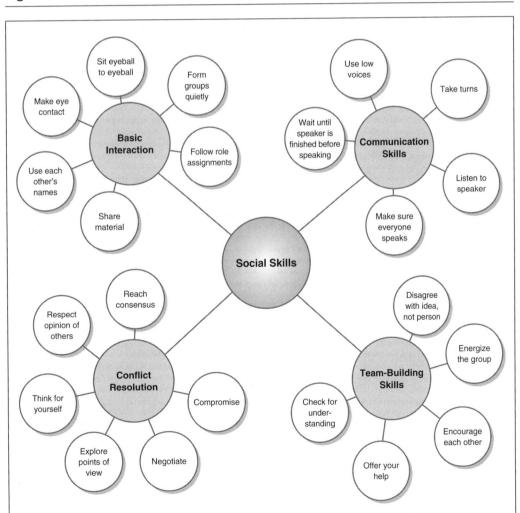

SOCIAL SKILLS IN THE CLASSROOM

Social skills are primarily developed in cooperative groups. These skills are the foundation for the management of cooperative classroom behavior and are needed for all interactions, large group and small. (Bellanca & Fogarty, 2003, p. 70)

Social skills provide the framework for effective classroom management. If students' social skills are well developed and appropriate to their age level, teachers can implement behavior management systems within the first few days of class with minimal instruction or practice. If, however, because of students' cultural or family backgrounds, they are not familiar with the social skills deemed important by the school culture, teachers must instruct students in the social skills that are necessary to function in a group, the class, and the school. Moreover, teachers must also reinforce the skills continuously and revisit them when necessary.

Goldstein and McGinnis (as cited in Wolfgang, 1999) have created a model called "skillstreaming," which is a skill-deficit model that views misbehaving students as lacking the necessary social skills—which they call *prosocial skills*—to function well with peers and adults. They believe that some students cannot handle stressful social interactions and conflicts; therefore, they only know how to respond by becoming passive, isolated, or violent. The designers believe that most students absorb prosocial skills through incidental learning, but more and more students are not acquiring these skills naturally and so must be taught them directly.

Skillstreaming attempts to teach skills directly related to classroom survival skills, friendship-making skills, alternatives to aggression, and dealing with stress (Goldstein & McGinnis as cited in Wolfgang, 1999, pp. 182–183). These prosocial skills and others need to be taught explicitly to students who have never acquired them, and these skills must be reviewed as necessary for students who have them but need more practice. All students could use a review of all social skills needed to function effectively in the classroom.

The Hidden Curriculum

Social skills aren't just important in the classroom. They are also important for how students relate to others outside the classroom. Students are subjected to the so-called "hidden curriculum" in schools. DeRoche and Williams (2001) discuss how values are taught both intentionally and unintentionally in the classrooms and in the hallways. They recommend looking at the climate (the hidden curriculum) and the actual lessons.

If your school climate is positive, it is likely the values learned by the students are positive personal and prosocial/civic ones. If your school climate is neutral or negative, it is likely that students are getting mixed messages about important values, behaviors, and expectations. (p. 15)

The hidden curriculum also consists of unstated behavior and social expectations, such as how to dress, how to act, and where to sit in the cafeteria as well as social interactions and popularity patterns. Most students learn the hidden curriculum by observation and trial and error. Many students, however, especially those with learning disabilities, behavior or emotional disorders, mental retardation, limited English skills, or communication disorders, may not be highly skilled in picking up on nonverbal and verbal cues. A great deal of the hidden curriculum involves complex social interactions that some students never master. These students may never gain social acceptance, because they cannot "engage appropriately in interpersonal interactions" (Gallagher as cited in Miller, 1998, p. 145).

For students with disabilities, students from different cultures, and students who have not been taught social skills at home or in their prior schooling, a lack of knowledge regarding how to function in social situations poses many barriers to functioning academically. Miller suggests that because research shows how important social skills are to classroom management, teachers should teach social skills to *all* students. "We know that students who have strong social skills tend to be friendly, have positive self-concepts, avoid angry reactions, and have good communication and conversation skills" (Reisman as cited in Miller, 1998, p. 145). Parker and Asher (as cited in Miller), add that "students who have well-developed social skills are less likely to drop out of school and become involved in criminal activities" (p. 145). The ability to practice prosocial behaviors not only helps students succeed in school but also transfers to life outside of school.

Anger Management

Students who don't have well-developed social skills tend to use anger as a response to others, because they are not able to interpret what their peers are saying or doing. Often these students react negatively to social situations, sometimes yelling or fighting (fight-or-flight syndrome) or withdrawing completely and becoming isolated or lonely. When a student develops a pattern of reacting inappropriately to other students' words or actions, that child soon gets labeled "weird" or "uncool" by the peer group. In addition, continuous negative social experiences may cause students to label themselves "failures." Poor social skills in school can lead to problems with drug abuse or suicidal tendencies later in life (Miller, 1998).

Dealing with students who are going through puberty presents social challenges. These students, ages 10 to 12, are going through changes in their reproductive systems. Armstrong (2006) says that when addressing the subject of young adolescents "with their mood swings, their impulsivity, their rebelliousness, their irritability, and their other troubles" (pp. 114–115), we must remember that these hormonal, neurological, and physical changes are taking place. It is important for educators to create an educational climate that will channel students' aggression into positive projects and proactive contributions to society.

Because so many students enter a teacher's classroom lacking fundamental social skills, it is important that teachers integrate the teaching of these skills into the curriculum. It is equally important that teachers not only teach the skills explicitly but also model the skills daily and continuously monitor their effectiveness.

Early Instruction in Social Skills

Wong and Wong (1998) emphasize the importance of starting each school year with a plan. "What you do on the first day of school will determine your success or failure for the rest of the school year. You will either win or lose your class on the first days of school" (p. 3). Social skills are one of the five components of the emotional intelligence discussed in Chapter 2. They also form the foundation for any type of interactive activity or group work that teachers use when they engage students in learning.

One way to justify the time spent teaching social skills to other teachers, parents, and administrators is their inclusion in most district, state, and national standards. Standards that address students' being able to contribute to the overall effort of a group, use conflict-resolution techniques, work well with diverse individuals in diverse situations, and display effective interpersonal communication skills and leadership skills have been adopted by many districts and states. As Goleman's (1995) emotional intelligence theory indicates, students who master social skills and gain acceptance by their peers are better able to achieve personal, social, and academic success for themselves as well as contribute to society.

Another important reason to take the time to teach social skills is that so many students come from diverse racial, ethnic, religious, social-class, and national backgrounds. San Antonio (2006) says that young people are becoming more aware of social status and their position in the social hierarchy. "Perhaps the most significant stress in a young adolescent's life is the sense of not fitting in. For most students, good adjustment and performance in school require some level of social comfort" (p. 10).

The Stages in Teaching the Social Skills

Bellanca and Fogarty (2003) describe six steps teachers can use to develop a lesson plan to teach social skills. The six steps include: create a hook lesson, teach specific behaviors, provide practice, extend practice, observe progress, and reflect on the activity. The following stages are an adaptation of their process.

1. **Create a hook.** This is a lesson or grabber that gets the students' attention and introduces the social skill.

Example: Three students engage in a group role-play of a discussion where everyone is arguing with each other. The students discuss a controversial issue like "drop-outs losing their driver's licenses," and emotions and tempers flair. Everyone is interrupting everyone else, and voices are getting louder and angrier. After the role-play, members of the role-playing group comment on how they feel and what specific actions or words upset them. Other hooks include video clips from movies, a prop, a question, a quote, an event from the news, a story, an anecdote, or a school event related to inappropriate social skills.

2. **Teach the skill.** Use a T-chart (see Figure 4.1) to have students generate specific behaviors of the conflict-resolution skill of "disagreeing with the idea—not the person."

Figure 4.1   Disagree With the Idea—Not the Person T-Chart

Sounds Like	Looks Like
"I hear what you are saying."	Looking at the speaker
"That's another way to look at it."	Taking notes
"Please repeat that idea."	Nodding head
"I have something to say when you're done."	Not interrupting
"Let's let Mary finish."	Using a speaker's gavel when a person "has the floor"

Select one or more social skills from Cluster of Social Skills Graphic Organizer on the Chapter 4 title page and have students complete the T-chart in groups or as a whole class. Then post the charts on the bulletin board or have students keep a copy in their notebooks to refer to whenever they engage in discussions. Use a web on a poster board to list characteristics or attributes of a social skill.

3. **Practice the skill.** Guided practice is necessary if students are to internalize the targeted social skill. Students select another controversial topic and discuss it in the group before presenting a consensus statement about the topic to the class. Brainstorm a list of controversial topics to use for the practice activity. Examples could include the following:

- School dropouts should lose their driver's license.
- Students who fall below a C average should not be able to participate in extracurricular activities.
- Students should have to wear uniforms.
- Soft drink machines should be banned from all schools.
- Students should have to wear ID badges.
- Cell phones should be banned from schools.
- Foods with trans fats should be banned from school lunches.

- Internet sites like YouTube should ban all video clips showing kids committing hurtful pranks, like throwing drinks back at fast-food workers.

4. Group members give each other verbal and written feedback.

> *Topic:* The district should adopt a "no pass, no play policy." Students who do not maintain an overall C average in school should not be able to participate in sports or other extracurricular activities.
>
> *Discussion:* (10 minutes) Refer to T-chart on "disagreeing with the idea—not the person."
>
> *Consensus Statement:* The "no pass, no play" policy should not be adopted by the district, because many students would drop out of school if they were not allowed to participate in extracurricular activities. Signed by the group members Joe, Donna, Mary Jo, and Gail.

5. **Observe the skill.** As students practice the targeted social skill, the teacher, a designated student observer, or the entire group should keep a behavior checklist to monitor positive behaviors (see Figure 4.2).

Figure 4.2   Behavior Checklist

Student \ Skill	Looks at speaker	Does not interrupt	Takes notes	Asks questions
Joe	✗	✗		✗✗✗
Donna	✗		✗	
Mary Jo	✗✗			
Gail		✗		

6. Students can self-assess their own skills or ask a peer to assess them. Figure 4.3 shows a sample checklist that teachers can use to observe the behaviors of students in their cooperative groups.

7. The group shares the results, and the checklist serves as a formative assessment describing which skills students still need to practice. Practice should continue until the skill becomes automatic. Group members should encourage students to engage in a controversial discussion without getting angry, rude, or loud. When group members speak while

Figure 4.3   Observation Checklist for Cooperative Group Work

Group Project: _____   Date: _____

Group Members' Names and #s:

1. _____   4. _____

2. _____   5. _____

3. _____

Behaviors	Group Member #				
	1	2	3	4	5
Follows assigned role assignments.					
Encourages others to succeed.					
Checks for understanding.					
Asks appropriate questions.					
Adheres to time limits.					
Stays on task.					
Allows each person to speak.					
Comments:					

someone else is speaking, other group members should gently remind them that only the speaker, who holds the group symbol (magic marker, gavel, or speaker's card), should be speaking. When finished speaking, that person passes the group symbol on to the next speaker.

8. **Reflect on the skill.** Students reflect on their use of the social skill by discussing their use of the targeted skill, what they learned about themselves and others, how much improvement they made, and what they still need to do. They should also reflect on their group's implementation of the skills and discuss the group's progress. Other methods of reflection could include logs, journals (see Figure 4.4), stem questions, self-evaluation checklists or rubrics, processing pieces, or discussion.

Figure 4.4   Double-Entry Journal

Initial Observation on Using a Skill	Upon Reflection
Date: September 16	Date: September 25
I always thought I kept my cool when I was in an argument, but my group members said I get red in the face and talk louder and faster when I want them to listen to me—I think I'm OK, but I'll try to be more careful.	After looking at our observer's checklist, I guess I do interrupt a lot—I guess I talk so fast that I can't sit still and listen to slower speakers—I'm going to have to be more patient and not try to "out-talk" everyone else. I make people nervous.

9. **Recognize and celebrate success.** As students internalize and practice the social skills, they receive recognition from their peers. Both the teacher and peers affirm positive behavior using specific feedback such as "I like the way you asked me questions about my views on the subject." The group members can also devise a team signal or cheer to energize the group and to encourage the members to celebrate their progress. Following are some examples (other examples of energizers are listed in Figure 4.32):

   - Group members give each other high fives after they finish a discussion where they respected each other's opinions.
   - The whole class raises their hands in the air and slowly lowers them, whispering, "Awesome, awesome."
   - Group members give themselves a "round of applause" by clapping and circling their hands over their heads.
   - Group members pretend they are playing the guitar and say, "Excellent," as they strum the guitar and bend their knees.

10. **Transfer skill outside the class.** If students have really internalized the social skill, they should be able to transfer the skill outside the classroom. If it is important to "disagree with the idea, not the person" in class, it is also important to do the same thing on the playground, in the cafeteria, at the bus stop, in the neighborhood, and in the home. Students should be encouraged to share their use of the skill outside the class. After all, social skills are really life skills. Each week, students take time to discuss how they used prosocial skills outside of class. Following are some examples:

- How did students use a targeted social skill at lunch or on the playground?
- What skill was used with a family member?
- What skill was used at work with a coworker or customer?
- What skill was used with a sibling?
- What skills are needed by certain sports figures, movie stars, or politicians in the news?
- What skill would help the school football team? (Bellanca, 1991)

Social skills could be the most important skills students learn in school. Therefore, teachers need to teach, reinforce, and assess social skills on a regular basis. Assignment #1 (Figure 4.5) helps plan for teaching a social skill in the classrooms. Assignment #2 (Figure 4.6) helps teachers develop a greater understanding of why social skills must be taught. Teachers can reflect on the importance of teaching social skills explicitly to their students.

This chapter deals with how social skills are prerequisites for students' becoming responsible members of the class and developing important interpersonal skills that will be discussed in later chapters. Even though the current educational environment places a tremendous emphasis on standards, standardized tests, rigorous curriculum, and accountability, educators must not lose track of the importance of both the cognitive and the affective domains of education. As Lantieri and Patti (1996) state,

Clearly, schools today must be committed more deeply than ever before to intentionally creating community and to paying attention to young people's social and emotional lives. We need a new vision for schools—one that includes educating the heart along with the mind. (p. 29)

The following scenarios address differing levels of students' appropriate social skills and specific strategies teachers can implement to help students improve their skills. The scenarios are followed by strategies, activities, and assignments related to the problem outlined in the scenario.

Figure 4.5   Stages in Teaching Social Skills

Assignment #1

ACTION

Directions: Select one social skill and plan how to teach it to your students.

Targeted Social Skill: _____

Stage 1—Create a Hook:

Stage 2—Teach the Skill:

Stage 3—Practice the Skill:

Stage 4—Observe the Skill:

Stage 5—Reflect on the Skill:

Stage 6—Recognize and Celebrate Success:

Stage 7—Transfer Skill Outside the Class:

Figure 4.6   Reflection on Social Skills

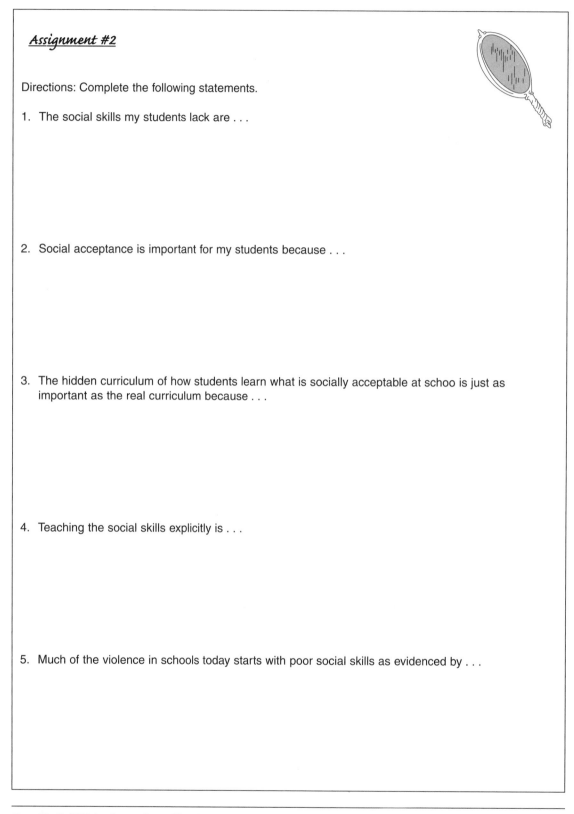

Assignment #2

Directions: Complete the following statements.

1. The social skills my students lack are . . .

2. Social acceptance is important for my students because . . .

3. The hidden curriculum of how students learn what is socially acceptable at schoo is just as important as the real curriculum because . . .

4. Teaching the social skills explicitly is . . .

5. Much of the violence in schools today starts with poor social skills as evidenced by . . .

BASIC INTERACTIONS

Scenario

> Miguel walks into the class the first day of school and quickly sits in the last seat of the first row.
>
> Alfie looks toward Miguel and tries to make eye contact, but Miguel continues to look down at his math book. When Mr. Otter, the teacher, walks in, the other students stand to greet him and introduce themselves.
>
> When Mr. Otter sees Miguel sitting at his desk, he approaches him and holds out his hand.
>
> "Hi, I'm Mr. Otter, your math teacher. Welcome to Park High. Where are you from?"
>
> Miguel barely glances at the teacher as he shakes his hand clumsily.
>
> "Mexico" mumbles Miguel under his breath.
>
> "Oh, I love Mexico," exclaims Jenny. "I went on vacation there last summer." Miguel turns sideways in his seat and doesn't reply.

Practicing Basic Skills

There is no one set of social skills that work for everyone. People from different cultures and even different communities observe different social skills. A social skill that is deemed important in one culture, such as looking directly at a person who is speaking to you, may be considered inappropriate in another culture. Because of the multicultural demographics of the classroom today, students may be academically prepared, but they also could lack the basic interactions or social skills that are deemed important by the dominant culture of the school. (Miller, 1998, p. 144)

Social skills help students interact with others both inside and outside of the classroom. While students may lack basic social skills, teachers set the stage for explicitly teaching them by modeling positive interactions. They "walk the talk" by beginning each day or class period with positive comments. Greetings such as "Good morning," "Welcome to class," "How did the game go last night?" "Tell me something about yourself," "How can I help you?" and "How are you doing today? establish a friendly classroom climate and set the tone for the day.

Emmer, Evertson, Clements, and Worsham (1997) encourage teachers to stand by the door at the beginning of class to help students find their room and to welcome them. It is also important for teachers to give students clear directions about finding their seat assignments on the first day of school (e.g., assigned seats or open seating). Students need to feel comfortable and feel they "fit in." Moreover, they do not want to do anything to embarrass themselves when they are meeting their new teacher and classmates for the first time.

The following chart (Figure 4.7) illustrates the social skills that are components of basic interactions.

Figure 4.7   Social Skills for Basic Interactions

- Use positive body language
- Make eye contact
- Listen to the speaker
- Respond appropriately
- Wait for your turn

The following activities help students develop interpersonal social skills and interact with one another. These activities promote effective communication and help students share ideas, ask questions, and listen to others.

Activity: Circle of Friends

This activity helps students practice using first names and finding out something about each other. Teachers assign each student a partner. Students spend five minutes talking to their partners and finding out things such as where the other student is from and what hobbies, sports, clubs, etc., the other student is interested in or involved with. At the end of the five minutes, teachers ask pairs of partners to join with another pair. This time, each person introduces his partner. Teachers should allow pairs eight minutes to exchange information. Ask for volunteers to share something interesting about their partners (see Figure 4.8).

This strategy provides a nonthreatening way for students to practice the basic interaction skills of introducing themselves, starting a conversation, smiling, carrying on a conversation, being polite, and using first names. At the end of the designated time, teachers ask students to give their new friend a compliment and to greet them by name whenever they see any of their circle of friends. This activity serves as an "ice breaker" and helps students begin to learn about their new classmates.

Figure 4.8   Circle of Friends Activity

1. Find a partner; someone you don't know well. (1 minute)

2. Interview each other to find out
   o hobbies,
   o sports,
   o clubs, and
   o travel interests. (5 minutes)

3. Each pair joins another pair. (1 minute)

4. Each person introduces his/her partner to the new pair. (2 minutes each; 8 minutes)

5. Call on volunteers to tell something interesting about their partners. (3 minutes)

Activity: Show and Tell

Teachers ask students to bring in three items that tell something about themselves. These items could be pictures, a trophy, a book, a letter, a souvenir, a CD of their favorite music group, or anything that provides insight into who the student really is. Teachers divide the class into groups of three and ask each student to spend five minutes introducing herself by showing and explaining the three items. Make sure students practice the following skills during their presentation:

- Introducing themselves appropriately
- Maintaining eye contact with other classmates
- Using positive facial expressions and body language
- Answering any questions posed by their peers
- Practicing good manners and being polite
- Using first names when they interact with their classmates

Process the activity by reviewing these six basic interactions and asking students how they think they did using all six during the conversations. This activity allows students to practice the components that make up positive social skills while sharing information about themselves. "Show and tell" is usually a popular activity in the early elementary grades, but students need to have these critical interpersonal skills revisited, reinforced, and sometimes reintroduced as they get older. Middle school and high school students need to revisit everything they first learned in kindergarten to survive and thrive in secondary school.

COMMUNICATION SKILLS

Scenario

"Shut up!" yells Martha as she leaps up from her desk. "You don't know what you're talking about!"

"Yes, I do," screams Joel. "You just never give me a chance to talk because you are always talking so much!"

"Martha, Joel! What's going on here? Why are you yelling? You are disturbing all the other students," says Mrs. Green.

"But Mrs. Green," Martha whines, "I am sick and tired of Joel mouthing off about something he doesn't know anything about. He never listens."

"Okay, Martha and Joel. I am going to let you two work this problem out," Mrs. Green says. "I am going to take the roll and check homework for a few minutes, but I'll be back!"

"You jerk. Now you got us in trouble. I need another partner," mutters Martha.

"You need a muzzle," laughs Joel. "Your mouth is never shut."

Martha turns away and covers her ears with her hands and tries to ignore Joel.

Practicing Communication Skills

Effective communication skills are critical for interpersonal relationships. Figure 4.9 lists some of the social skills students need to practice to feel comfortable when they are communicating with others.

Figure 4.9   Social Skills for Communication

- Don't interrupt.
- Listen to the speaker.
- Give feedback.
- Ask appropriate questions.
- Use appropriate language.
- Make sure everyone speaks.

Activity for Role-Playing Social Skills

Students can role-play various social situations. Volunteers rehearse scenarios that include basic interactions to reinforce the social skills. Scenarios might include the following:

- Meeting a blind date (high school students)
- Meeting a new teacher or principal
- Meeting a new boss at work
- Asking Santa for presents at the local mall
- Convincing the "Tooth Fairy" to leave money under the pillow
- Welcoming a new student to the school
- Meeting students from another team who won the game
- Debating other students running for a student council office
- Congratulating a cheerleader or athlete who made the squad by beating you

Ask the rest of the class to critique the role-playing scenarios by commenting on how well each student did at using basic interactions effectively. Taking part in and watching a role-play gives students a chance to see how interaction skills can apply to different situations as well as giving them a chance to rehearse life skills.

Activity: Fishbowl and T-Chart

One way to hook students is to use a "fishbowl" technique. Teachers ask two students to move their desks into the center of the room so everyone in the class can see them (thus, the fishbowl effect). Teachers ask students to role-play a typical conversation. Before the conversation starts, teachers call one student aside and tell him to talk about an interesting place he went or something fun he did that really excited him. Then, call the other student aside and ask her *not* to listen to the speaker. (In other words, the student should be asked to demonstrate inattentive listening strategies.) The other students in the classroom should observe the two students carefully. After the activity, teachers ask the speaker how he felt about the conversation. Then the speaker and the rest of the class can use a T-chart to list what nonlistening sounded like and looked like. The students complete the T-chart in groups and then share the characteristics by creating one unduplicated list on a big piece of paper for the class.

Some characteristics of nonlistening are listed in the T-chart in Figure 4.10.

Figure 4.10 T-Chart: Nonlistening

Sounds Like	Looks Like
Tapping pencil	Darting eyes
Winding watch	Fidgeting
Saying "uh-huh" a lot	Playing with hair
Saying "really"	Putting on lipstick
Sighing	Going through a folder
"What's for lunch today?"	Looking down
"Are you going to the game?"	Turning away
	Not facing the speaker
	Looking at the clock

Once the students have listed all their ideas, tear up the list and put it in the trash to symbolize that the class will not tolerate nonlistening habits.

Then, ask two more student volunteers to act out good listening skills in a fishbowl role-playing activity. Once again one student will talk about a movie, a sports game, or a trip or vacation. The other student will demonstrate attentive listening skills. Following this activity, the whole class brainstorms ideas for the Attentive Listening T-Chart (see Figure 4.11). Then, either in small groups or as a class, students complete a T-chart for attentive listening on a piece of poster paper or on the blackboard.

Figure 4.11 T-Chart: Attentive Listening

Sounds Like	Looks Like
"Tell me that again."	Nodding
"I know what you mean."	Making eye contact
"Tell me more."	Sitting eye to eye, knee to knee
"What you're saying is . . ."	Positive body language
"That's a good idea . . ."	Smiling

This list should be posted in the room to remind everyone of the importance of listening to others. If a student isn't listening during a group activity, often all teachers need to do is merely point to the Attentive Listening T-Chart as a gentle reminder of the exemplary characteristics expected from all group members. Teachers could also distribute additional social skills to cooperative groups and ask them to complete a T-chart to share with the whole class (see Figure 4.12).

Figure 4.12   T-Chart: Making Sure Everyone Speaks

Sounds Like	Looks Like
"Okay, now it's your turn."	Smiling
"Who haven't we heard from?"	Nodding
"We haven't heard from Doug yet."	Eye contact with speaker
"Let's rotate speaking."	Speaker's symbol (magic marker, token) passed around so that only one person speaks at a time
"Who's next?"	
"It's my turn now."	Checker keeping track of who speaks
"You're next."	Group using positive gestures

Web for Social Skills

Another activity involves a graphic organizer called a "web." Write the target social skill in the middle of the web and ask the students to brainstorm behaviors that would demonstrate the skill. Students may not know what the abstract skill of "listening" really means, but they know specific attributes of listening, such as "nod your head" or "ask good questions." Figure 4.13 shows a "Web for Effective Listening."

Activity: Round-Robin Listening Circle

Another activity that emphasizes good listening is the round-robin listening circle. Teachers assign three students to a group. The roles rotate so that each person gets a turn as the speaker, the listener, and the observer. Teachers assign a controversial topic or give the group a controversial article to read. Next, the speaker is given five minutes to discuss the topic with the listener. The listener responds during the time provided to simulate a regular conversation. The observer takes notes on what the listener is doing and saying.

At the end of the five-minute round, the observer shares feedback with the listener. The roles then rotate, and the same procedure is used. Students use Figure 4.14 to record their observations. It is important that teachers process each round by asking the observers what they observed so that students are aware of what they do and say that might demonstrate poor listening traits.

Figure 4.13 Web for Effective Listening

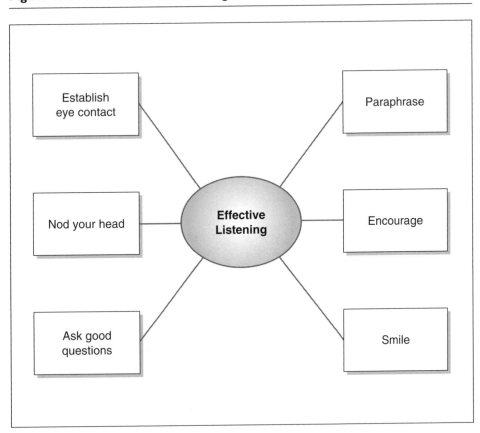

Some thought-provoking topics include the following:

- The effects of secondary smoke on nonsmokers
- Restricting students who don't pass all their classes from participating in extracurricular activities
- The negative effects of the Internet (YouTube, MySpace)
- Requiring all students to do volunteer work in their community to graduate
- Eliminating all snack and soft drink machines from the school
- Eliminating high-fat foods from school lunches
- Eliminating recess from elementary schools so students have more time to prepare for standardized tests

Ask students to reflect on their own listening abilities and ask them if they listen better when they *agree* with the speaker. Often, people who *disagree* with a speaker do not listen as well because they are so busy thinking of ways to rebut the speaker's ideas.

Processing the Use of Social Skills

Individual students and groups reflect on their use of the targeted social skill by using some of the following strategies (see Figures 4.15–4.18) to process how well they are using the skill.

Figure 4.14 Round-Robin Listening Circle

Topic: _____ Time Limit: _____

Speaker: _____

Listener: _____

Observer: _____

The speaker should start the round by giving his or her an opinion on the topic, and the listener should join in the conversation and respond to the speaker's opinion. The observer should take notes on what the listener says and does by making comments or making checks every time a behavior is observed.

Observation of the Listener

Put a "✓" each time a behavior occurs and write down specific comments.

Listener: _____

	CHECKS	COMMENTS
Gives Feedback	_____	_____
Asks Questions	_____	_____
Paraphrases	_____	_____
Uses Positive Body Language	_____	_____
Uses Appropriate Facial Expressions	_____	_____
Other	_____	_____

Observer: _____

Figure 4.15   Indy 500 of Social Skills

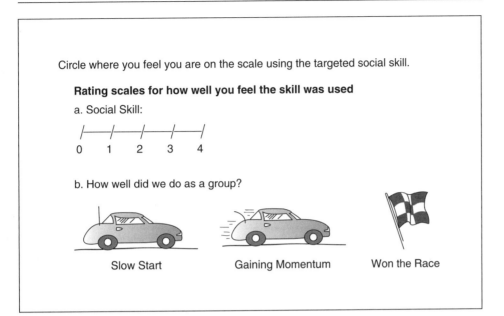

Circle where you feel you are on the scale using the targeted social skill.

Rating scales for how well you feel the skill was used

a. Social Skill:

```
|———|———|———|———|
0    1    2    3    4
```

b. How well did we do as a group?

Slow Start   Gaining Momentum   Won the Race

TEAM BUILDING

Scenario

"Good morning class," says Mr. Parks as he greets his students.

"Today we will try something new. We will work in cooperative groups to solve our word problems in math. I'd like everyone to number off from one to eight—ready? Tim, you start...

"Okay, now that you all have your numbers, I would like all the students with the same numbers to get into a group. The person who lives the farthest from school will be the organizer. The person who lives the next farthest will be the reporter. And the person who lives the closest to school will be the materials manager. Ready? Go!"

"Number three," yells Billy. *"Where are the other threes?"*

"Sixes," shouts Mary. *"Where are we going to sit?"*

"Over here," bellows Ann. *"Bring your desk over by me."*

"I can't find any twos, Mr. Parks. I think some people changed their numbers to go with their friends. I am all alone," wails Albert.

"What were we supposed to do?" whines Elizabeth. *"I don't know if I live the farthest or not, and if I did, what do I organize?"*

"What materials do I need?" shouts Sidney. *"And where are they?"*

"I still can't find my group," sobs Albert.

(Ten minutes later...)

"Okay," says Mr. Parks. *"Now that everyone has found a group and figured out roles, we can begin our assignment."*

Figure 4.16 PMI Chart for Processing Use of Social Skill

Use de Bono's PMI chart to process the pluses, minuses, and interesting points about using the targeted social skill.

Social Skill: _____

_____

P (Pluses) of using the social skill	M (Minuses) of using the social skill	I (Interesting Points) about using the social skill

Figure 4.17 Reflective Log on Using a Social Skill

Targeted Social Skill: _____

Initial observation about using the targeted social skill . . .	*Upon reflection . . .*
Date: _____	Date: _____
When I first started practicing using the targeted social skill, I . . .	After having used the targeted social skill, I . . .

Signed: _____

Figure 4.18 Self-Evaluation Observation Checklist

Use an observation checklist to complete a self-evaluation on your use of social skills.

Group Member	Skill	Feedback Symbol
Mary Smith	Taking Turns	0
	Listening	√+
	Encouraging	√
	Staying on Task	0

Scale: 0 = Not Yet,   √ = In Progress,   √ + = Mastery

Comments:

Facilitating Cooperative Group Activities

"Getting into groups" may seem like a basic social skill that all students from Grades 1 to 12 could master in a few minutes of practice—right? Wrong! Every teacher has experienced the "controlled chaos" of desks being dragged across the floor and students scattered in mass confusion as they attempt to find their groups. Getting into groups should take only a few minutes of precious class time; however, some classes spend as much as 10 minutes just forming their groups, thus losing valuable time to accomplish their goals. Teachers at all grade levels should demonstrate to their classes the appropriate procedures. Working in *cooperative* groups is not just working in groups. A great deal of preparation and training must precede the first cooperative learning attempt.

How often have teachers said, "I tried cooperative learning with my students, but it just didn't work. This year, I had a lot of kids with behavior problems, and the students got too loud and nothing got done." After one or two unsuccessful forays into cooperative learning, many teachers simply abandon the practice and return to more traditional methods of teaching. After all, students separated by rows of chairs are less likely to talk. Cooperative group activities fail if the teacher does not take the time to set up the groups properly. There are no shortcuts in the cooperative classroom. If time is not taken to establish the climate for cooperation (bulletin boards, themes, bonding activities), to set up the procedures (how to get into groups, room arrangements, signals, assigned roles), to establish the groundwork (rules and consequences), and, most important, to teach students social skills (listening, sharing, taking turns, helping one another), then the cooperative group activity is doomed from the start.

Cooperative Learning Basics

A good hook or motivator to introduce cooperative learning is to have the class complete a K-W-L sheet (Ogle, 1986) on cooperative learning. The students list what they *Know* about cooperative learning in the first column and what they *Want* to know about cooperative learning in the second column. Later in the year, they fill in the last column about what they *Learned* about cooperative learning (see Figure 4.19).

Figure 4.19 Cooperative Learning K-W-L Chart

Use Ogle's (1986) K-W-L Chart to process your feelings about cooperative learning.

K	W	L
What I *know* about cooperative learning . . .	What I *want* to know about cooperative learning . . .	What I have *learned* about cooperative learning . . .

Most cooperative learning experts recommend that teachers wait three or four weeks after the school-year begins before assigning students to their heterogeneous base groups. These base groups are groups the students should return to on a regular basis. They are composed of students of different races, sexes, and ability levels who work together for as long as a quarter, semester, or year. Teachers need to get to know the students' ability levels, personalities, learning modalities, and behavior patterns before assigning them to a base group.

It is essential that students be placed in base groups before they begin practicing social skills. Students interact with all the students in the class during formal and informal group activities, but they should always return to their base group when specific social skills are introduced and taught. Base groups are like homerooms. Students go to other classes, but they always return to their homeroom group sometime during the day or week. They begin to bond with familiar students and feel more secure with them.

Teachers who respect the dignity and individuality of students allow the students to help formulate the rules and consequences that govern group activities. If students decided the classroom rules and consequences for their classroom at the beginning of the school year, students can replicate the same process later in the year when it comes to determining the rules that will govern their group interactions.

Figure 4.20 demonstrates the social skills that are needed for cooperative group activities.

Figure 4.20 Social Skills for Cooperative Groups

- Follow role assignments.
- Encourage others.
- Stay on task.
- Offer to help.
- Check for understanding.
- Make decisions.
- Respect others' opinions.

The teacher can call a class meeting to discuss cooperative learning and to tell the students about the philosophy behind cooperative groups, what their roles will be, and how the groups will function. The students should then brainstorm the types of roles the class needs and define the duties assigned for each of the roles. Some possible roles include those listed in Figure 4.21.

Figure 4.21 Cooperative Group Roles

• Organizer	• Recorder	• Sergeant at Arms
• Timekeeper	• Encourager	• Bookkeeper
• Materials Manager	• Checker	• Editor-in-Chief
• Discussion Leader	• Observer	• Traveler
• Reader	• Umpire	• Summarizer
• Keyboarder	• Scout	• Reporter

The students and the teacher decide which roles are most useful and then list the tasks for each of those roles. The following roles and tasks (see Figure 4.22) could be used in cooperative groups in different classes and at different grade levels.

Figure 4.22 Example of Cooperative Group Roles and Tasks

Cooperative Group Roles	Tasks
Materials Manager	1. Finds out what materials are needed 2. Makes sure all students have what they need 3. Returns materials after the activity
Organizer	1. Assigns students their parts 2. Watches time 3. Makes sure all tasks are completed
Recorder	1. Writes down what the group decides is important 2. Reads ideas to the group 3. Checks for spelling and accuracy
Encourager	1. Compliments group members 2. Leads the group in a cheer 3. Energizes the group
Clarifier	1. Makes sure everyone understands the directions 2. Checks for understanding 3. Checks with other groups or the teacher if no one in the group understands
Scout	1. Checks what other groups are doing 2. Brings back information
Editor-in-Chief	1. Assigns the members their work 2. Makes sure the deadline is enforced 3. Turns in the group's work
Reporter	1. Makes sure he or she understands information 2. Reports group ideas to class 3. Answers questions from the rest of the class

After the roles and responsibilities have been established, students brainstorm some cooperative group rules and some possible consequences if students do not function well in groups. The teacher initiates a class brainstorming session to ask about the types of problems that could occur. Write each problem on the board as students think of it. Some problems might include the following:

- Students who prefer to work alone
- Students with whom no one wants to work
- Students who talk all the time
- Students who take over the group
- Students who text-message their friends rather than contributing to the group
- Students who are absent all the time and get behind
- Students who don't have their work
- Students who use inappropriate language or put-downs

It is beneficial to anticipate problems that might arise when students are placed in cooperative groups to study and learn before students form such groups.

Activity: Brainstorming Problems and Solutions

After the class has generated a list of possible problems, the teacher divides the members into groups of three or four, assigns each group a specific problem, and asks the groups to brainstorm possible solutions using a web graphic organizer. Some examples of possible solutions to a problem are diagrammed in the web in Figure 4.23.

Each group shares its web with the whole class. Class members add, delete, and revise possible solutions after thoughtful discussions. They post the webs around the room so they serve as reminders and resources for potential problem-solving strategies.

Figure 4.23 Generating Possible Solutions to a Problem Web

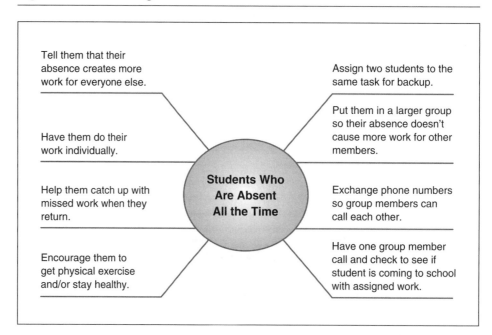

Activity: Constructing Consequences

After the class discussion of all the problems and possible solutions, they vote on a list of possible consequences for each of the problems. See Figure 4.24 for an example. Students need to know ahead of time the consequences they might experience if they violate the protocol.

Figure 4.24 Possible Consequences for Group Member's Behavior

Group Member's Behavior	Possible Consequences
Student forgets his or her part of group project.	Teacher gives the group an extension but deducts points from the grade of the student who forgot his or her part of the project.

Some sample consequences might include the following:

- Group members discuss student's behavior with that student.
- Teacher talks to student about the problem.
- Student must discuss his behavior with teacher and group members before returning to group.
- Student signs "social contract" describing what she will do to improve behavior.

Because students are individuals, a prescriptive formula does not fit all situations. Teachers must make it very clear that they always reserve the right to select or alter the consequences depending on individual students and cases. Through these exercises, students become aware of the types of problems that might occur in group situations, and, more important, they become aware of how their peers feel about specific behaviors. Peer pressure to perform cooperatively in groups is a powerful incentive.

Discussing potential problems and possible solutions before students are placed in base groups or form learning groups could help eliminate problems or at least focus the students on becoming student problem solvers who don't always have to yell "Teacher, teacher!" to solve their group problems. Assignment #3 (Figure 4.25) provides webs to brainstorm solutions to problems related to cooperative learning.

Behavior Checklists

Many standards or goals include communications skills related to speaking and listening. In addition, some standards include skills related to team building, consensus, and conflict resolution. Other districts include standards related to attitudes, dispositions, and character. It is important to use the terminology in your district's or state's standards so the assessments are valid.

Figure 4.26 shows a "Cooperative Social Skills Checklist" that group members could use to self-assess themselves. Figure 4.27 shows an "Observation Checklist for Cooperative Group Work" that emphasizes specific characteristics of encouragement, communication, and problem solving. Figure 4.28 is a "Clustered Criteria Checklist" to use to target different social skills as needed.

(*Text continues on page 124*)

Figure 4.25 Problem-Solving Web for Group Problems

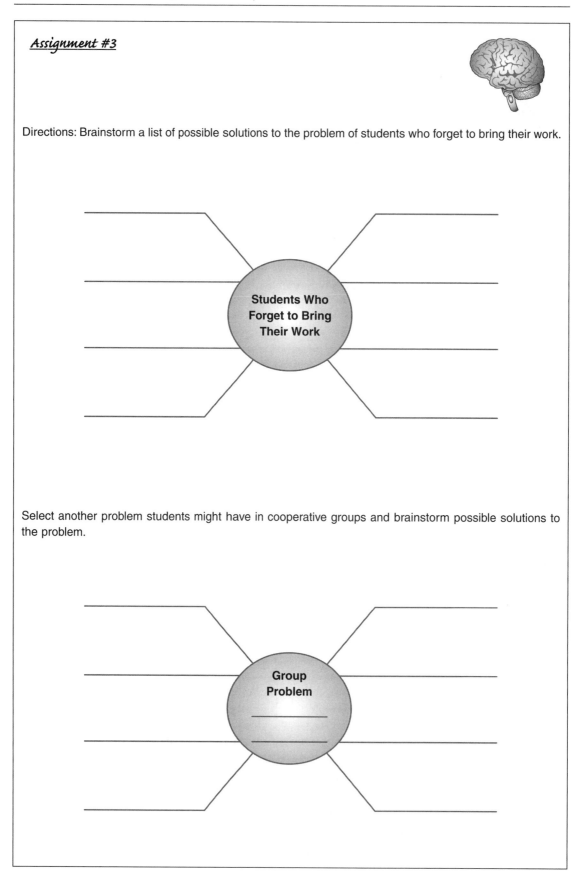

Figure 4.26 Cooperative Group Social Skills Checklist

Group Name: _____   **Date:** _____

	Observed	Not Observed
Basic Interaction: *The students . . .*		
• Formed their group quietly		
• Followed their role assignments		
• Shared their materials		
• Used each other's first names		
• Made appropriate eye contact with each other		
Communication Skills: *The students . . .*		
• Listened to the speaker		
• Took turns speaking		
• Made sure all students contributed their views		
• Used their low (12") voices		
• Waited until speaker finished before speaking		
Team-Building Skills: *The students . . .*		
• Encouraged other group members		
• Checked for understanding		
• Offered their help to others when needed		
• Energized and celebrated the group		
Conflict Resolution: *The students . . .*		
• Disagreed with the ideas—not the person		
• Respected the opinions of others		
• Reached consensus through negotiation		
• Explored different points of view		
• Compromised when necessary		

Figure 4.27 Observation Checklist for Cooperative Group Work

Group Project: _____ Date: _____

Group Members' Names

1. _____ 3. _____

2. _____ 4. _____

	Observed	Not Observed
Encouragement: *The students . . .*		
• Restate (paraphrase) the ideas of others		
• Check for understanding		
• Provide positive verbal feedback (encouraging words)		
• Provide positive nonverbal reinforcement (facial expression, gestures, eye contact)		
Communication: *The students . . .*		
• Speak clearly		
• Speak with appropriate volume (12″ voices)		
• Allow others to speak without interrupting		
• Listen attentively to other group members.		
• Respond appropriately to comments		
Problem Solving: *The students . . .*		
• Begin work promptly on the project		
• Brainstorm various ideas		
• Seek input from all team members		
• Explore multiple solutions to problem	/	
• Encourage creative options		
• Help build team consensus		
	Total:	

What team members did well?

What needs more work?

Scale:

14–15 = Dynamic Group

12–13 = In Progress

10–11 = Not Yet!

Teacher's signature: _____

Figure 4.28 Clustered Criteria Checklist

Social Skill: _____

Assignment: _____

Criteria/Performance Indicators	Not Yet 0	Some Evidence 1
•		
•		
•		
•		
•		
•		
•		
•		
•		
•		
•		
•		
•		
•		
•		
Total Points:		

Bonding Activities

The concept of team building is critical to the success of cooperative groups. Even though taking time from the content and the textbook to practice "bonding activities," which build trust and rapport, may seem frivolous to some, its importance cannot be emphasized enough.

Bonding activities allow students in a group to get to know each other better by discovering common likes and dislikes as well as similar hobbies, talents, tastes, and other things that create lasting friendships. To have students forge friendships is important in all group activities, but it is essential to forming base groups. The following bonding activities help bring students closer to their fellow group members and make them more willing to provide each other with help, encouragement, and support.

Activity: True-False Quiz

1. Teachers pair two students in the group and give them each 10 minutes to interview each other. Students should be encouraged to ask lots of "far out" or creative questions so the class can get to know the real person.

2. After the students have interviewed their partners, tell them to construct a five-item, true-or-false quiz about their partners. Students should be reminded to include questions that could stump the rest of the class.

3. Have students introduce their partners to the class and read the questions aloud. The class votes true or false on each question. Here is an example.

Mike has just returned from visiting his uncle in Australia.	T	F
Mike's favorite singer is Bruce Springsteen.	T	F
Mike loves writing research papers.	T	F
Mike's mom is a former Miss America.	T	F
Mike has won five tennis trophies.	T	F

4. After the class votes on each question, the partner tells the right answer and a little bit about the question.

Question #4: Mike's mom is a former Miss America.	T	F
Answer: False. In fact, Mike's mother protested the pageant as being demeaning to women.		

Students have fun with the quiz and find out something intriguing about each other without giving speeches. This activity can be used with groups of three, but it takes longer to make sure all three students have been interviewed so that each group member can introduce one of the other members to the group.

Activity: The Venn and the Triple Venn Diagrams

This activity works for two, three, or four people in a base group. If there are four students, teachers can put them in pairs and have each pair complete a Venn diagram stating how they are different and how they are alike. Groups of three can do a triple Venn diagram. Groups use big poster paper or transparencies so the Venn diagrams can be shared with the entire class. Students feel more comfortable introducing each other when they have the graphic organizer to help them. The Venn diagram constructed by Sally and Mike is shown in Figure 4.29; Figure 4.30 contains forms for both a regular Venn and a triple Venn diagram.

Activity: Create a Business

Give each group of four a piece of poster paper and ask students to draw a picture frame. Consider the following options:

- Ask each student in the base group to write down a list of all his strengths in his corner of the picture frame. Make sure students include everything they do well (sports, shopping, artwork, computer skills, public speaking, dancing, singing, etc.).

Figure 4.29 Partner Introduction Activity Using the Venn Diagram

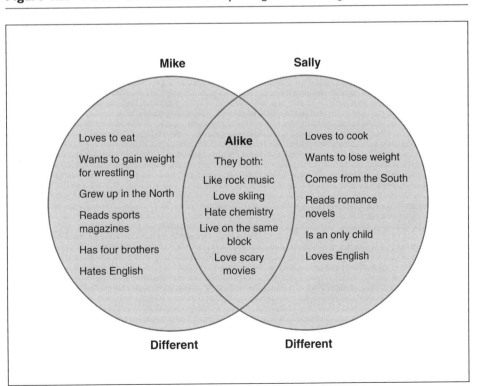

Figure 4.30 Triad Introduction Activity Using the Triple-Venn Diagram

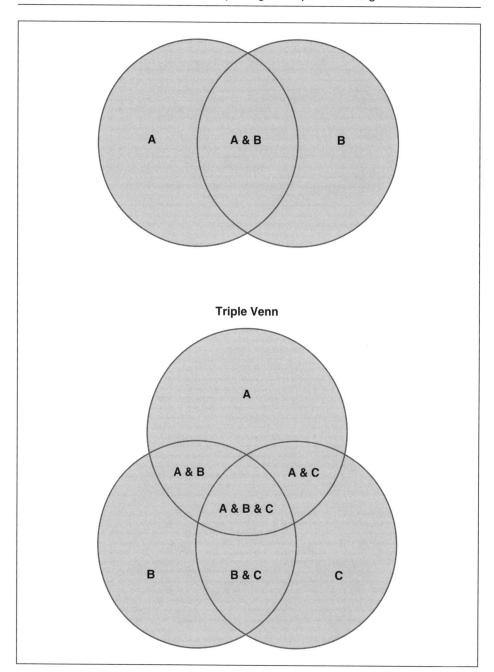

- Ask each group member to share the list with her group.
- Ask students to check whether any strength appears several times.
- Ask students to write the strengths they have in common in the middle of the picture frame.
- Ask teams to invent businesses their team could start based on the strengths of the team members listed in the middle of the frame.
- Ask teams to name their businesses.
- Ask teams to create business cards they can use.
- Ask teams to write a television, radio, or Internet commercial advertising their businesses.

- Ask teams to create a Web site for their group.
- Ask teams to write a poem, jingle, song, or rap to advertise their businesses.
- Ask teams to share one or two of their ideas with the entire class.

This activity promotes bonding by asking students to share their strengths with each other and having them acknowledge and appreciate each other's strengths when working together to complete a project. The students will become more attuned to what they have in common and more likely to talk to one another outside of class because they know each other's interests. They do not have to complete all the activities at once. Sometimes, the group can present ideas throughout the year as its business plan evolves into a marketing campaign. When new students join the class, they should be added to a base team so they contribute their strengths and also feel part of the group and the class. Figure 4.31 shows an example of one student group's "business plan."

Figure 4.31   Create a Business Bonding Activity for Teams

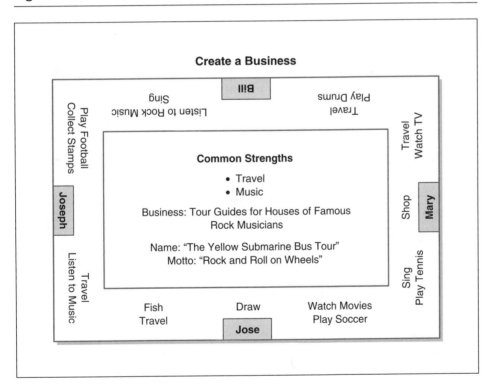

Activity: Creative Energizers

It is amazing how close students become once they have gone through a risk-taking ordeal together. Teachers ask students to "take a risk" by sharing their creative talents with the class by performing their interpretation of two of the activities listed below. Although some older students may look at the teacher like he is crazy when this activity is assigned, deep down, many of them relish the idea of presenting their talents to an audience of their peers.

Each base group is assigned a presentation to make in front of the class. After the group has a chance to talk, get to know one another, and discover each other's likes and dislikes, they are ready for another bonding activity. They need to decide on a group name based on their personalities, come up with a motto, and create a sign with their group logo. They then must select two of the following items to present to the class:

- An Internet commercial
- A poem depicting the group's goals, expectations, fears, etc.
- A cheer that epitomizes their team spirit
- A TV commercial that depicts the outstanding merits of the group
- A rap song that describes the group in musical verse
- A radio jingle advertising their unity
- A short video for Internet sites
- A group dance or cheer
- An ad that captures the essence of the group spirit
- A pantomime that symbolizes togetherness

Students must also create an "energizer" or sign of encouragement to use when their entire group or a member of their group does something well. Creativity and originality are encouraged, but the list in Figure 4.32 contains some common energizers, created by the Boy Scouts and Girl Scouts and others, which students can adopt. Students need to celebrate when they do a good job of using their special skills. More importantly, positive recognition from their peers is probably more effective in building their self-esteem than recognition from the teacher.

The students share their signals with the class, and the teacher tells groups when they are allowed to honor and celebrate other class members with their official seal of approval. Students enjoy receiving recognition and encouragement from each other, and sometimes the traditional smattering of applause just doesn't convey a true sense of appreciation or excitement. Group energizers let students personalize their recognition and encourage their continued participation. Students and adults love recognition and encouragement, and receiving attention from one's peers motivates and stimulates positive interaction.

Having students evaluate their own behavior, social skills, and group work is part of Glasser's (1990) quality school concept. He feels that students should evaluate their own work for quality to see how satisfying quality can be. When students appraise their own performance and assess the quality of their own work, they are well on their way to becoming self-sufficient and responsible adults. Assignment #4 (Figure 4.33) encourages teachers to create more bonding activities to introduce to their students. Students will generate many more energizers throughout the year, and these can be shared with the whole class to build a community of enthusiastic learners.

Figure 4.32 Group Energizers

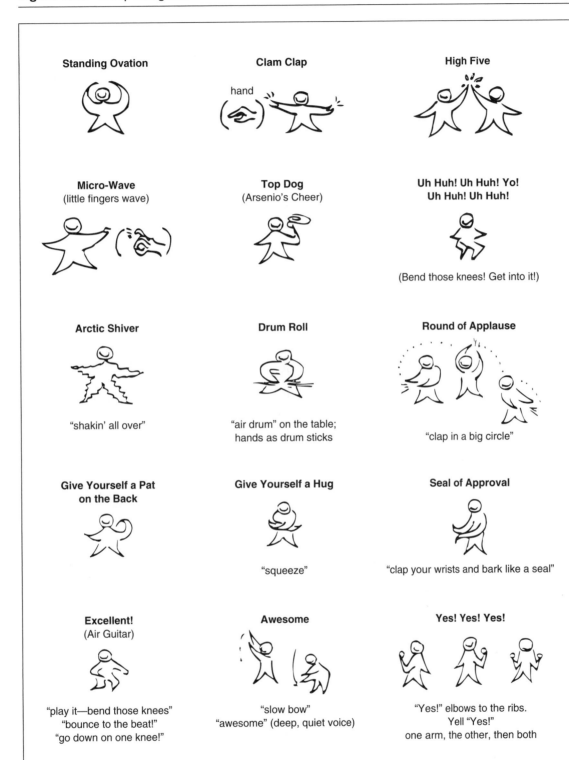

Figure 4.33 Brainstorming Energizers

Assignment #4

Directions: Brainstorm six more group energizers students can use to celebrate their success and their enthusiasm. Draw pictures that describe the energizer.

CONFLICT RESOLUTION

Scenario

> "Yeah, right, Sarah," Jack says. "What kind of idiot would ever consider voting Democratic. Are you crazy?"
>
> "Jack," Rose implores. "We are supposed to be working on a Venn diagram comparing one Republican candidate with one Democratic candidate for the next presidential election. Don't get hysterical."
>
> "I'm just amazed that someone is stupid enough to ever consider Sarah's candidate," says Jack.
>
> "Thanks for listening, Jack," Sarah says sarcastically. "I really appreciate your open mind and willingness to listen. You're such a supportive person."
>
> "Well, you don't know anything about the candidates," says Jack. "You are just voting the way your parents vote!"
>
> "I am not going to sit here and listen to that know-it-all analyze my life," Sarah says with emotion.
>
> "Okay you guys. We need to finish this social studies assignment in 20 minutes," interrupts Rose. "You two need to cool it."

Handling Conflict

Contrary to the beliefs of many teachers, students should be encouraged to disagree and argue with each other. Teachers who spend time bonding groups and getting them to conform often become upset when the group members begin to engage in disagreements or express opposite points of view. They sometimes refrain from introducing controversial topics because the arguments that ensue may cause discipline problems. Controversy should be encouraged, however, because it leads to students' using higher-order thinking skills to solve problems and higher-level social skills to handle confrontation.

The key is not to avoid conflict but, instead, to teach students how to handle conflict. The social skills related to conflict resolution need to be taught, retaught, reviewed, and taught again until they are embedded in students. Everyone knows of people who possess many other wonderful social skills, but their inability to listen and respect others' opinions or reach agreement on any divisive issue often causes them immeasurable problems in their personal and professional lives. Students should be taught how to engage in controversy or conflict by listening to others' ideas, respecting their opinions, and learning how to disagree with the idea—not the person.

These social skills are especially important for students in gifted programs. Exceptionally intelligent students may try to be the center of attention and dominate the group. They can sometimes be assertive about their own beliefs and dismissive of the ideas of others. These students may not function well in cooperative groups unless they are in charge, and they may withdraw or get angry if others disagree with their ideas.

In the course of the discussions outlined in activities in this chapter, students will disagree with each other. However, if students have internalized the social skills that go along with conflict resolution, they will know how to disagree with the idea without alienating or insulting the person with whom they disagree. They will also develop the critical thinking skills that help them to listen to the opinions of others, analyze a problem by examining all sides, form an intelligent opinion, and persuade people to agree with them by using logical arguments and effective communication skills.

Vitto (2003) believes that teachers make assumptions that students should know *how, when,* and *why* to behave appropriately, but they may, in fact, lack this knowledge or lack self-control. When students yell inappropriately or engage in name-calling during an argument, he says teachers need to treat the "behavioral deficits" as they do academic deficits.

> If a student is struggling with mathematics facts, we assume that remediation is necessary, or if a student is struggling with staying in his or her seat or is disrupting class, we assume that the student knows fully how to act but is deciding not to. We need to give behavior the same educational benefit of the doubt that we give academics. (p. 189)

One of the goals of cooperative learning is to help students make appropriate decisions. If students are to achieve this goal, they need to be exposed to people who think differently than they do and to ideas that are contrary to their beliefs. Students need to learn how to formulate and defend their beliefs rationally, intelligently, and calmly in a global society. They need to prepare to live in a diverse world where differing opinions cause controversy. Their willingness to recognize and understand different points of view and their ability to negotiate compromises or solutions are critical skills for the twenty-first century.

Figure 4.34 shows the social skills that can help students engage in successful conflict resolution when they interact with others.

Students who always agree with the crowd and never question their teachers or authority figures may not become independent thinkers who can later make critical and creative decisions on their own. Use the following activities to encourage students to form and defend opinions and to show students they can do so within the framework of trust, respect, and courtesy—not anger and violence.

Figure 4.34 Social Skills for Conflict Resolution

- Disagree with the idea—not the person.
- Respect other's opinions.
- Explore different points of view.
- Think for yourself.
- Negotiate and/or compromise.
- Reach consensus.

Activity: Agree/Disagree Chart

Give a diagnostic quiz to students prior to studying a unit to see how each group member feels about an issue. Distribute the same quiz at the end of the unit to see if students have changed their minds. This graphic organizer is similar to a pretest and a posttest. Consider the following:

1. Introduce the Agree/Disagree Graphic Organizer Chart (see Figure 4.35). Students note that the chart has a BEFORE column and an AFTER column. They use the BEFORE column before the activity or lesson and the AFTER column after the activity or lesson. Prior to studying a topic, distribute copies of the chart and ask each group's reader to read the statements out loud. Ask the recorders to write the names or initials of each group member under either the Agree or Disagree column, according to their opinion about each statement.

2. Have the class listen to a lecture, view a film, read an article, study a unit, attend an assembly, read a book, or go on a field trip that is related to the topic.

3. Have the group's reader read each of the statements again after the learning activity. The team members think about the new information they have received and write their name in the AFTER column of the agree/disagree chart.

4. Encourage students to discuss with the other team members their views and why they did or did not change their opinions.

Notice that Figure 4.35 shows an example of an agree/disagree chart for a course on classroom management.

This activity helps students learn the importance of gathering facts and information when taking a stance on a subject. It also helps them listen to information and other people's views and justify their own opinions based upon facts—not just emotion, which tends to "hijack" the intellect.

An agree/disagree chart, such as the example shown in Figure 4.36 for a drug and alcohol unit, could be used at the beginning of a unit to check for prior knowledge. It could also be used again at the end of the unit to see if students have changed their opinion of each statement based upon the information they learned. Encourage students to discuss their opinions before they write their initials in either the Agree or Disagree box.

Assignment #5 (Figure 4.37) asks teachers to create an agree/disagree chart for a curriculum unit. The unit could be on deserts, spiders, Spain, right angles, or anything the students will be studying. Assignment #6 (Figure 4.38) deals with the classroom organization. Teachers could make statements such as "Students receive a detention for their first tardy" or "Five points are deducted for late assignments." The chart will help students review class procedures and rules. It could be given to the students prior to creating the rules with the class or as a review any time students become "rusty" in their attention to procedures, rules, and consequences.

(Text continues on page 138)

Figure 4.35 Agree/Disagree Chart Graphic Organizer

Topic: Classroom Management

Directions: Create eight statements to introduce a unit on classroom management.

Statement	Before		After	
	Agree	Disagree	Agree	Disagree
1. Classroom procedures are the same as classroom rules.				
2. Consequences are just another form of punishment.				
3. Social skills should be taught to students explicitly.				
4. Students should help develop classroom rules.				
5. Cooperative learning is the same as group work.				
6. Teachers should not lower students' academic grades because of their behavior.				
7. Cruelty to animals is predictor of potential violent behavior in students.				
8. Competition should be emphasized over cooperation.				

Figure 4.36 Agree/Disagree Chart

Drug and Alcohol Unit

Directions: Write your name in the Agree or Disagree box *before* you study the unit and *after* you study it.

Example:

Statement	Before		After	
	Agree	Disagree	Agree	Disagree
1. Marijuana is a safe drug.		Jose Mary Dave Monica		Jose Mary Dave Monica
2. Alcoholism is a disease.	Dave	Jose Mary Monica	Jose Mary Dave	Monica
3. Coffee can reduce alcohol in the body.	Jose Mary Dave Monica			Jose Mary Dave Monica
4. Men can drink more than women.	Jose Mary	Dave Monica		Jose Mary Dave Monica
5. Steroids are legal in pro sports.		Jose Mary Dave Monica		Jose Mary Dave Monica
6. Crack is not as lethal as cocaine.	Mary Dave	Jose Monica		Jose Mary Dave Monica
7. Heroine is always addictive.	Jose Mary Dave Monica		Jose Dave	Mary Monica
8 Alcoholism runs in families; it's in the genes.	Jose Dave	Mary Monica	Mary Dave	Jose Monica

Figure 4.37 Agree/Disagree Chart on Classroom Principles and Procedures

In the Learning Center . . .	Agree	Disagree	Not Sure
1. There should be "rules" that outline the behavior/work habits that are expected.			
2. If there are going to be rules, I want to have a say in what they are.			
3. I should respect the adults I work with.			
4. I should respect the other students in the Learning Center.			
5. Teasing, of any kind, is just fine.			
6. Humor is okay and a welcome "stress reliever."			
7. I should be able to speak as loudly as I want.			
8. Teachers are responsible for knowing all of my assignments and due dates.			
9. "Fair" means everyone will be treated exactly the same.			
10. "Fair" means that each person will get what he or she needs.			
11. It's okay to come unprepared.			
12. It's perfectly acceptable to "slack off."			
13. The consequences for misbehavior should be stated ahead of time so students know what to expect.			
14. Teachers can read my mind, so they will know when I need help.			
15. It's fine to wait until the last minute to get help from the teacher.			
16. It is necessary for me to clean up and put supplies, etc. away before leaving the room.			
17. I am responsible for knowing and understanding my individualized educational program, modifications, etc.			
18. I will be able to get the help I need, but I am encouraged to work independently as often as possible.			
19. I will have a great time and look forward to coming each period I am assigned here!			

Name _____

What do you expect from the teachers in the Learning Center? Please be as specific as you can.

_____

Created by Lorrie King, Yarmouth High School, Yarmouth, ME. Used with permission.

Figure 4.38 Agree/Disagree Chart on Classroom Organization

Assignment #6

Directions: Create statements to review classroom procedures, rules, and consequences. Example "We receive a tardy if we are not in our seat when the bell rings."

Statement	Before		After	
	Agree	Disagree	Agree	Disagree
1.				
2.				
3.				
4.				
5.				
6.				
7.				
8.				

Activity: Consensus Chart

This activity helps students reach consensus. Consider the following steps:

1. Students have the task of choosing their group's choice for top three television shows.

2. The recorder writes down 10 programs from the titles that the group members brainstorm.

3. To help reach consensus, have the groups take a "reading" of each person's rating of the television shows by doing a "five to fist" (see Figure 4.39) as the title is announced. (This is not a vote!)

4. If a student holds up a fist, that student must provide an alternative title.

5. Students who want a show to be on the list can try to persuade other students who show two fingers (let's talk more) or three fingers (okay with me) to agree with the choice.

6. The consensus cycle of talk-discuss-persuade-justify should be used until the group can reach consensus on its choice of the top three shows.

This activity teaches students the importance of compromise and listening to others during a discussion. Also, group members learn that one cannot veto an idea without supplying an alternative. Use assignment #7 (Figure 4.40) to do a consensus activity about the top three foods in the cafeteria, the best music group, the best movie, or the best book. Ask students to brainstorm a list of 10 possible choices and then arrive at the top three.

Figure 4.39   Consensus Chart—Five to Fist

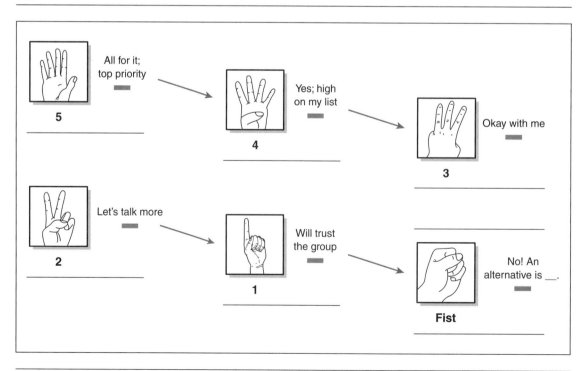

Figure 4.40 Consensus Chart

Assignment #7

Directions: Ask students to use the process to come to consensus about their top three choices of foods, music groups, movies, or books.

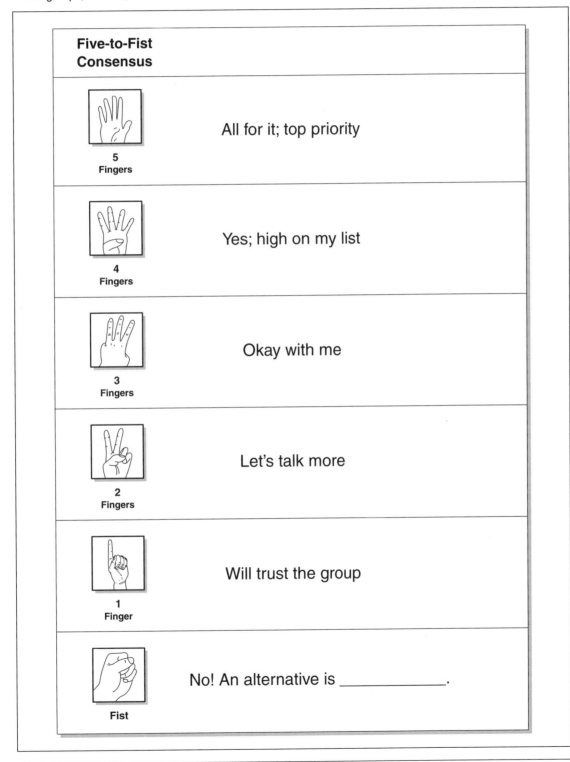

Activity: Human Graph

The human graph is an interactive opinion poll. Consider the following steps:

1. The teacher selects several controversial topics before engaging in the human graph experiment. Topics might include the following:
   - Making the school year 12 months long instead of 9
   - Eliminating many standardized tests
   - Raising the driving age to 18
   - Lowering the drinking age to 18
   - Unannounced drug testing in schools
   - Requiring all high school students to complete 60 hours of community service as part of their graduation requirements
   - Eliminating recess or physical education from school schedules
   - Requiring all students to take at least one foreign language
   - Not allowing sweets in schools for birthday parties
   - Banning all peanut products from school to accommodate students who have allergies

2. The teacher then makes a statement about the topic. For example, the teacher might say, "All public school students should be required to wear uniforms to school." Then the teacher stands in the middle of the room to indicate the neutral position. Students in favor of the statement stand to the right of the teacher; students opposed stand to the left (see Figure 4.41). The position students take indicates how strongly they feel about the topic. Students can line up in front of one another if they share the same opinions. Students can remain neutral in front of the teacher if they don't know anything about the topic or if they don't have an opinion.

3. The teacher calls on students to explain why they feel the way they do about the topic. Only one person speaks at a time. Everyone listens to all arguments.

4. After several students have expressed their opinions, the teacher gives a signal to allow everyone to change positions in the human graph to represent their changed opinions on the topic.

5. The teacher asks students why they changed their opinions.

The human graph activity allows for a great deal of interaction, and it allows students to use their facts and ideas to persuade others to side with their view. It also emphasizes effective listening skills and the importance of keeping an open mind. Students often change their position, literally and figuratively, by listening to arguments and reassessing their stance on a topic. This kinesthetic discussion can serve as a hook to introduce an issue or as a review after a controversial topic has been studied.

Activity: Conflict Resolution

This activity helps students to recognize a variety of ways to handle disagreements.

Figure 4.41 Human Graph

From *Blueprints for Achievement in the Cooperative Classroom* by James Bellanca and Robin Fogarty. © 2003 by Corwin Press. Used with permission.

1. The teacher explains the roles of court reporter, judge, and bailiff to the cooperative teams. The court reporter writes down all the group's ideas on the team sheet. The judge makes sure each team member agrees and explains the teams' ideas to the class. The bailiff makes sure the team finishes on time and looks up words in the dictionary.

2. Assign roles by alphabetical order. The person in each group whose first name comes first in the alphabet will be the court reporter, the second person will be the judge, and the third person will be the bailiff.

3. Ask the bailiff of each group to read the rules for working together in the courtroom to that group:
   - Listen carefully to all arguments.
   - One person talks at a time.
   - Stay with the team.
   - Do your job well.
   - Be positive.
   - Tell the truth; you are under oath.

4. Remind the court reporter to have the team's dictionary ready.

5. Ask the students to look over the words in Figure 4.42 and tell them to discuss each of the words and make sure everyone in the group understands their definitions. Students check off each word after everyone understands it.

Figure 4.42   What Do You Do When You Disagree?

❏ *Argue*—repeat the same ideas and stand firm

❏ *Persuade*—justify; provide reasons to back up your ideas or appeal to emotion

❏ *Vote*—count votes to select the majority

❏ *Compromise*—combine and/or modify ideas

❏ *Mediate*—find a neutral party to facilitate or judge

❏ *Arbitrate*—agree to abide by decisions of an assigned person who takes the best from both sides

❏ *Delay*—table it, sleep on it, wait

❏ *Reconceptualize*—rethink, find new angles

❏ *Negotiate*—give and take

❏ *Give in*—give up, cave in, play martyr

❏ *Seek Consensus*—talk, juggle, adjust, modify, and find an agreement both sides can live with

❏ *Humor*—veer away from confrontation

❏ *Avoid*—ignore or postpone indefinitely

6. Have each person in the group select one of the strategies for conflict resolution listed above and tell about a time when she used that strategy effectively.

7. Have students rank the three strategies their group feels are most effective for solving conflicts.

This activity helps students learn to work together to help each other and prompts them to reflect on effective problem-solving skills. This activity also helps students understand the importance of communication in solving conflicts. It is important that they understand that one cannot always "win" in all situations and that there are alternative ways to arrive at a solution.

SETTING THE STAGE

The strategies, activities, and assignments in the first four chapters of this book have set the stage for learning. Use assignment #8 (Figure 4.43) to reflect on what was discussed in these chapters. Establishing procedures, rules, and consequences forms the foundation of an effective classroom management program. Establishing a caring climate and a warm and nurturing environment sets the tone of a class. Teaching social skills explicitly and building camaraderie among students establishes expectations for acceptable behavior. And engaging in cooperative learning activities helps bond the students and make them feel part of the classroom team.

Figure 4.43 Reflection on Chapters 1–4

Assignment #8

Directions: Spend five minutes reviewing Chapters 1–4.

1. Write down five new things you have learned.

    1. _____

    2. _____

    3. _____

    4. _____

    5. _____

2. Find a partner for sharing.

3. **Partner A** talks for **one minute**—then switch and let **Partner B** talk for one minute (you cannot repeat anything your partner said!)

                                         Switch!

4. **Partner A** talks for **30 seconds**—Switch. Partner B talks for **30 seconds.** (You still cannot repeat anything you or your partner said.)

                                         Switch!

5. **Partner A** talks for **15 seconds**—Switch. **Partner B** talks for **15 seconds.**

                                         Stop

6. With your partner, write a one-sentence summary to synthesize what you have learned.

_____

_____

_____

Figure 4.44   Cooperative Group Activity Template

Assignment #9

Directions: Create a cooperative group activity using this template. Fill in the directions to help students understand the expectations of the assignment.

1. Formation of groups: _____

   _____

2. Role assignments: _____

   _____

Organizer/Timekeeper:

Materials Manager:

Recorder:

Reporter:

Encourager:

3. Task: _____

   _____

   _____

4. Time limit: _____

5. Social skill: _____

6. Processing: _____

7. Energizer: _____

Assignment #9 (Figure 4.44) provides a template for organizing a cooperative group activity. Create this chart on a large piece of paper, a transparency, or a handout and fill in the directions to help students understand what they are expected to do for each cooperative learning activity. It can serve as a visual reminder for students who have trouble remembering and following verbal instructions.

These proactive steps provide the groundwork for conducting engaging and meaningful lessons that help students learn. Despite all the preparation and all the attention to social interactions, some students will still have problems accepting responsibility, interacting with peers, or fitting in with others. The next four chapters will address strategies to handle "the square pegs who are trying to fit in the round holes," offering scenarios and strategies focused on helping the students who either cannot or will not assume responsibility for their own behavior and refuse to cooperate with their peers or their teacher. As one educator noted, "We prepared for everything, but then they sent us the wrong kids!"

Helping Students Who Won't Accept Responsibility 5

Figure 5.0 Responsible Students Fishbone Graphic Organizer

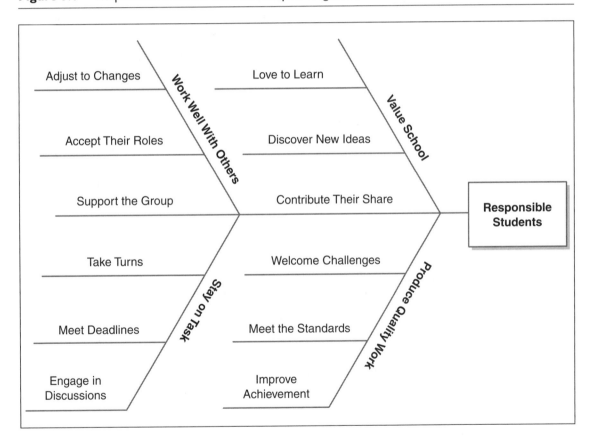

TEACHING RESPONSIBLE BEHAVIOR

When students are upset, they are never responsible; they are always victims of someone who has caused their misery. (Glasser, 1986, p. 47)

Many students have difficulty accepting responsibility for their own actions. They choose instead to blame someone else—another student, their parents, society, the dog (as in "the dog ate my homework"). Unfortunately, this pattern of students' never accepting responsibility for their own actions follows them throughout their lives if it is not addressed. This pattern starts in early grades, when a student begins shirking her responsibility to take tests, to perform in school, or to complete projects by staying home from school. Too often, parents contribute to the problem by either completing the work for the student or writing a note to the attendance office to excuse the child for the "absence."

In addition to teaching social skills explicitly, teachers also have to teach and model responsible behavior to maintain effective classroom management. DiGiulio (2000) advises teachers that commercial programs do not work. He says, "In such packaged plans, the teacher is promoting not prosocial behavior but conformity to reactive, impersonal rules" (p. 12). Classroom management packages ignore the fact that teaching influences student behavior. The teacher's behavior sets the expectation for the student's behavior. Moreover, students may comply because of fear of punishment, yet the good behavior has not necessarily been internalized so that it carries over to other settings outside the classroom. He says that "worst of all, these plans can turn a teacher into a dizzy robot whose time and attention are more focused on detecting and reacting than on teaching" (p. 12).

Some students may have developed a sense of irresponsibility at home by not being able to follow directions from parents or remembering to do things in a timely manner. These early behavior patterns transfer to their performance in school. These students constantly forget their lunch or lunch money; lose their books, glasses, and homework; forget their locker combinations, bus numbers, and field trip forms; and misplace their supplies. Rather than use the excuse "He's just not responsible," DiGiulio (2000) recommends that teachers practice five instructional interventions (see Figure 5.1) that allow students to develop prosocial behaviors and improve learning.

Teacher Behavior

Even though teachers set the stage for encouraging student responsibility with their expectations, sometimes students are not even aware they are not accepting responsibility for their own actions. Albert (1989) discusses the importance of pinpointing and describing the student's behavior by writing it down. She suggests that teachers observe and record the student's behavior objectively. It is then easier to discuss the behavior with the student and the parent if necessary. "A comprehensive description includes exactly *what* the student does to misbehave, *when* the student usually does it, and approximately

Figure 5.1 Instructional Interventions that Result in Prosocial Student Behavior

1. The teacher clearly communicates instructional expectations for students.
2. A teacher conveys enthusiasm for the subject and for teaching that subject to students.
3. A teacher holds students accountable for their work. Once dates and requirements are clearly established, the teacher then proceeds to hold students to those dates and requirements.
4. A teacher is aware of what's happening in the classroom.
5. A teacher teaches for success.

Adapted from *Positive Classroom Management: A Step-By-Step Guide to Successfully Running the Show Without Destroying Student Dignity* (2nd ed.), by Robert C. Di Giulio (1999). Thousand Oaks, CA: Corwin Press, www. corwinpress.com. All rights reserved.

how often the student does it" (p. 21). This description is an objective way of opening up discussions with students about their behaviors.

The ultimate goal of behavior management is to help students become more self-controlled and self-directed. Kauffman, Mostert, Trent, and Hallahan (1998) believe that after a student engages in a major acting-out incident, the teacher should have a conference with the student to debrief the event and discuss ways to avoid future upsets. They recommend that "during de-briefing, you will want to discuss what led up to the incident, what the student might have done instead of act out, and how future incidents can be avoided" (p. 83). They suggest that the teacher and student make a plan that will lead to the student's learning new strategies to self-manage behavior independently.

Using I-Messages

Another strategy teachers use to let students know they are not behaving responsibly is the I-message. Wolfgang, Bennett, and Irvin (1999) define the I-message as "a technique of expressing to a student that a behavior is having a negative effect on you. This statement must contain three elements: the student's *behavior*, its *effect* on you, and your *feeling* as a result of the behavior" (p. 63).

The I-message is a way for the teacher to inform the student of the problem the teacher is facing. The I-message is not saying, "You are absent too much," or "You didn't do your work." Those are "you-messages" that assess blame or guilt. The I-message lets the student know how what he did affects the teacher (see Figure 5.2).

Figure 5.2 You/I-Messages

You-Message	I-Message
"You are absent all the time. You're going to flunk this course."	"I feel upset that you are missing so much school and may not be able to go to college as you'd planned."
"You didn't do your group work."	"I feel bad that the rest of your group has worked hard on the project, and now they'll have to do your part also to get their grade."
"Jeff, quit running in the hall."	"When I see you running down the hall, I'm concerned that you will fall and get injured."

You-messages delivered publicly also put the student in an awkward situation in front of her peers. The teacher has just thrown down the gauntlet—issued a challenge and embarrassed the student. Some students accept the you-message quietly, while others experience an emotional "flood" and go into a fight-or-flight response. Wolfgang et al. (1999) offer examples of specific students' actions and appropriate I-messages teachers can give to make students aware of their thoughtlessness or irresponsible acts, without alienating the student or causing a showdown in front of the whole class (see Figure 5.3).

Gordon (1974) says that "you" statements or "you understood" statements, such as "Quiet down," or "The groups are too loud," become ultimatums issued by an authority figure. Students often feel embarrassed, put down, or angry when teachers send you-messages, making students less likely to accept responsibility for their actions. Students also become defensive about their actions and may act out to cover up their anger, rebellion, or embarrassment in front of their peers.

When teachers use I-messages, however, they appeal to a student's good nature and spirit of cooperation. When teachers say things such as "I'm upset," or "I am very concerned about your grades," teachers take responsibility for their own feelings and at the same time leave the students to worry about their own behavior.

Figure 5.3　I-Messages

Student's Action	Teacher's I-Message
Joe starts to talk during seat work while the teacher is reading to a small group. He talks loudly enough that it starts to disrupt everyone listening to the story.	"When someone talks during seat work (*behavior*) I have a hard time reading so everyone can hear (*effect*), and that makes me feel frustrated (*feeling*).
After getting up from the art table, Joanne leaves her supplies and trash behind.	"When students leave their supplies behind (*behavior*), I'm concerned (*feeling*) that these materials will be lost or broken (*effect*)."
Kate finishes eating and departs, leaving behind her trash.	"I get frustrated (*feeling*) when I have to clean up the lunch table (*effect*) after trash is left behind (*behavior*)."
When the door is opened to go to the next class, Jeffrey runs through the door and down the stairs.	"When students run down the stairs (*behavior*), I'm concerned (*feeling*) that people will fall and get injured (*effect*), and my job is to keep people safe."
Sara is taking a test when she stops, begins to cry, and comes to talk to the teacher through the crying.	"When students cry and talk to me at the same time (*behavior*), I can't understand what is being said (*effect*), and I am disappointed (*feeling*) that I can't help."
The teacher is talking to a parent when Tim interrupts and starts talking.	"It makes me sad (*feeling*) when I cannot understand two people who are talking to me at the same time (*behavior*), and I become confused (*effect*)."

Adapted from Wolfgang et al. (1999). *Strategies for teaching self-discipline in the middle grades*, pp. 65–66. Boston: Allyn & Bacon.

Students are often surprised when they hear teachers express personal feelings or concerns without placing blame on students. The key to successful I-messages, however, lies in sincerity, tone of voice, and depth of feeling. "I-messages laced with anger (or with similar hostile feelings like annoyance, hurt, disgust) have the same effect as you-messages" (Dinkmeyer, McKay, & Dinkmeyer, 1980, p. 99). When teachers are too angry to approach the student coolly and calmly, they should wait to address the problem, or they should delay their reaction until they are calm. Likewise, when teachers give encouragement and positive feedback, they show they recognize effort and improvement, value self-evaluation, allow students to be imperfect, and challenge students to be willing to try new ideas and take risks.

Link Between Standards and Discipline

Responsibility is not something teachers require students to bring to class the first week of school along with their notebooks, supplies, and immunization records. Students need to develop responsibility as early as kindergarten and practice it throughout school. One of the major goals of the business world is to hire responsible workers. Students who are not taught to be responsible for their own learning and for their own behavior will probably have a difficult time accepting responsibility later in life. The student who forgets to bring his homework, supplies, and textbooks to class; has frequent absences and tardies; and misses every project deadline might well become the adult who does not finish business reports or projects, frequently misses work, and often arrives late or leaves early. The referrals, detentions, and suspensions in school can translate to unsatisfactory performance reviews and pink slips later in life.

In addition, many state and district standards address life skills. Students must demonstrate they can regulate themselves by setting and managing goals, performing self-appraisals, considering risks, demonstrating perseverance, maintaining a healthy self-concept, and restraining impulsivity (Kendall & Marzano, 1997). Teachers, therefore, can justify taking measures to embed responsibility in their lessons because the standards regarding self-reflection reinforce the Responsibility Model of classroom management.

Teachers are understandably focused on teaching academic standards because that's how students, teachers, schools, districts, and states are assessed. Standardized tests have become the yardsticks for accountability, but the new emphasis on performance learning requires students to spend more time engaged in activities to measure their learning. These activities include cooperative group work, in which they must demonstrate their ability to accept responsibilities for their actions and their performance.

Cummings (2000) believes that the teacher must anticipate what skills and work habits students will need so they can demonstrate high levels of performance to meet and exceed standards. The proactive teacher teaches self-control first—before content standards. Effective discipline is teaching students how to maintain their self-control. "Our goal is to establish a community of learners who feel bonded and connected: such a community exhibits self-discipline and perseverance and takes responsibility for learning" (p. 2).

The following scenarios depict students who have trouble accepting their responsibilities. The scenarios show how irresponsible behavior on the part of one or two students makes groups of students or even the whole class dysfunctional. Ideas and strategies are offered following the scenarios for teachers to use with their students. Teachers can also brainstorm additional tactics that can help not only the students described in the scenario but also their own students who may have similar problems.

STUDENTS WHO ARE FREQUENTLY ABSENT

Scenario

Juan saunters into class—late as usual—and stops to high-five two of his buddies as he strolls slowly to his seat. Mrs. Gray watches Juan out of the corner of her eye but doesn't want to confront him and start the class with an altercation.

"Please take out your books and your homework," Mrs. Gray says as she checks attendance.

The students begin rustling their papers and searching for the autobiographies they started in class yesterday and finished for homework.

"Please move your desks into triads and exchange your autobiographies with a person in your group. I am distributing a rubric that you are to use to evaluate your partner's paper. Review all the criteria and provide feedback to your partners."

"What the hell is going on?" Juan growls just loud enough to be heard by the whole class.

Mrs. Gray moves closer to Juan and whispers, "Settle down."

Juan shouts, "What am I supposed to do? I wasn't here yesterday so I don't have anything to share."

"Juan, you are absent a lot," Mrs. Gray replies. "You'll have to make up the work because the autobiography counts for 20 percent of your grade. You also will lose points on your peer-editing grade because you cannot participate in today's activity. You see how frequent absences cause you problems? At this rate, your grade will suffer because you miss so much work!"

"I'd come to class if it wasn't so damn boring!" shouts Juan. "I'm going to see my counselor."

He picks up his books and storms out of the room, slamming the door behind him.

Solving the Problem

Many teachers have experienced the frustration of working with students who are chronically absent from class. Students develop their attendance patterns as early as kindergarten. Generally speaking, a senior in high school who is frequently absent was probably also frequently absent in kindergarten.

In the traditional classroom, the teacher must spend time helping absentee students understand the material they missed, keep up with their work, and make up assignments and tests. The student and perhaps the parents are also involved in the process, but the other students in the class are usually not involved.

In the cooperative classroom, however, the other students are also affected by another student's absence. Poet John Donne's (as cited in Bartlett, 1980) famous line, "No man is an island, entire of itself; every man is a piece of the continent, a part of the main," is applicable to the cooperative group. If one member is absent and doesn't pull her weight, everyone suffers. When a group member does not fulfill his obligations, "never send to know for whom the bell tolls; it tolls for thee" (p. 254). The cohesiveness of the group can break down, and the other students can begin to feel resentful and frustrated because of a member's apparent lack of interest.

When a student is frequently absent, the teacher's first priority is to determine the real cause of the student's chronic absenteeism. Is the student prone to illness? Does he have a serious medical problem? Is she bored with school? Do his parents need him to babysit at home or work to help pay the bills? Is she overwhelmed by the class work? Does he feel embarrassed by his lack of skills or his weaknesses? What is the real cause of the problem? Use the focus strategy demonstrated in Figure 5.4 to ascertain the root of the problem described in the scenario, and use the Problem-Solving Model Template in Figure 5.5 to practice the strategy. Once a teacher has determined the problem, the teacher can work with the student to find ways to solve it. Sometimes teachers have to ask good questions and become attentive listeners to cut through the "kid talk" and determine whether or not the real problem has been identified.

Other Strategies Teachers Can Use With Students Who Are Frequently Absent

- Review the absentee patterns of all students before assigning groups. Put an extra person in the groups that contain a student who is frequently absent.
- Talk privately to the student who is frequently absent to find out if personal or family problems are causing the absences.
- Initiate a one-on-one conference with the absentee student to find out if she feels inadequate because of a learning disability, low-ability skills, or a lack of understanding of the material.
- Interview the student to find out if there is a personality conflict with one or more group members.
- Organize a makeup work system where absentee students are responsible for doing the same amount and caliber of work as other members of their group.
- Organize a class phone tree where a student can call a buddy to find out what work he missed if he was absent.

Add some of your own solutions for helping students who are frequently absent:

_____

_____

_____

_____

_____

Figure 5.4 Problem-Solving Model

The student meets with the teacher and fills out the following problem-solving sheet to try to discover the cause of the problem and develop a mutual plan of action.

Focus Strategy

Student: _____Juan_____   Date: _____Sept. 6_____

Teacher: _____Mrs. Gray_____

Student's Description of the Problem:

I hate going to your English class because I'm not a good writer and I don't want other kids to read or valuate my work. My Dad says his taxes pay your salary and you should grade kides work—not have other students do it.

Teacher's Description of the Problem:

I am frustrated because I'm trying to teach you writing but since you miss about two days a week, you never learn enough. And then you can't move on because you haven't learned the basic skills.

Identify the Real Problem

Student:

It might be that my English is so bad I don't want kids making fun of me. I've learned to speak good enough to get by since I've moved from Mexico, but my writing is filled with grammer and spelling errors. I'm embarased to have other kids giggle when they correct my stuff.

Teacher:

I feel the real problem concerns your behavior when you enter the class. It seems like you cause so much confusion by showing off that I read it negatively and I start the class in a bad mood. I admit I don't help you as much as I should because I don't feel you're putting forth enough effort.

Possible Solutions:

1. _Juan can use the class computer to write his papers and use spell check and grammar check to correct his work._

2. _Mrs. Gray will pair Juan with another bilingual student, Marie, whom he feels comfortable with, until he feels confident about his writing._

3. _Juan will make a big effort to come to class more or to call Marie to get his homework if he is absent._

Signed: _____Mrs. Gray_____   _____Juan Martinez_____   _____Sept. 6_____
                    Teacher   Student   Date

Figure 5.5 Problem-Solving Model Template

ACTION

Student: _____ Date: _____

Teacher: _____

Student's Description of the Problem:

_____

_____

Teacher's Description of the Problem:

_____

_____

Identify the Real Problem

Student:

_____

_____

_____

Teacher:

_____

_____

_____

Possible Solutions:

1. _____

2. _____

3. _____

Signed: _____   _____   _____
          Teacher   Student   Date

STUDENTS WHO DON'T DO THEIR WORK

Scenario

"All right students," Mr. Fetzer announces. "Please pass up the scientific reports you did for homework. I need to grade them and average them into your final grades before report cards are issued."

Meggie looks down and doesn't add her report to the stack as the students pass them up the row.

Mr. Fetzer notices that Meggie did not hand in her work.

He calls Meggie to his desk and says, "Why didn't you complete your work? You know how close it is to the end of the quarter. Why would you jeopardize your grade and risk not passing this course? Why don't you care?"

"I do care," Meggie retorts with difficulty. "I just decided not to waste my time since there is no way I'm going to pass this course anyway. I may not know science, but I do know math. I calculated my average and those two zeros I got early in the quarter just killed me. Even if I get a 100 percent on the last two tests, which I know I won't, I'll still get a 68 percent average—an F. What's the use of trying? I'll be taking biology in summer school. I'm not going to waste my time on this class anymore!"

"Please come see me after class." Mr. Fetzer whispers to Meggie.

Meggie puts her head down on her desk and covers her face with her hands.

Solving the Problem

All students forget things and don't turn in work occasionally, but some students tend to forget things on a regular basis. They often grow up to become adults who forget things and don't do their work or meet deadlines on a regular basis. In a traditional classroom, students who don't do their homework or forget something necessary for class are usually penalized by losing points, getting a detention, or receiving a zero.

Teachers can suggest a series of organizational tips to help students who consistently forget their work. Students can learn to use a to-do list by writing down all the things they have to do in a day planner or notebook. They also can put sticky notes inside their lockers, on their bedroom doors, or on their car dashboards to remind them of important things. Or they can keep a weekly or monthly calendar with an assignment sheet for all of their classes, so they can write down assignment due dates. These strategies might work if a student is forgetful or disorganized. However, if a student is not turning in work for more serious reasons, the teacher must try to ascertain the real problem to develop a solution.

Teachers might want to examine their grading policies to see if they can develop some options to provide hope to students whose low grades have doomed them to failure early in the quarter. The following grading options are possibilities:

- Allow students to drop one or two of their lowest grades at the end of the grading period.
- Give credit for improvement over the grading period (progress).

- Give some credit for using the correct process, even though the answer may be wrong.
- Avoid using a zero for a grade; use an "Incomplete" instead.
- Weigh the work at the end of the quarter more to reflect growth.

Reeves (2006) and others are concerned about the grading systems used in schools. He is concerned when teachers give high grades to students who are friendly, cooperative, trying hard and who turn in their homework but are not proficient at the standards of their grade level. He asks whether we are rewarding students for being "quiet, compliant, polite, and acquiescent to the authority figures around them" (p. 119). By the same token, teachers who take off points for bad handwriting, messy papers, late work, or missing homework may assign low grades to students who are proficient and can meet all the standards on both formative and summative assessments. There can be a huge disconnect between the grades assigned by teachers and the scores earned by students on standardized tests. Parents and administrators are justifiably concerned when students receive either low or high grades in their class work and receive totally different scores on state and national standardized tests.

Reeves (2006) is also concerned by the most common grading errors, which include zeroes, averages, and misleading labels. A zero would be appropriate on a 4-point scale where $A = 4$, $B = 3$, $C = 2$, $D = 1$, and $F = 0$ because the interval from one grade to the next is 1 point. But on the 100-point scale used by many teachers, there is usually a 10-point interval between 90, 80, 70, and 60 for A, B, C, and D, respectively. When the zero is preserved in a 100-point system, the interval between D and F is not 10 points but 60 points.

> To insist on using zero on a 100-point scale is to assert that work that is not turned in is worthy of a penalty that is six times greater than work that is done wretchedly and worthy of a grade of D. (p. 121)

Current grading practices do not consider the principles of ratios and unfairly penalize students who miss a few assignments.

Kohn (2006) says that the research on the benefits of homework are inconclusive. He is concerned that even though some assignments might be meaningful and necessary, teachers and administrators have decided that children must do something every night, but later on "we'll figure out what to make them do." He adds,

> This commitment to the idea of homework in the abstract is accepted by the overwhelming majority of students—public and private, elementary and secondary. But it is defensible only if homework, per se— that is, the very fact of having to do it, irrespective of its content—is beneficial. (p. 13)

And yet, homework grades can make or break a student's grade in the class. A string of missing homework assignments and subsequent zeroes may lower a student's grade so much that no amount of improvement will help him.

Moreover, students who don't do their homework (whether or not it is meaningful homework) and who receive a series of zeroes in the grade book may give up, withdraw, miss school, resort to misbehaving, or even drop out. Alternatively, a teacher who values engagement in the lessons and uses a fair and equitable grading policy and standards-based instruction could mean the difference between success and failure for many students.

Figure 5.6 shows an example of a focus strategy teachers can use with students to find a solution for the problem of work not being completed. Figure 5.7 contains a template that teachers can use with their students. The Point/Counterpoint Strategy demonstrated in these figures gives students a chance to present their ideas in response to the issues raised by the teacher. The strategy also empowers students to raise issues in a one-on-one conversation with the teacher. It is important for teachers to admit when the grading and make-up policy they use could be improved.

The two-way open communication used in this focus strategy helps the student feel important and the teacher feel flexible in meeting the needs not only of the student but also of others in the class who may have similar feelings of frustration and powerlessness.

Other Strategies Teachers Can Use
With Students Who Don't Do Their Work

- Give students time to work on assignments in class.
- Don't penalize the student without discussing the situation first.
- Talk to the student who did not do the work to determine how his grade will be affected (minus points, late grade, lower grade, chance for extra credit, etc.).
- Talk privately with the student who forgot her work to find out if any personal or family problems are involved.
- Talk privately with the student to make sure he is aware of how the group members feel when one of the members is not prepared.
- Remind the student that her grade will be affected by her inability to meet deadlines or complete her work in a timely manner.
- Talk with other teachers about how they average grades.
- Consider dropping the lowest grade or grades of students.
- Avoid zeroes. Assign 60 percent as the lowest grade (which is failing). This allows students to pull up their grade if they begin getting A's, B's, or C's.

Add some of your own solutions for helping students who don't do their work:

_____

_____

_____

_____

_____

Figure 5.6   Point/Counterpoint Strategy

The teacher and student meet to discuss the issue using the point/counterpoint strategy. The teacher first fills out his or her points, and the student responds to those points in the counterpoint section.

Focus Strategy

Student: _____Meggie_____   Teacher: _____Mr. Fetzer_____   Date: _____Dec. 15_____

Teacher's Points	**Student's Counterpoints**
1. *I prepare meaningful assignments.*	1. *I had some personal problems at the beginning of the quarter.*
2. *I can't help you if you do not try.*	2. *I received two zeroes on work I did not do.*
3. *When you get zeroes on work, it does hurt your average.*	3. *I was not allowed to make up the two zeroes.*
4. *You have given up and become a behavior problem.*	4. *I have tried hard recently, but what's the use when I can't pass?*
5. *I don't know what to do next.*	5. *I won't waste my time in this class if I'm going to flunk anyway.*
6. *I have to be fair to other students too!*	

Compromise Solution

Teacher: I realize that I should consider allowing students to make up their work if they talk to me and explain why they didn't do it. Also, since I have 25 grades for the quarter, I will consider allowing each student to drop their lowest three grades. Therefore, I won't just be helping Meggie—all the students will benefit.

Student: If Mr. Fetzer adopts the make-up and drop-three-grades policies, I will promise to do a better job of completing my work on time. I will also talk to the teacher if something personal keeps me from doing my work.

Signed:_____Mr. Fetzer_____   _____Meggie_____   _____Dec. 15_____
         Teacher   Student   Date

Figure 5.7   Point/Counterpoint Strategy Template

Student: _____   Teacher: _____   Date: _____

Teacher's Points	Student's Counterpoints
1.	1.
2.	2.
3.	3.
4.	4.
5.	5.

Compromise Solution

Teacher:

Student:

Signed: _____   _____   _____
Teacher   Student   Date

STUDENTS WHO ARE OFF TASK

Scenario

"Today, students, we will start our unit on dinosaurs. How many of you know something about dinosaurs?"

"Good, I see that many of you have your hands raised," says Ms. Jones. "We are going to find out just how much you do know by doing something called a K-W-L.

"When I give you the signal, I want you to get into your groups and brainstorm all the things you think you know about dinosaurs in the left-hand column of your chart under the letter K.

You already have your role assignments, so timekeepers need to remind their group members when 10 minutes are up. You may begin!"

The students quietly form their groups and begin brainstorming what they know about dinosaurs.

Timmy, however, starts drawing his favorite football player while the other members in his group work on their K-W-L.

"Timmy," Ann calls, "You are the organizer this time. Put away your picture and help us with this. We'll never finish in 10 minutes."

Timmy shrugs his shoulders and continues to draw, oblivious to the other group members and the K-W-L.

Frustrated, Ann and Mary Jo start brainstorming on their own. Pretty soon, Ms. Jones comes up to the group and asks how many ideas they have brainstormed.

"Only five," cries Ann. "Timmy isn't helping us."

"Make him help us, Ms. Jones. We always end up doing his share. Everybody else always gets better grades and finishes before us. Put him in another group," says Mary Jo.

Timmy smiles sweetly and continues coloring in the player's helmet.

Solving the Problem

Students have gotten off task in school since the first school was built. Teachers since Aristotle have observed students daydreaming, writing notes, staring into space, completing homework for another class, or sleeping—some with their eyes wide open. The current challenge for teachers is to monitor students' use of cell phones, iPods, and other technological tools that many teachers don't even know about. Off-task behavior is not new, but it can become more noticeable and more frustrating when it is experienced in a cooperative group setting or in a whole-class activity on a regular basis.

It is evident that Timmy is engaged, but he is not engaged in the assigned task. Obviously, the more students practice a skill such as reading, writing, or problem solving, the more proficient they become with appropriate feedback. But as McCarthy and Kuh (2006) write, "In addition to these important behavioral components, however, engagement has an affective dimension, involving such issues as whether students get along with their peers and how they feel about the school environment" (p. 665).

Because Timmy is not cooperating with his peers, he is not engaged in the cognitive skills or activities that he needs to learn. His emotions have "hijacked his intellect," and his interest in football supersedes his interest in dinosaurs.

Off-task behavior affects students in the cooperative classroom because one of the members of a group is not engaged in the group's work. In the previous scenario, the other group members do not tolerate Timmy's love for football at the expense of their dinosaur assignment. Their low tolerance may turn to anger and more serious behavior problems if Timmy's off-task behavior is not addressed and corrected.

Glasser and others have commented on the importance of "choice" in a democratic classroom. It is obvious that the teacher cannot give students free choice on all matters, but students feel more empowered and in control if they have some options. In this scenario, Ms. Jones could pull Timmy aside during or after class and help him brainstorm different ways he could handle the problem. Timmy, with the help of his teacher, could brainstorm alternative actions as well as potential consequences that could be either positive or negative. This type of decision-making process is demonstrated in Figure 5.8, the Decision-Making Model. This focus strategy helps students analyze the pros and cons of all decisions. Their final decision will still be their own, but it may be more rational and logical than a decision made quickly while under emotional pressure. A Decision-Making Model Template that teachers can use with their students is offered in Figure 5.9.

Other Strategies Teachers Can Use With Students Who Are Off Task

- Walk over to the student who is off task and stand there quietly (proximity).
- Quietly lean over and ask the off-task student what he is "supposed to be doing."
- Review the responsibilities of the role the off-task student was assigned to make sure she understands what is expected of her.
- Whisper in the student's ear to get on task and quickly walk away.
- Talk privately with the student to see if he is upset with one or more group members about something.
- Call the parents of a student who is constantly off task to see if there is some explanation for the behavior.
- Check with the school counselor, administrator, or special education teacher to have the student tested for learning or behavior disabilities.
- Allow five minutes of free time at the end of each activity for students to socialize, draw, or read if they perform their assigned tasks according to the directions.

Add some of your own solutions for helping students who are off task:

_____

_____

_____

_____

Figure 5.8   Decision-Making Model

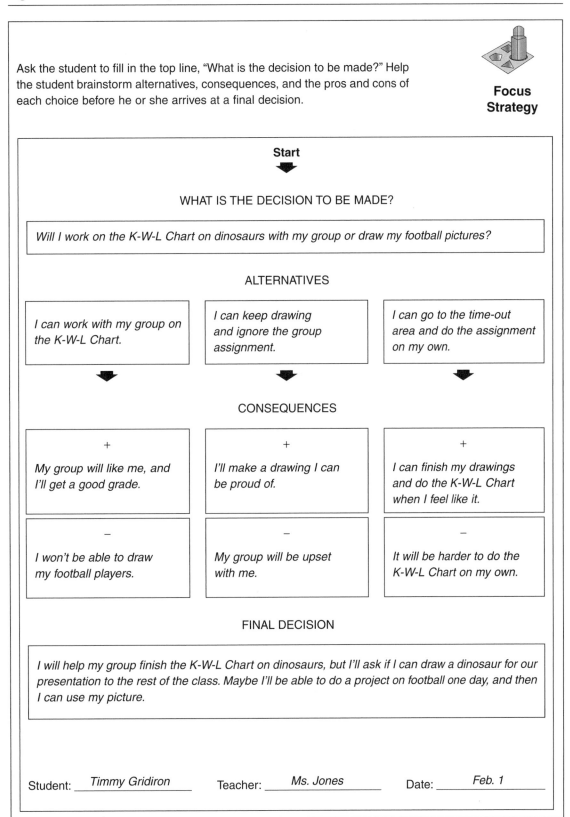

Ask the student to fill in the top line, "What is the decision to be made?" Help the student brainstorm alternatives, consequences, and the pros and cons of each choice before he or she arrives at a final decision.

Focus Strategy

Start

WHAT IS THE DECISION TO BE MADE?

Will I work on the K-W-L Chart on dinosaurs with my group or draw my football pictures?

ALTERNATIVES

I can work with my group on the K-W-L Chart.	*I can keep drawing and ignore the group assignment.*	*I can go to the time-out area and do the assignment on my own.*

CONSEQUENCES

+	+	+
My group will like me, and I'll get a good grade.	*I'll make a drawing I can be proud of.*	*I can finish my drawings and do the K-W-L Chart when I feel like it.*
−	−	−
I won't be able to draw my football players.	*My group will be upset with me.*	*It will be harder to do the K-W-L Chart on my own.*

FINAL DECISION

I will help my group finish the K-W-L Chart on dinosaurs, but I'll ask if I can draw a dinosaur for our presentation to the rest of the class. Maybe I'll be able to do a project on football one day, and then I can use my picture.

Student: ___*Timmy Gridiron*___   Teacher: ___*Ms. Jones*___   Date: ___*Feb. 1*___

Figure 5.9   Decision-Making Model Template

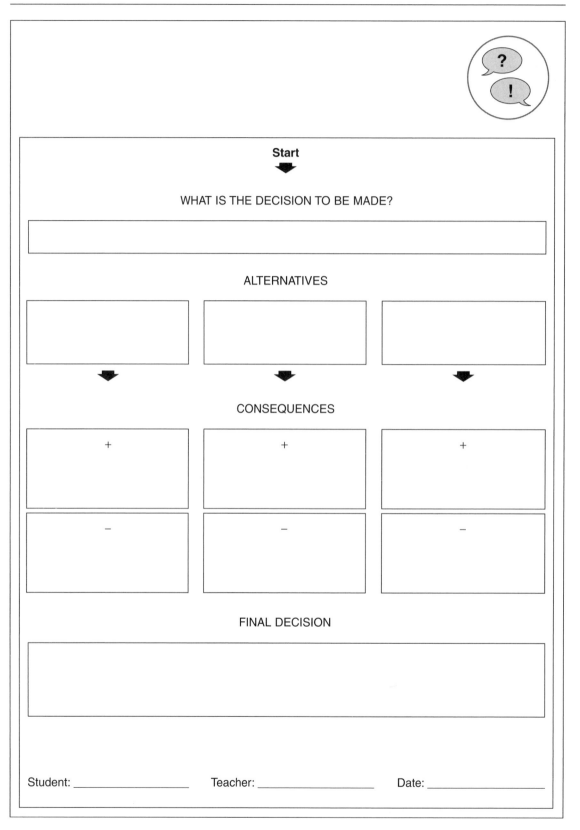

STUDENTS WHO DO NOT CONTRIBUTE TO THE GROUP

Scenario

The students in Ms. Swartz's American literature course move into their base groups to continue working on their research papers about major literary figures of the twentieth century. Each group has been assigned an author's life to research together. Each member is responsible for writing her own paper showing how aspects of the author's life are reflected in one of the author's novels.

Nancy, Doug, and Jeff move their desks together and get out their note cards, notebooks, and the research books they are using.

"Okay, group," Nancy says, "I have twenty note cards on Gertrude Stein's early life. Doug, what do you have about her years in France?"

"I have lots of information about the people she hung around with," says Doug. "I've got great quotes from Stein about Hemingway and F. Scott Fitzgerald."

"Great, Doug. We should be ready to start our individual papers soon. What do you have about Stein's life with Alice B. Toklas, Jeff?"

"Nothing," Jeff shrugs. "I had to work last night so I didn't get a chance to go to the library. I'll try to go this weekend when I'm off work."

"This weekend!" shrieks Nancy. "Our paper is due next week. We can't wait until Monday to get your information. We'll never finish our own papers in time. You know that Ms. Swartz will lower our grades one letter grade if our papers are late."

"Thanks a lot," mumbles Doug. "Nancy and I will just have to do the research ourselves. I'm not going to let you ruin my grade in here. What a loser!"

Solving the Problem

One of the major criticisms of cooperative learning is that some students do all of the work while others just "ride their coattails." What adult has not been a victim of a group project, a community fundraiser, a school project, or an office proposal where someone came late, left early, and did nothing? That same person often receives the same grade, same reward, or same salary increase or promotion that the others do. Sadly, sometimes the one who does the least even receives more than everyone else! Needless to say, students in cooperative groups experience the same negative feelings when one of their members is not carrying his weight.

Many proponents of cooperative learning do not recommend giving all the members of the group a single grade for their project or performance. Kagan, as cited in O'Connor (2002), believes that group grades can penalize students who work hard but have group members who don't, and they can reward students who do not work hard but have hard-working partners. Legal questions about group grades have also arisen. Several issues are involved with giving a group grade. First, students may not want to work with group members because they have behavior problems, are special education or English-language-learner students, are not popular, are of either high or low ability, or are just "different." By forcing students to work for a group grade, teachers may inadvertently cause personality conflicts.

Group work should be a means to an end—and the end is individual accountability. Many teachers encourage group work and grade it on the basis of participation, completion, effort, daily work, or progress but then assign individual grades for individual work based on meeting the standards. In today's standards-based classroom, each student is responsible for meeting the standards, and it is not fair either to "ride the group's coattails" to a higher grade or "get torpedoed" by one member who causes everyone to get lower grades. The original philosophy of "we sink or swim together" is no longer as accepted as it once was because of the emphasis on standards-based account-ability for all students.

When a student does not contribute to the group, teachers first must talk with that student to find out whether the problem is laziness, inadequacy, time constraints, home problems, or work demands. The cause could also be some-thing much deeper that must be identified if the student is to become a func-tional group member and a respected team player. Then, after the teacher and the student have identified the causes, they can brainstorm solutions together. After the problem has been addressed, the teacher may want to implement a strategy to "rebond" the group. One possible technique teachers use to rebond the group is to have the students write Mailgrams, short journal entries, to each other, explaining their feelings.

In the situation outlined in this scenario, the teacher might want to talk to the group members and ask them to think about what they said to Jeff when they were angry at him. They called him "a loser" in the heat of the moment, and their put-down may have made Jeff even more upset. The Mailgram Strategy (Figure 5.10) can help students reflect on their actions. Obviously, the students could discuss how they feel, but their emotions could get out of control and escalate rather than resolve the problem. Instead, they exchange Mailgrams and write responses prior to their discussion. The teacher acts as the intermedi-ary to deliver the messages. Mailgrams can be successful because writing usu-ally has a calming effect and allows students more time to reflect on their actions and process their feelings.

Figure 5.11 contains a Mailgram Template that teachers can use to resolve conflicts among students in their classrooms. The Mailgram allows students to present their side of the story after they have had time to calm down. The writ-ten word is usually more objective and sometimes more honest and thoughtful than verbal comments hurled in the heat of an argument.

Figure 5.10 Mailgram Strategy

Distribute a copy of the Mailgram form to the students involved in the discussion or problem. Ask them to write down their feelings or concerns and send the Mailgram to the other group members.

Focus Strategy

MAILGRAM

Date: _____January 3_____

Message to: _____Jeff_____

From: _____Nancy and Doug_____

We didn't mean to get mad at you and call you a loser yesterday. It's just that we have been working so hard on this paper because it counts a lot. We got upset because you are not pulling your weight and we are going to suffer.

MAILGRAM

Date: _____January 3_____

Message to: _____Nancy and Doug_____

From: _____Jeff_____

I am sorry I didn't have my portion of our research ready yesterday. I just got a new car, and I've been working extra hours to make the payments. I'll talk to my parents and boss and try to reduce my schedule. I'll have my section tomorrow.

Figure 5.11 Mailgram Template

MAILGRAM

Date: _____

Message to: _____

From: _____

MAILGRAM

Date: _____

Message to: _____

From: _____

Other Strategies Teachers Can Use With Students Who Do Not Contribute to the Group

- Don't give group grades.
- Assign individual work after the group work and grade that to make sure every student meets the standards.
- Assign major individual and group assignments several weeks before due dates, allowing students to arrange their work schedules and delegate group tasks so they have plenty of time to finish them.
- Discuss effective study skills and time management strategies with the entire class. Teach these strategies.
- Use the Swiss-cheese approach. Break down major assignments into smaller tasks and have due dates for each segment. For example: outline due October 4, introduction due October 6, rough draft of body due October 10.
- Monitor due dates for each segment of a major assignment to find out which students or groups are having trouble. Use a checklist to keep track of who is behind in turning in segments.
- Structure group assignments so that one student cannot lower the group's grade. When this happens, students resent the group member, and bonding in the group erodes. Also, lawsuits could occur.
- Encourage group members to discuss their individual assignments and get help from fellow group members prior to the final deadline.
- When processing group activities, allow students to write their evaluation of the group's work. Monitor groups whose written evaluation indicates problems with a particular group member's work.
- Give students some choice in their individual and group assignments. Students who select topics that interest them are more likely to contribute more of their time and effort.

Add some of your own solutions for helping students who do not contribute to the group:

_____

_____

_____

_____

_____

Helping Students Who Lack Effective Interpersonal Skills

6

Figure 6.0   Students Who Have Effective Interpersonal Skills

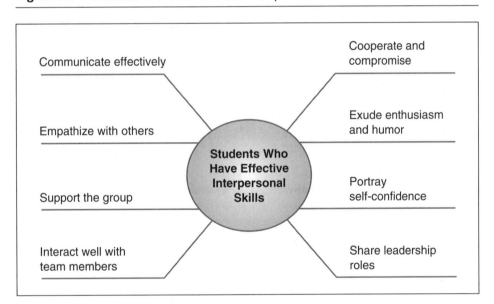

FOSTERING INTERPERSONAL SKILLS

Many at-risk and antisocial children simply do not have the school readiness skills and preschool experiences that would allow them to be successful as they begin their school careers. (Walker, Colvin, & Ramsey, 1995, p. 35)

The term *interpersonal* is defined as "being, related to, or involving relations between persons" (*Merriam-Webster's Collegiate Dictionary,* 2003).

Gardner (1993) defines interpersonal intelligence in his theory of multiple intelligences as "the ability to understand other people: what motivates them, how they work, and how to work cooperatively with them. Successful salespeople, politicians, teachers, clinicians, and religious leaders are all likely to be individuals with high degrees of interpersonal intelligence" (p. 9).

Interpersonal skills are essentially life skills. Effective educators know that getting along with others is critical for academic and social success; therefore, they integrate teaching "people skills" throughout their content lessons. Interpersonal skills are included in many state standards or national competencies. Sometimes, the standards are listed under "good citizenship," where students are expected to show respect for different languages and cultures as well as tolerance and understanding toward other individuals and groups. Interpersonal skills may also be addressed in standards related to "communication" or "participation," where students are expected to demonstrate respect for the rights and opinions of others. Teachers are even beginning to assess social skills and interpersonal skills so that students and their parents realize their importance. Current research focuses on the idea of the "whole child," encouraging teachers to emphasize curriculum goals, standards, and problem solving to address students' cognitive domains and interpersonal skills, the arts, and outside interests to address their affective domains.

With-it-ness and Overlapping

Even though teachers may teach social skills explicitly, students often forget these skills when they engage in activities. The prosocial skills taught in the cooperative group settings need to be retaught as needed, reinforced when necessary, and most important, monitored. When teachers have "eyes in the back of their heads" and can see which student appears agitated and ready to "lose it" or what student is on the verge of tears and about to leave the room, they have what the experts call "with-it-ness."

In a series of classroom studies conducted by Kounin and his colleagues (as cited in Sternberg & Williams, 2002), researchers videotaped classroom lessons and analyzed teacher behaviors to determine which ones predicted classrooms that demonstrated high amounts of student involvement and low levels of deviant behavior. Two concepts that Kounin found to be critical for classroom management were what he labeled "with-it-ness" and "overlapping." According to Kounin, with-it-ness means that teachers are observant and attentive to everything going on around the teacher in the classroom.

Because a classroom is a complex setting, teachers deal with many things simultaneously. Teachers who focus on only one element and ignore the rest often find that the problem they are ignoring is the one that escalates into something bigger. With-it-ness is the degree to which the teacher corrects misbehavior before it intensifies or spreads. It is also the degree to which the teacher targets the correct student for misbehaving.

Sternberg and Williams (2002) report that Kounin's research showed that teachers who demonstrate they are "with it" have fewer discipline problems than teachers who are either unaware or do not react to what is going on in their classroom. When teachers monitor the entire classroom, they spot signs of disruption, make eye contact with students, call them by their names, and let then know they are fully aware of what each student is doing at all times. "When multiple problems arise, with-it teachers always deal with the more serious problems first. You can increase your with-it-ness by making maximal use of your voice, eyes, and body language to remain simultaneously in contact with different students" (p. 389).

Overlapping is the term Kounin uses to describe how a teacher supervises several activities at once. A teacher who is adept at multitasking can be interrupted by a visitor at the door but still notice Teddy's grabbing another student's pencil out of "the corner of her eye." Effective teachers know almost instinctively when to give the class a task to keep them focused if they need to deal one-on-one with a student who is upset or causing a disturbance. They also don't interrupt a lesson to deal with a student who enters the room late without a pass. They wait until there is a natural break in their teaching and until the students are engaged in a task before they address the tardy student privately and calmly (Sternberg & Williams, 2002).

These two concepts, labeled with-it-ness and overlapping by Kounin and his associates, show how teachers who react promptly to problems without overreacting, prevent simple disturbances from escalating into a major disruptions. By using a "teacher look," behavior redirection, and proximity to the offending student effectively, teachers continue the ongoing activities without antagonizing the "interrupter" and distracting the rest of the students (Evertson, Emmer, Clements, & Worsham, 1997). Students are always looking for anything to take themselves and the teacher off track—teachers need to remember not to get hooked and play the students' game.

Strategies for Minor Misbehaviors

Sending a student to the principal's office for making a face or for not bringing his notebook to class is not a good idea. First, the teacher has just given up her authority. Second, the principal will not want to deal with such a minor infraction. Third, the teacher could have addressed the problem quickly and easily by utilizing a few strategies. Fourth, the student may be sitting in the principal's office for as long as an hour and miss valuable class time. Often, the students who need the most academic help spend the most time outside the classroom awaiting disciplinary action.

Koenig (2000) describes 13 strategies designed to address common disruptive behaviors that any student might exhibit. He labels these "Strategies for Minor Behaviors (Plan A)," because they are quick and easy to use and they usually produce immediate results by redirecting the misbehaving student with a minimum of disruption. Little, if any, teaching time will be lost, and teachers can experiment with which techniques work best with different students. Figure 6.1 describes three of these strategies.

Figure 6.1 Three of Koenig's Strategies for Minor Misbehaviors (Plan A)

- **Use Friendly Evil Eye**—Make eye contact with the misbehaving student, smile, and shake head slightly.

Note: Keep this nonthreatening by smiling. Don't let it interrupt your teaching.

- **Invade Space**—Keep teaching while you walk over and stand by the offending student. Don't bother to make eye contact, but smile and continue teaching.

Note: A majority of students will stop misbehaving just so you will vacate their space.

- **Whisper Technique**—Walk close enough to the student to whisper something like, "Cindy, would you please spit out your gum?" Don't wait for a response. Assume the answer is yes by quickly saying "Thank you," breaking eye contact, and moving away.

Note: The whisper technique conveys to the student the following messages:

1. You are not afraid.

2. You care about the student.

3. You don't want to embarrass anyone.

4. You accept the student but not the behavior.

5. You don't want to get into an argument.

6. You trust the student to comply willingly.

Adapted from *Smart Discipline for the Classroom: Respect and Cooperation Restored* (3rd ed.), by Larry Koenig (1999). Thousand Oaks, CA: Corwin Press, www.corwinpress.com. All rights reserved.

Prosocial Behavior

The limits and boundaries that DiGiulio (2000) discusses are similar to the rules and consequences discussed earlier. However, there could never be enough rules to govern prosocial behavior or to make students sensitive to the needs and wants of others. This ability to empathize with the feelings of others correlates with Goleman's theory of emotional intelligence discussed in Chapter 2. It is evident from reading news accounts about the students who have shot other students at school that the shooters did not possess this sensitivity to others' needs or the inclination toward the collective group. In addition to teaching social skills or common courtesies explicitly, teachers can continually focus on the interpersonal skills the students need by modeling and reinforcing thoughtful, caring, and courteous behavior every day in their classrooms.

Most students need to be taught how to socialize. The first time toddlers meet, it is not uncommon to hear a mother say, "No, it's not nice to hit Amy with your rattle," or, "You need to share your toys." As students get older, they learn higher-order social skills similar to higher-order thinking skills. Life necessitates that students learn a gradual hierarchy of appropriate interpersonal skills to survive and thrive in an increasingly complex and diverse society. Students who have trouble dealing with other people need to learn how to recognize, and hopefully solve, their own problems independently.

Gootman (1997) discusses how students can use a problem-solving model to figure out how they can assume some responsibility for changing their inappropriate behavior to more appropriate behavior.

By guiding the students to figuring out what they can do, rather than threatening them about what we will do, we help them develop responsibility for their own behavior. The burden is placed on the student rather than on us to change the behavior, and the student is more likely to take ownership of the solution. (p. 133)

Students who have poor interpersonal skills will no doubt encounter more social and behavior problems as they go through school and life. These students will not always have their parents, teachers, coaches, or other authority figures to help them solve either their immediate or long-term problems. The ultimate outcome of education is for students to be able to make decisions and solve problems on their own. Problem solving goes far beyond simply dealing with behavioral disturbances.

Gootman (2001) describes what students learn from social problem solving and outlined seven steps that students can use to handle problems they may have interacting with other people (see Figure 6.2). Students who can analyze their own behavior and, more important, recognize the effects their behavior has on others are perhaps on their way to controlling their behavior and self-conditioning their responses to be more socially acceptable.

This chapter presents scenarios about students who don't get along well with others, who don't care about school, or who are always trying to show off or get extra attention. The focus strategies at the end of each scenario can be added to a teacher's toolkit of potential methods to use when addressing students with poor interpersonal skills.

STUDENTS WHO DON'T LIKE TO WORK WITH OTHERS

Scenario

Mr. Totts tells his class, "As part of our unit on health, we will be engaging in a performance task that requires our seventh-grade class to prepare a presentation to city council advocating banning smoking in all public places in our city. I have divided the class into four groups. You may sign up to work in one of the following groups:

Group A—Research the effects of smoking on individuals who smoke and of second-hand smoke on others; Group B—Prepare a pamphlet to distribute to the community; Group C—Prepare a PowerPoint presentation for members of city council; Group D—Conduct a poll of 100 community members and create a pie graph depicting their responses."

As soon as Mr. Totts finishes speaking, the students rush to the sign-up sheet to select the projects they want. "Now form your groups, and I'll distribute the criteria you'll need to create your projects," directs Mr. Totts.

Belinda joins her group and announces, "I have been creating my own PowerPoint presentations for three years. I don't need your help to do this one. I don't want to spend my time training the rest of you to keep up with me. My mom hates group work, and she'll probably complain to the principal again that I'm not being challenged, and as usual, I carry the group!"

The other group members look at each other and roll their eyes.

Figure 6.2   What Students Learn From Social Problem Solving

1. **State the problem.** Often students aren't even aware of the problem that their behavior may be creating. This may be the case with a student who hums absentmindedly to herself. Other times, they are fully aware of what they are doing but are unaware of its effect on others, such as the student whose nervous tapping distracts those around him. Some may not realize, until we point out how their feelings and actions are influenced by the feelings and actions of others, how they can get "hooked" into misbehaving. At this beginning step of problem solving, we can heighten our students' awareness and sensitivity to the nature and causes of the problem.

2. **Brainstorm solutions.** Often children see no other path than the one they are taking, such as the child who sees hitting as the only option when she is insulted. Through brainstorming, we can open their eyes to other solutions, and they can develop the capacity to generate a variety of alternative solutions to a problem.

3. **Evaluate solutions.** Many students don't think beyond what they are doing and the pleasure it may bring them. They don't think of the effects of their actions on others, such as the child who keeps tapping on his desk. By discussing each of the solutions brainstormed in step 2 and evaluating the ramifications of each, students learn to consider the consequences of their actions. They also learn empathy as they discuss how other people might respond to each solution that they are evaluating.

4. **Select a mutually acceptable solution.** By working to find an idea mutually acceptable to all parties concerned, students learn the art of give-and-take and, consequently, the art of compromise.

5. **Try out the solution.** After students have chosen a solution, we can help them articulate, step by step, how they will carry out the solution. Some children have no idea how to proceed to change. Specifying the details, step by step, gives them a map to guide themselves and teaches them how to plan in the future.

   As we teach them problem solving, we can help our students understand why "I promise I'll never do it again" or "I'll be good" are unacceptable solutions. These are empty words with no actions planned to back them up. Students need to have a plan of action for carrying out the solution. They need to choose exactly what appropriate behaviors they will use to replace inappropriate behaviors.

6. **Evaluate the solution.** By discussing with students how well they think their solution is working, we are teaching them to be reflective about their actions.

7. **Decide.** The most critical piece of information that students learn from this step is that if they don't succeed at first, try and try again. Although this solution did not work out, another might. This is a message of hope and accountability. Even if they mess up, they can go back and figure out another solution to the problem.

Solving the Problem

Some students prefer to work alone. They don't want to take the time to learn how to socialize, or they would rather do the work themselves than have to compromise with others. Jenkins (1989) describes the learning style of this type of conscientious student. The student's priority is the task or the process, and he loves correctness and thoroughness. This type of student gains security by intense preparation and precision and equates grades with self-worth. Conscientious students hate surprises and inaccuracy and may withdraw under tension. They want quality, privacy, accuracy, and credibility and would just as soon work alone, so they have control of the final product, than work in a group, where their high standards might be compromised.

One tactic that might be successful with such students is for teachers to develop a Social Contract (see Figure 6.3). The Social Contract establishes appropriate behaviors as well as positive consequences if students fulfill the contract obligations and negative consequences if they do not adhere to the contract. The student in the scenario, Belinda, as well as many students like her, needs to recognize how important group work is in school and in life. Students like Belinda need to recognize that they will have to make compromises in their quest to become the quintessential student and those compromises will continue to be necessary in college and the workforce.

The Social Contract can be filled out by both the student and the teacher. The "steps taken" part of the contract should be discussed in a supportive, one-on-one setting. Ideally, the student should also have input into the "consequences" part of the contract to ensure that she agrees that the consequences are fair, or at least logical. Students are far more likely to adhere to the contract if they feel they have had a say in its construction.

There is a line at the end of the contract for the parent's signature. It is best if parents have the opportunity to support and reinforce students as they strive to fulfill their part of the contract. In this scenario, the parents may be contributing to Belinda's belief that she does not do her best working in groups, and as such, they need to be included in the contract. The teacher might want to meet with the parents to discuss the rationale for assigning group projects. Parents need to know the specific standards that emphasize interpersonal skills in collaborative efforts. In addition, some high-stakes tests require students to solve problems in groups. Parents need to see the value of group work and cooperation as important life skills. Many parents oppose any type of cooperative efforts because they feel life is basically competitive. They don't see why their child should share his ideas with others when he competes for grades, academic honors, class rankings, jobs, and scholarships. The parents' anti-group philosophy and their comments about "talking to the principal" or pursuing legal action could be the "real problem" in this case study.

A Social Contract Template is offered in Figure 6.4 for teachers to use with their students.

Figure 6.3   Social Contract Strategy

Arrange a conference with the student who prefers to work alone. Fill out the Social Contract form with the student and then send it home for the parent's signature or include parents in the conference.

Focus Strategy

Student: _____Belinda_____   Teacher: _____Mr. Totts_____   Date: _February 26_

Teacher: Describe the problem.
Belinda does not help her group members in health class. She prefers to work alone on her own projects. She does an excellent job on all her individual assignments, but her behavior in her group is antisocial and the group members do not want her in their group. I believe some group work is essential.

Student: What is your reaction to the problem your teacher has described?
I don't want to be in the stupid group in the first place. Pete is sloppy and can't even draw a square. Sandy spends more time putting on her lipstick than she does drawing. I enjoy PowerPoint, and I love doing a good job on all my projects. I know I can do better work by myself than I could do in a group of technophobes!

Teacher and Student: Decide on a social contract to help solve the problem.
Steps taken by the teacher:
1. *I will assign more individual projects so Belinda can have more opportunities to do her own work.*
2. *I will monitor Belinda's group more carefully to make sure each group member is on task.*
3. *I will rotate groups more frequently so Belinda has a chance to work with other students.*
4. *I will allow Belinda to do enrichment health projects on her own and allow her to share them with the whole class.*

Steps taken by the student:
1. *I will be more tolerant of my group members' artistic talents.*
2. *I will contribute to the group more and try to share my technology skills.*
3. *I will try to be more friendly and cooperative with my group.*
4. *I will help my group on the big projects so we can all be proud of our work when we display it.*

Positive consequences of fulfilling the social contract.
1. *Belinda can have a showing of her own PowerPoint presentations.*
2. *Belinda can be a "buddy" to students in the lower grades by tutoring them in technology.*
3. *Belinda can demonstrate how to design a PowerPoint project to the whole class.*

Negative consequences of not fulfilling the social contract.
1. *Belinda will be penalized in her grade for not demonstrating social skills and accepting responsibility.*
2. *Belinda will lose the friendship and respect of her classmates.*

Timeline for contract: _____March 8_____

Signed: _____Belinda_____ (student)   Signed: _____Mr. & Mrs. Moss_____ (parents)

Figure 6.4 Social Contract Template

Student: _____   Teacher: _____   Date: _____

Teacher: Describe the problem.

_____

_____

Student: What is your reaction to the problem your teacher has described?

_____

_____

Teacher and Student: Decide on a social contract to help solve the problem.
Steps taken by the teacher:

    1. _____

    2. _____

    3. _____

Steps taken by the student:

    1. _____

    2. _____

Positive consequences of fulfilling the social contract.

    1. _____

    2. _____

Negative consequences of not fulfilling the social contract.

    1. _____

    2. _____

Timeline for contract: _____

Signed: _____   Signed: _____

*Other Strategies Teachers Can Use With
Students Who Do Not Like to Work With Others*

- Review social skills with the class and emphasize the importance of everyone's contributing his fair share.
- Use a jigsaw activity, where every member of the group is assigned a part of an assignment to share with the rest of the group.
- Assign the reluctant worker a special privilege that she will especially enjoy if she cooperates with the group (e.g., a pass to the computer lab).
- Assign students to groups of two for certain activities. Make sure to pair the student who prefers to work alone with a nurturing and supportive student who will encourage him to cooperate.
- Talk with the student individually to find out if the problem is personal or group related.
- Talk to the other group members confidentially to find out if they know why the student does not like working with the group.
- Call the parents of the student who is withdrawing from group interactions to find out if they know why she doesn't like working in a group.
- Include the parents in the social contract process.

Add some of your own solutions for helping students who do not want to work with others:

_____

_____

_____

_____

_____

STUDENTS WHO DON'T CARE

Scenario

Mr. Barke distributes copies of questions from the state test to the class. "Let's practice some of these reading passages since the school's scores were lowest on the inference section."

"What is inference?" asks Bob.

"Inference is when the passage doesn't tell you something directly. You have to interpret the meaning by reading 'between the lines,'" replies Mr. Barke. "Let's try a timed reading because the test allows 10 minutes for this section. Ready—begin reading the first passage."

All of the students begin reading the passage, but John lays his head down on his desk. Mr. Barke walks slowly to John's desk.

"Aren't you feeling well, John?" he asks.

"I feel fine," John answers.

"Well, why aren't you practicing? You want to pass the state test, don't you?"

"Not really," mumbles John. "I really don't care if I pass the test or if I pass this year. I'd rather sleep."

Solving the Problem

Unfortunately, teachers tend to ignore apathetic students because they are so quiet and unobtrusive. But a teacher's silence is a subtle form of discouragement. Dinkmeyer and Losoncy (1980) believe that "human beings increase their self-esteem, self-confidence, and feelings of worth when they are recognized" (p. 59). If teachers do not provide feedback to an individual who appears to be uninterested, bored, or apathetic, the student could "slip through the cracks."

Teachers always seem to notice the attention seekers, the troublemakers, and the "star students." It's the nameless quiet ones who don't get recognized, even though they probably need the most attention.

Students who choose to ignore their work need to examine their choices and the consequences these choices have for themselves, their fellow students, and their parents. Teachers can use the Decision-Making Model (see Figure 6.5) to help students reflect on their choices and perhaps examine the real problem to make better choices. A Decision-Making Model template is offered in Figure 6.6 for teachers to use with their students.

Other Strategies Teachers Can Use With Students Who Don't Care

- Assign the student an easier task to build his self-esteem and self-confidence.
- Talk to the parents to find out if the student has had problems that have caused her to withdraw or "tune out."
- Discuss privately with the student his reasons for not participating.
- Orchestrate group work so that the apathetic student gets into a group of students who will support and encourage her.
- Discover any special talents the student has and make sure he can display them in the group setting (e.g., artwork, computer use, speaking, props, and so forth) to raise his self-esteem.
- Talk to the parents or counselor to see if alcohol or drugs could be causing the student's lack of interest.
- Talk to the parents or counselor to find out if family problems or girlfriend/boyfriend problems are causing her apathy.
- Recognize the symptoms of depression or suicide signals and monitor the student's behavior over a few weeks.
- Notify a counselor if symptoms of depression continue.

Add some of your own solutions for helping students who don't care:

_____

_____

_____

_____

Figure 6.5   Decision-Making Model Strategy

Focus Strategy

Fill out your view of the problem and ask the student to fill out the rest of the form.

Student: _____*John*_____   Date: _____*March 3*_____   Teacher: _____*Mr. Barke*_____

Teacher's View of Problem
John is not applying himself in my class, nor is he preparing for the state test he needs to pass.

Student's View of Problem
I really don't care about a state test. I plan to race cars when I grow up so I don't need to "infer" reading passages. Reviewing for a test is boring!

Solutions to Problem	Pros and Cons
Solution #1 *I could continue to blow off the test review.*	**Pro** *I can sleep, and I won't be so bored.* **Con** *I'll probably flunk the test and repeat fourth grade.*
Solution #2 *I could get some extra help in reading after school. I feel nervous about the test. I don't want to fail.*	**Pro** *I know reading is very important for life. I'd rather pass the test.* **Con** *I don't want to give up my afterschool time to get extra help.*
Solution #3 *I need to get help taking tests. I always fall apart during tests. I get so nervous.*	**Pro** *If I stay in school, I will be taking lots of tests. I'd better be prepared.* **Con** *I don't believe in tests. My class work and portfolio should count more than a test.*
Final Decision *I will talk to the teacher and ask for extra help in reading after school. I will also ask for tips to calm down during tests.*	**Reasons** *I really do care. I just pretend I don't care because I don't want to have the lowest score in the class. I also don't want to repeat fourth grade.*

Figure 6.6   Decision-Making Model Template

1, 2, 3

Student: _____   Date: _____   Teacher: _____

Teacher's View of Problem

Student's View of Problem

Solutions to Problem	**Pros and Cons**
Solution #1	**Pro**
	Con
Solution #2	**Pro**
	Con
Solution #3	**Pro**
	Con
Final Decision	**Reasons**

STUDENTS WHO DOMINATE THE CLASS

Scenario

As Mrs. Jackson writes the solution to the math problem on the blackboard, Michael blurts out, "That's a stupid way to solve the problem."

Flustered, Mrs. Jackson tries to contain her anger and calmly replies, "Do you have a better way to solve the problem, Michael?"

"Yeah, you bet I do. Give me the chalk," Michael says.

He gets out of his seat and walks to the blackboard. Mrs. Jackson moves aside as Michael starts crossing out her answer and writing in his own.

The students start to snicker, but a few roll their eyes at their friends and whisper, "Here he goes again!"

Mrs. Jackson nervously waits as Michael completes the problem, throws down the chalk in triumph, and saunters back to his seat.

"Thank you for your contribution," Mrs. Jackson mumbles through clenched teeth.

"No problem, Mrs. J.! I am here to help you."

Solving the Problem

Dominating students love being the center of attention and being in control. Jenkins (1989) describes the dominant child as having a choleric personality and as being a student who takes risks. The dominant child likes leadership, competition, and control and is irritated by indecision and inefficiency. When confronted by deadlines, this student will "dictate and assert." The dominant child intimidates teachers and often destroys class discussions.

Dominating students may offer their academic strengths, knowledge, and organizational skills ostensibly to "help" others, but sometimes the real motive is to control the task because they feel the other students or the teacher won't do it as well as they can. Dominating students also offer their expertise at the expense of others. This may then cause other students to lose their self-confidence and feelings of self-worth (Dinkmeyer & Losoncy, 1980).

One of the major problems with dominating students is that they often do not realize the effect their behavior has on others. A graphic organizer, such as the Cause-and-Effect Model (see Figure 6.7), might help dominating students reflect on their behavior and see the effect their actions have on themselves, their teachers, and other group members. The student can fill out this model with the teacher or with his group. A Cause-and-Effect Model Template is offered in Figure 6.8 for teachers to use with their students.

Even though dominant students may think they know all of the answers, they may need some help from the teacher or counselor to evaluate the effects their behaviors have on others. They probably lack empathy with others; therefore, they may not have a clue that their actions are upsetting anyone. Some students may be capable of psychologically analyzing their actions. Others may need some assistance from a responsible student, student aide, counselor, or teacher to arrive at the insight necessary to change their inappropriate behaviors.

Figure 6.7 Cause-and-Effect Model

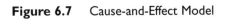

Focus Strategy

Ask the student to list his or her behaviors and the effect those behaviors have on the teacher and other students.

Student: _____Michael_____ Date: _____October 15_____ Teacher: _____Mrs. Jackson_____

Specific Behavior	Effect It Could Have on Others
I interrupted the teacher and showed her up.	Mrs. Jackson could be embarrassed because I am smarter than she is in math.
I say that I am smarter than the rest of the class.	My class members could begin to resent me because I get all the attention. They love it when I make a mistake.
I try to upstage the teacher.	Mrs. Jackson could send me to the office or try to lower my grade.

Reflection on Behaviors _____I guess I can get pretty pushy at times. I'm usually right, but I guess what I say hurts people's feelings. Maybe I shouldn't be so cocky. When I get to Stanford, smarter students could make me feel stupid, too._____

Targeted Behavior to Change _____I'll work on listening to others and taking turns. I think I can do it. I'll try to wait until I'm asked to answer questions and prblems._____

Signed: _____Michael_____ Date: _____Oct. 15_____

Figure 6.8   Cause-and-Effect Model Template

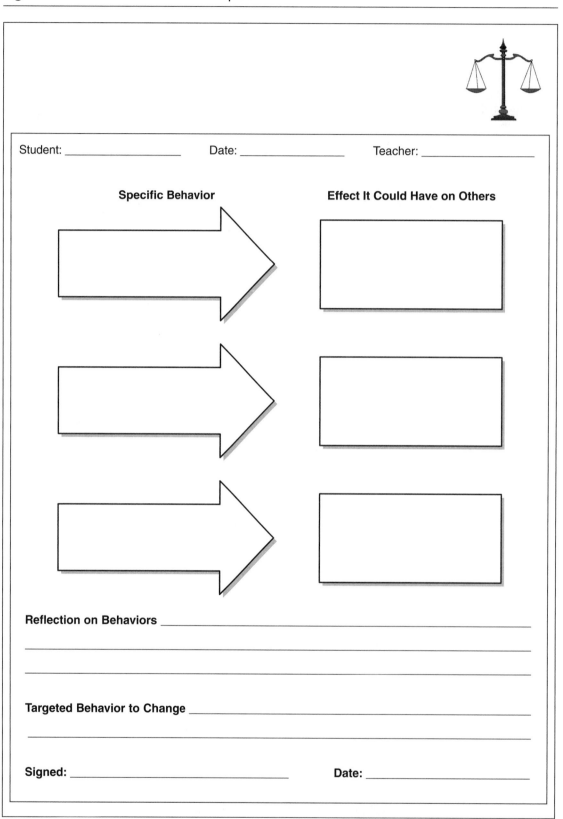

Other Strategies Teachers Can Use With Students Who Dominate the Class

- Review social skills of sharing, taking turns, contributing, and helping others.
- Review class rules about respecting people.
- Talk privately with the dominating student to determine why he has to be in control.
- Practice five-to-fist consensus building (see Chapter 4) with the class and groups.
- Do exercises on conflict resolution to show students how to disagree with ideas, not people.
- Make the dominating student an observer so she has to remain quiet throughout the activity.
- Allow the student to prepare and teach a lesson to the class to showcase his expertise in one area legitimately.

Add some of your own solutions for helping students who dominate the class:

_____

_____

_____

_____

_____

STUDENTS WHO CANNOT GET ALONG WITH OTHERS

Scenario

Paul sits at his desk, tapping his pencil louder and louder until Brittany, who sits in the seat in front of him, turns around angrily and yells, "Will you quit it, you creep!"

"Shut up!" Paul yells back at her. "If you turn around again I'll stick the lead in your neck. Nothing like a little lead poisoning to start your day," he quips.

"Oh grow up," Ron calls to Paul from across the room. "You're such a jerk!!"

"I'll show you who the jerk is. Let's step out in the hall and go one-on-one," Paul retorts. "I won't even use my weapon out there," he says, holding up his pencil and pointing it at Ron.

"I wish you weren't in our class," Sally mumbles under her breath.

Sammy overhears Sally and says loudly, "I wish he wasn't in our school!"

Paul smiles sarcastically and begins tapping his pencil again as Brittany covers her ears and puts her head down on her desk.

Solving the Problem

Every classroom teacher has a few students who just don't get along with anybody. These students are usually socially immature, hyperactive, antisocial, obnoxious, or off task. They try very hard to show off and get attention, but their efforts are usually rebuffed and even scorned by teachers and students. When these types of students are assigned to groups, the reactions of the other group members may include the following:

- "Oh, no! Now we'll never get anything done."
- "Please, Miss Jones, we had him last time."
- "Great, now we have that kid again."
- "I want to go to the Time-Out area and work on my own."
- "It's not fair. Now we have to do twice as much work to make up for her."

Teachers complain that having a few students with weak interpersonal skills can make small groups and even entire classes dysfunctional. And they really complain when they check their class rolls at the beginning of the school year and see six or seven of these "pariahs" scheduled in one classroom. Unfortunately, word gets out in the faculty lounge, and many students don't start the year with a "clean slate" when they matriculate in the same school. Teachers wonder: Should I put them all in the same group and hope for the best? Should I spread them out to divide and conquer? Should I not use cooperative groups because of the potential for behavior problems?

There is no "quick fix" for handling the diverse personality types that comprise the category of students who don't get along well with others. Underneath all the smart remarks, peer put-downs, social blunders, and bravado, many of these students feel inadequate and use negative behaviors as a smokescreen to hide their basic insecurities. They want to be popular, but their poor grades and sometimes obnoxious behaviors often make them unpopular with both teachers and other students.

It is evident that young people today are strongly influenced by their peers. So even though it may appear that a student is deliberately trying to alienate everyone, the reality is that he wants to be included by the group.

> Young people have a strong desire to be liked, and the easiest way to be liked by others is to be like them. The most obvious example is the adoption of particular clothing styles, peer influence, and the desire to conform are so strong that some students will not take books home because studying and achievement in school rank low in their subculture. (Marshall, 2004, p. 499)

Often these children start violating social norms early in their school careers, and the other students label them "weird," "geeky," or "gross" in kindergarten or first grade. Kids can be ruthless when it comes to making fun of other kids. Moreover, the label or reputation often follows the student throughout school. These students are frustrated by the knowledge that they are capable of doing much better and the knowledge that no matter how hard they try, they are not popular with their teachers or peers. In their minds, negative attention is better than no attention.

Whatever the cause of the problem, the student with poor interpersonal skills who doesn't get along with anybody often needs guidance to redirect her efforts toward positive rather than negative relationships. The Social Contract With an Action Plan (see Figure 6.9) is a tool the teacher can use to help the student think through the consequences of his behavior and, as a result, possibly improve relations with his group, the teacher, and the class. A Social Contract With an Action Plan template is provided in Figure 6.10. It is important to involve the parents in the social contract. There is a good chance that the student has had problems relating to other students her entire school life.

Other Strategies Teachers Can Use With Students Who Cannot Get Along With Others

- Review the social skill of offering encouragement versus giving put-downs. Make a T-chart and have groups brainstorm what put-downs look like and sound like.
- Review the social skill of "doing your share" to make sure all students realize the importance of contributing to the class and the group.
- Review the characteristics of ADD and ADHD to see if the student should be referred to special education.
- Monitor the class carefully to see if the students are secretly antagonizing the student who cannot get along with them. Then talk to the antagonizers.
- Move the entire group that is having problems closer to the front of the room to monitor put-downs and negative conversations more closely.
- Place the student whom no one likes with a supportive and nurturing partner rather than with a group of three or more so he can feel more a part of the activity.
- Rotate groups frequently. Other students may be more accepting of the student who doesn't get along with anybody if they know they will not have to work with her too long.
- Have the group write about their group interactions in a log or journal that only the teacher will see. Sometimes, students will share their problems in writing more honestly than when they have to speak in front of group members. The teacher can then monitor the group more carefully based upon students' feelings.

Add some of your own solutions for helping students who cannot get along with others:

_____

_____

_____

_____

Figure 6.9 Social Contract/Action Plan

Meet privately with the student who is alienating himself or herself from the class and the group and develop a social contract to monitor the problem.

Focus Strategy

Student: _____Paul_____ Date: ____Mr. Boden____ Teacher: ____Feb 3____

Teacher's Perception of Problem: _I think you are trying so hard to be popular that you are using the wrong tactics to get the attention of the other students. You need to stop saying and doing immature things and start trying to be nice to other kids._

Student's Perception of Problem: _The kids always make fun of me or ignore me. I'm not going to back down. You don't see what they say to me in the halls or at the bus stop. I'm just defending myself from their comments._

Possible Strategies:
1. _Avoid making comments to my peers for one week.—Paul_
2. _Change the group so Paul starts fresh with new students.—Mr. Boden_
3. _Try to say at least one nice thing a day to someone in class.—Paul_
4. _Spend more time bonding the groups.—Mr. Boden_
5. _Try to be polite and ignore comments they make to me.—Paul_

Create an Action Plan: The student will do the following:

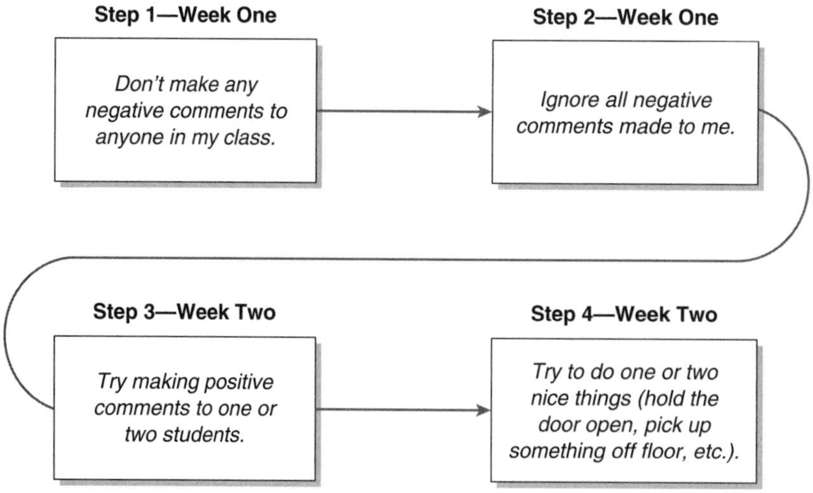

Step 1—Week One

Don't make any negative comments to anyone in my class.

Step 2—Week One

Ignore all negative comments made to me.

Step 3—Week Two

Try making positive comments to one or two students.

Step 4—Week Two

Try to do one or two nice things (hold the door open, pick up something off floor, etc.).

What the teacher will do to assist the student in following the action plan:

I will rotate the groups so Paul can start fresh with new peers. I also will change my seating charts every few weeks and do more team-building activities.

Signatures: _____Paul_____ _____Mr. Boden_____ _____Mr. Brown_____
              Student   Teacher   Parent (optional)

Date to Review Progress: _____Feb. 17_____

Figure 6.10 Social Contract/Action Plan Template

Student: _____   Date: _____   Teacher: _____

Teacher's Perception of Problem: _____

_____

_____

Student's Perception of Problem: _____

_____

_____

Possible Strategies:

1. _____

2. _____

3. _____

4. _____

5. _____

Create an Action Plan: The student will do the following:

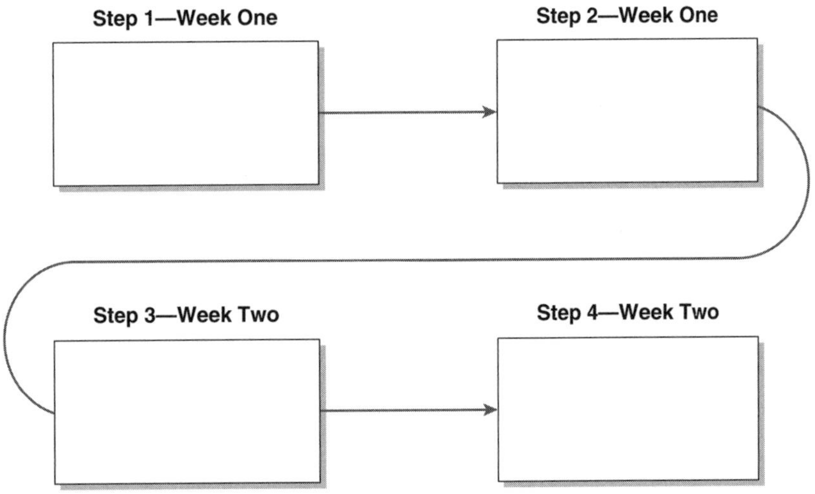

Step 1—Week One   Step 2—Week One

[ ] → [ ]

Step 3—Week Two   Step 4—Week Two

[ ] → [ ]

What the teacher will do to assist the student in following the action plan:

[   ]

Signatures: _____   _____   _____
                    Student   Teacher   Parent (optional)

Date to Review Progress: _____

Addressing Students Who Cause Class Disruptions **7**

Figure 7.0   Phases of a Power Struggle Explosion

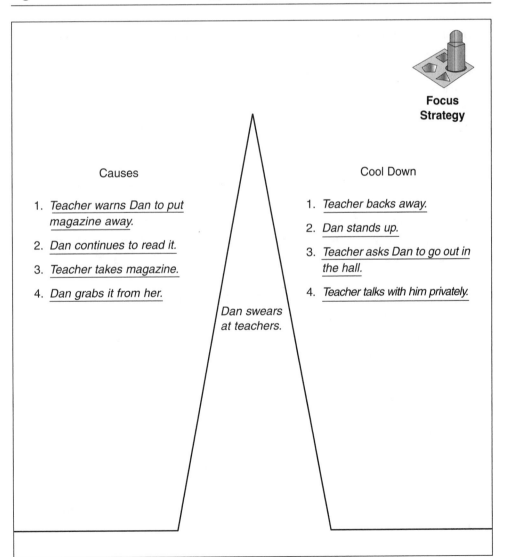

Focus Strategy

Causes

1. *Teacher warns Dan to put magazine away.*
2. *Dan continues to read it.*
3. *Teacher takes magazine.*
4. *Dan grabs it from her.*

Dan swears at teachers.

Cool Down

1. *Teacher backs away.*
2. *Dan stands up.*
3. *Teacher asks Dan to go out in the hall.*
4. *Teacher talks with him privately.*

ADDRESSING BEHAVIOR PROBLEMS

> *When students display inappropriate behavior, they do so because they have the* **mistaken goal** *that it will get them the recognition and acceptance they want.* (Dreikers, Grunwald, & Pepper as cited in Vaughn, Bos, & Schumm, 2000, p. 81)

Behavior problems constitute student behaviors that cause disruptions in the class. Such behaviors can be directed at other students or the teacher and may include talking when another student or the teacher is talking, name calling, fighting, arguing, throwing things, or getting up out of one's seat. Although any of these behaviors is enough to disrupt a classroom, most of them can be controlled by a proactive teacher.

Curwin and Mendler (1988) propose the 80-15-5 model, in which they estimate that 80 percent of students in most classes never or rarely break the classroom rules and cause disruptions. They estimate that about 15 percent of students break rules on a regular basis and 5 percent are chronic rule breakers. Walsh (as cited in Levin & Nolan, 1996) reports that some teachers spend as much as 30 to 80 percent of their time addressing discipline problems. It is evident that the successful teacher of the twenty-first century needs to be able to manage students to maximize the time spent on learning. With the increased emphasis on high-stakes standardized tests, standards, and accountability, teachers must increase time-on-task to prepare students to meet rigorous academic goals.

Most children lack the skills to handle the conflict situations they face. DeRoche and Williams (2001) say these skills include communication skills (listening and verbal/nonverbal messages), problem-solving skills (identifying problems, brainstorming solutions, finding win-win solutions), and cooperative skills (working collaboratively to complete tasks). They say that

> these conflict resolution skills should be taught to students through situations that allow them to practice using the skills in realistic contexts. Students need frequent guided practice in these skills to make them feel comfortable enough to use them to resolve conflicts when they arise. (p. 30)

Because many students lack these conflict resolution skills, they sometimes resort to the only methods they know to try to solve conflicts. Often their methods involve inappropriate behaviors.

Ripple Effect

Teachers are concerned not only with addressing student disruptions but also with the "ripple effect" (Kounin as cited in Levin & Nolan, 1996). The ripple effect results from the initial misbehavior, the methods the teacher uses to curb the misbehavior, and the resultant behavior of the targeted student.

Studies have shown that rough and threatening teacher behavior causes student anxieties, which lead to additional disruptive behaviors from on-looking students. However, students who see that disruptive students comply with the teacher's control technique rate their teacher as fairer and are themselves less distracted from their classwork than when they observe unruly students defying the teacher." (Smith as cited in Levin & Nolan, p. 29)

Many complex dynamics come into play when a teacher addresses even a minor behavior disruption.

At-Risk Students

Educators often use the term *at risk* to describe a particular category of students. A profile of at-risk students has evolved that helps educators make predictions regarding a student's self-concept, behavior, and educational needs. Barr and Parrett (2003) say this profile often describes the

low socioeconomic students living in homes of poverty, often with only a single parent, grandparent, or a foster parent. These students, often identified prior to arriving at school through interactions with social agencies or identified through free and reduced lunch program applications, often constitute a significant percentage of the school's enrollment. (p. 39)

Poverty

Educators need to learn more about how these students live to anticipate their behavioral and academic needs. These students can achieve both social and academic success, but they may need more help.

Payne (as cited in Tileston, 2004) defines poverty as being more than just money. She says poverty is the extent to which an individual does without resources. She defines resources as the following:

- Financial—Money to purchase goods
- Emotional—Ability to respond appropriately to situations and having the role models to demonstrate this
- Mental—The mental abilities and skills needed in daily life
- Spiritual—Belief in a divine purpose and guidance
- Physical—Good health
- Support systems—Friends and family and backup resources in times of need
- Role models—Frequent and appropriate role models who are adults
- Knowledge of hidden rules (p. 71)

Moreover, children who are poor may be at greater risk of failing their classes, dropping out of school before graduation, and turning violent.

The added pressure on these at-risk students to meet high academic standards under the No Child Left Behind Act compounds their problems. Rothstein, a research associate at the Economic Policy Institute, is concerned that students from all demographic groups must meet high academic standards without regard to their poverty, substandard housing, and inadequate health care. In his 2004 book, *Class and Schools,* he writes, "the influence of social class characteristics is probably so powerful that schools cannot overcome it, no matter how well-trained are their teachers and no matter how well-designed are their instructional programs and climates (as cited in Holland, 2007, p. 54).

Labeling students is a challenge because at-risk conditions are not clear-cut and what causes one student to be at risk may not affect other students the same way. Short, Short, and Blanton (1994) discuss how students who are low achievers in school activities are described as at-risk students. Some of the characteristics they describe for an at-risk child include not having mastered basic skills, having been retained, being below grade level on test scores, having a poor attendance record, having a record of suspensions, qualifying for free or reduced lunch, or having a history of high mobility. In addition, at-risk students could have experienced child abuse or neglect; abused substances; have experienced racial, cultural, or gender bias; or come from a dysfunctional family. "A large proportion of school-age children either are or will be poor, multicultural/minority, and from nontraditional homes—all characteristics that have been related to school and social failure" (p. 75).

Even though the characteristics of at-risk students are mostly extrinsic to the child, they still have a profound effect on the development and performance of the student in school. Moreover, at-risk students often display characteristics that distinguish them from the rest of their peer group. This difference can cause tremendous social pressures that result in their not fitting in with the social structure of the class and exhibiting recurrent discipline problems in school (Short et al., 1994).

Teachers have to be aware of the "baggage" many students bring to school each day. They need to be as fair and consistent as possible in maintaining high expectations for all students and enforcing classroom procedures, rules, and consequences. They must also, however, be aware of students' situations and the philosophical idea that "fair is not always equal." Moreover, each student should be handled with some consideration, respect, and flexibility, if possible. Kati Haycock, the director of Education Trust, believes that skilled and dedicated educators can succeed with disadvantaged children and close the achievement gap if they provide rich curricula and quality instruction. "There is no question when you look at both research and our experience around the country that expert teachers are the heart of any solution" (Haycock as cited in Holland, 2007, p. 57).

Identifying Antecedents

The events or conditions that immediately precede instances of problem behavior are called antecedents (Kauffman, Hallahan, Mostert, Trent, & Nuttycombe, 1993). Teachers can keep an anecdotal record or written notes to describe a pattern of when, where, and under what conditions the behavior most often occurs.

For example, if Jimmy usually becomes rude and obnoxious right before a major test, the teacher might have a private conference with him to find out why. Maybe he can't read the directions or he feels inadequate. Maybe he can't handle the time constraints of a test and would like more time. Maybe he can't understand the multiple-choice format and would do better on a performance task that demonstrates what he actually knows rather than how well he guesses.

Effective teachers look for patterns to identify specific events, times of the day, or activities that cause students to act out. One event that often causes disruptions is assigning students to groups. If Kathy hates Jenny because of a problem with an old boyfriend, she may cause a disruption to avoid working with Jenny on a cooperative project. Obviously, teachers cannot anticipate every potential problem, but the proactive teacher can diffuse potential problems before they become major disruptions.

Coercive Interaction

Kauffman et al. (1993) discuss the typical situations that occur when a pupil finds a teacher's expectations and demands aversive or unpleasant. The teacher, in turn, finds the student's refusal to follow his order also aversive and, therefore, restates the demand and adds a threat or punishment as an "incentive." The student then feels challenged in front of her peer group and becomes even louder, more obnoxious, and more threatened, causing the teacher to respond with more severe threats of punishment. This type of coercive interaction continues until the teacher "wins" and the student backs down. This retreat is sometimes temporary, lasting only until the student seeks revenge on the teacher for "beating" her in public. Another typical situation results in the teacher's backing down and not following through with the threat, in which case the student wins. In this case, sometimes the teacher is "out to get the student" the rest of the year because he lost face in front of the class. The best situation is a win-win outcome where both parties compromise, save face, and address the real cause of the problem and possible solutions in private.

Figure 7.1 represents a typical coercive classroom interaction. Skillful teachers can avoid such coercive interactions and recognize when students are baiting them to seek attention or engage in a power struggle.

Figure 7.1   Coercive Interaction

- Teacher asks student to complete page of math problems.
- Student says, "I don't know how to do this crap!"
- Teacher says, "Yes you do, we just did some problems like these yesterday. Get started now."
- Student slams book closed, saying, "Ain't doin' it!"
- Teacher goes to student's desk, opens book, hands student pencil, says in angry tone, "Get started now!"
- Student shoves book off desk.
- Teacher squeezes student's shoulder, growls, "Pick that book up, young man!"
- Student jumps to feet, says, "Get your hands off me, b——— ! You pick it up! You can't make me do nothin'!"
- Teacher yells, "That's it! I've had enough of this! Pick that book up and get to work now or you're outta here to the office!"

Reprinted with permission from Kauffman et al. (1993). *Managing classroom behavior: A reflective case-based approach*, p. 31. Needham Heights, MA: Allyn & Bacon.

STUDENTS WHO SEEK ATTENTION

Scenario

Glenn gets up from his desk, slowly walks down the aisle to the pencil sharpener, and starts sharpening a long pencil. Each time he finishes sharpening, he puts the pencil inside the sharpener again and again until it becomes a stub.

"Sit down," yells Mrs. Martinez. "We're trying to work here, and you're not supposed to be out of your desk."

"I'm just trying to sharpen my pencil," Glenn announces loudly to the entire class. "Is that a crime? Excuse me for living!"

Mrs. Martinez walks over to Glenn and whispers quietly, "Glenn, the class is working on their group art project, and your group really needs your help."

Glenn reluctantly rejoins his group and proceeds to draw a happy face on the back of Mary's black sweater with a piece of hot-pink colored chalk.

"You idiot," shrieks Mary. "When are you going to grow up?"

Glenn laughs and looks around the room to see all the students and Mrs. Martinez staring at him.

Mrs. Martinez walks over and taps Glenn on the shoulder, and they both walk into the hall.

Solving the Problem

Misbehaving students are often seeking *extra* attention. Albert (1989) says that all people need a certain amount of attention to feel as though they belong and are an important part of the social group. "In contrast, students who misbehave for attention are never satisfied with a normal amount. They want more and more, as if they carry around with them a bucket labeled 'attention' that they expect the teacher to fill" (p. 26).

Attention seekers are students who seek independence but spend a great deal of their time complaining to others that they cannot control what is happening in their lives. "They see themselves as victims of circumstance and strive to gain attention by keeping adults busy with them" (Dinkmeyer, McKay, & Dinkmeyer, 1980, p. 252).

Many attention seekers are discouraged students who may become obnoxiously loud and silly or resort to immature acts, like pushing books off a desk or trying to trip someone, to get noticed. Attention seekers are like stage performers; they require an audience. They do get noticed, but many of them eventually get rejected by their peers and their teacher, who grow tired of their constant attempts to be in the limelight. The attention seeker's idea of success is to be on stage, even if their actions violate the dignity and rights of other students and earn her the hostility of those who feel attacked or violated (Dinkmeyer & Losoncy, 1980). In the elementary grades, attention seekers usually gear their performance toward the teacher, but as they move to upper grades, they prefer a wider audience that includes their classmates, guidance counselors, administrators, and sometimes the entire school community (Albert, 1989).

Appropriate Attention

The origins of attention-seeking behavior range from students' not receiving enough attention at home to students' not knowing how to ask for attention in an appropriate manner. The greatest challenge for teachers is to change the behavior of the attention seeker by giving him as little attention as possible when the misbehavior occurs. Bellanca and Fogarty (2003) recommend the following strategies:

- Highlight other students who are behaving appropriately.
- Move the student out of the spotlight by giving him an errand to run.
- Distract the student with a question.
- Attend to the attention seeker positively when she is on task.

By encouraging attention seekers to succeed in individual or group work and by noticing and encouraging their accomplishments, teachers and students reinforce appropriate behavior with positive attention. The goal is to encourage attention seekers to strive for positive attention, rather than negative attention, from peers and teachers to fulfill their needs.

Because one method to prevent students from seeking attention is to identify the goal of the misbehavior, teachers should help students to analyze their own behavior. The Newspaper Model (see Figure 7.2) allows attention seekers to analyze their actions and reflect on the causes and effects of their behavior. Figure 7.3 offers a Newspaper Model template that teachers can use with their students. Teachers should work with students to fill out the form and discuss and reflect on the process.

Educators must remember that the number of students seeking attention will probably increase commensurate with the lack of attention they may be getting from their families at home. Large class sizes and big schools can cause many students to feel lost in the crowd. Some larger secondary schools have adopted the "school within a school" structure or Freshmen Academies to provide smaller learning communities, so students feel more connected to their peer group and teachers. When students have to compete for attention each day, they may resort to more disruptive or even violent ways to capture the attention of their parents, teachers, and classmates—even the media.

Other Strategies Teachers Can Use With Students Who Seek Attention

- Help the student find an area where she can shine. Find a specific interest or strength she can use to get attention in a positive way.
- Find the student a study buddy. Sometimes a student who lacks friends tries to compensate by acting out.

Figure 7.2   The Newspaper Model

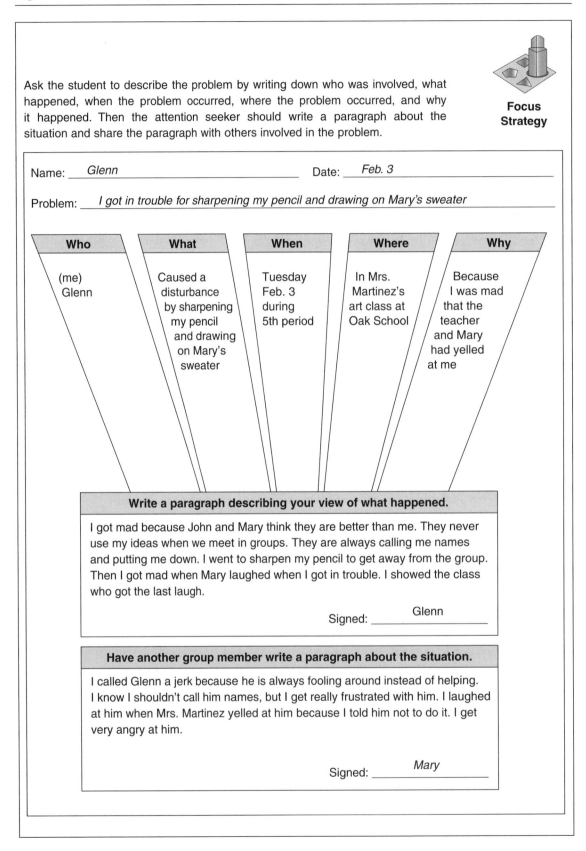

Ask the student to describe the problem by writing down who was involved, what happened, when the problem occurred, where the problem occurred, and why it happened. Then the attention seeker should write a paragraph about the situation and share the paragraph with others involved in the problem.

Focus Strategy

Name: ____Glenn_____   Date: ___Feb. 3_____

Problem: ____I got in trouble for sharpening my pencil and drawing on Mary's sweater_____

Who	What	When	Where	Why
(me) Glenn	Caused a disturbance by sharpening my pencil and drawing on Mary's sweater	Tuesday Feb. 3 during 5th period	In Mrs. Martinez's art class at Oak School	Because I was mad that the teacher and Mary had yelled at me

Write a paragraph describing your view of what happened.

I got mad because John and Mary think they are better than me. They never use my ideas when we meet in groups. They are always calling me names and putting me down. I went to sharpen my pencil to get away from the group. Then I got mad when Mary laughed when I got in trouble. I showed the class who got the last laugh.

Signed: ___Glenn_____

Have another group member write a paragraph about the situation.

I called Glenn a jerk because he is always fooling around instead of helping. I know I shouldn't call him names, but I get really frustrated with him. I laughed at him when Mrs. Martinez yelled at him because I told him not to do it. I get very angry at him.

Signed: ___Mary_____

Figure 7.3   The Newspaper Model Template

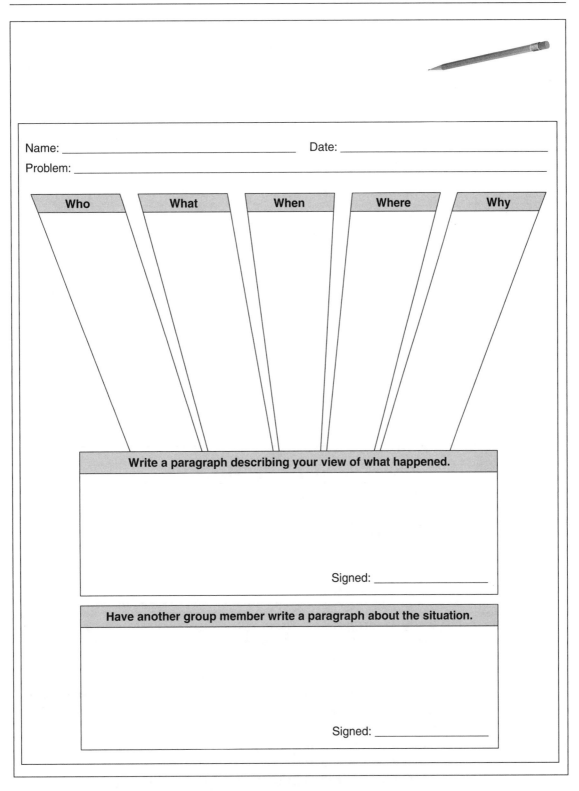

- Give the student an option of a short time-out period. He can go to a corner of the room to cool down or write in a journal about his feelings.
- Analyze the Newspaper Model to see when, where, and why most incidents occur. Remember to review the antecedents or context. If incidents usually arise from the student's being involved with certain people or situations, try to avoid placing the student in those situations.
- When a student does something well, encourage her.
- When a student raises his hand, call on him quickly to give him positive attention for an answer or for trying to answer a question.
- Give the student legitimate positive attention by allowing her to go to the Media Center, lead the "Pledge of Allegiance," or conduct an Internet search. Be careful to rotate these privileges regularly so the other students don't resent her.
- Have a secret signal to give the student from across the room to remind him when he is doing something to get attention.

Add some of your own solutions for helping students who seek attention:

_____

_____

_____

_____

_____

STUDENTS WHO SEEK POWER

Scenario

Mrs. Bradley returns the students' English tests and then asks if there are any questions.

"This sucks!" exclaims Brian. "You can't take off points for misspellings. We weren't allowed to use dictionaries!"

"You should know how to spell the words you write. I take off five points for every error."

"You can't do that!" Brian yells, moving forward in his desk. "This test was on short stories, and we were supposed to describe the plots. Who cares if we misspelled a few words. You missed the point of the test! We didn't get to use spell check!"

"Excuse me, young man," Mrs. Bradley snarls as her face turns red. "This is my class, and I will be the one who decides what I will and will not grade!"

"This sucks," mutters Brian. "I want to go to my counselor to get transferred to Mrs. Brown's English class."

"You're not getting a pass from me," counters Mrs. Bradley.

"I don't need a pass—I'm outta here." Brian grabs his backpack and kicks his desk before he bolts from the room.

The other students glare at Mrs. Bradley in silence.

Solving the Problem

"I believe that the need for power is the core—the absolute core—of almost all school problems" (Glasser as cited in Gough, 1987, p. 658).

Students who seek independence sometimes engage in power conflicts with adults because they are determined not to do what adults want. Curwin and Mendler (1988) warn teachers not to get caught in a power trap:

> Commit yourself to avoiding power struggles, even if it means initially backing down. Remember that continuation of a power struggle makes you look foolish and out of control. You must be prepared to see long-term victory (a cooperative, positive classroom climate) as more important than short-term winning. (p. 105)

Glasser (1986) feels that students, even good students, don't feel important in school because no one listens to them. Moreover, students who receive poor grades and are considered discipline problems cannot feel important from the standpoint of academic performance and acceptance. Glasser asserts that students would work harder in school if they had more freedom and fun. Mendler (1997) says, "It is estimated that 70 to 80 percent of challenging student behavior in school is primarily attributable to outside factors such as dysfunctional families, violence in our culture, the effects of drugs and alcohol, and fragmented communities" (p. 4). Yet teachers cannot relinquish their responsibility for controlling student behavior in their classrooms by blaming it on outside forces. The challenge is to teach all students.

Most often, the power base in schools is tilted in favor of teachers. Teachers have the power to threaten students and can back up those threats with minus points, minutes in the time-out area, detention, notes to parents, suspensions, expulsion, and the ultimate weapon—failure. Despite all the power teachers have, Glasser (1986) says that half the students still won't work because they don't feel they have any control over their lives. They are discouraged because they have so little to say about what they learn, when they learn it, and how they learn it. Students are discouraged, and they don't have the patience to wait it out until teachers and the school system give them more say in their education. Power seekers vent this frustration through temper tantrums, verbal tantrums, and quiet noncompliance (Albert, 1989).

More and more schools recognize the need to empower students by allowing them to be involved in setting classroom rules and having some choice in what they study and how they will be assessed.

> Students also need to learn to look for more effective behaviors while they wait, but they have less power over their lives than adults and little confidence that the school will change for the better. If we can restructure schools so that they are more satisfying, we can expect many more students to be patient when they are frustrated. (Glasser, 1986, p. 55)

The tactics in Figure 7.4 can be used by teachers to avoid getting pulled into a power struggle.

Figure 7.4   Tactics Teachers Can Use With Power Seekers

- Don't grab the hook. Teachers should not fall into the power trap, especially in front of the class.
- Avoid and defuse direct confrontations.
- Listen to the problem in private.
- Recognize the student's feelings.
- Privately acknowledge the power struggle.
- Do not embarrass students publicly.
- Give the students choices in their academic work.
- Place the power seeker in a leadership role.
- Encourage independent thinking—but not anarchy!

Students who seek power often try to dominate the entire class and their groups. If they cannot control the class, the teacher, or the school, they might consider their cooperative group as their personal power base. Teachers should monitor the roles assigned to group members and make sure that power seekers are fulfilling their assignments without trying to take control of the entire group.

Teachers should also review the specific roles assigned to each group member and the responsibilities of each of these roles every time they assign cooperative group work. Remind students that group roles are rotated so everyone will have a chance to be the organizer or the group leader. If the tasks are structured so that they allow a great deal of choice, creativity, and freedom, power seekers should be satisfied that they do, in fact, have some control over their lives. Hopefully, they will develop positive leadership qualities rather than negative dictatorial traits. Figure 7.5 shows the phases in a power struggle.

The most difficult behavior for teachers to model when engaged in a power struggle with a student is self-control. Jones and Jones (2001) warn teachers to guard against their vulnerabilities and be "smarter than a trout." They warn, "Like the wily trout who knows better than to strike at every imitation lure, we

Figure 7.5

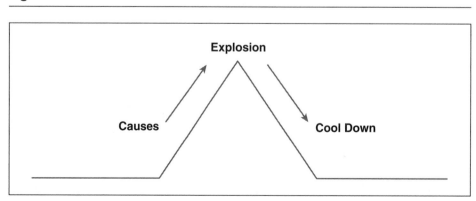

must be careful not to become snared by students' attempts to gain control or negative attention by making inappropriate comments" (p. 309).

Teachers need to be proactively aware of when students become upset, look angry or frustrated, depressed or anxious. If teachers practice their best "with-it-ness" strategies, they will be able to select the most appropriate option to deescalate the behavior thoughtfully and purposefully.

Figure 7.6 shows how the student and the teacher in this scenario can use Phases of a Power Struggle to analyze what they could have done differently to prevent a power struggle. Figure 7.7 is a Phases of a Power Struggle Template that teachers can use with their own students. The graphic organizer and strategy developed by Bob Wiedmann shows the initial causes that escalate the problem, the explosion, and the cooldown phases of a power struggle. This graphic organizer helps both the teacher and the student analyze the "hot points" or "key words and actions" that cause a minor comment or incident to escalate into a full-scale power struggle from which neither the teacher nor the student emerges victorious.

Power-seeking students constantly challenge teachers by trying to prove they are in control of issues such as tardiness, incomplete work, making noises, gum chewing, or muttering under their breath. Albert (1989) reminds teachers,

> Often power-seeking students don't act out until they're assured of an audience. We fear that if we lose a public battle, we'll be labeled a "loser" by the entire class until school is out in June. The pressure of having to handle such a difficult situation with so much at stake in front of an audience adds greatly to our discomfort. (p. 44)

Urban Teaching

Weiner (1999) discusses how young teachers going into urban schools, who have not lived in the communities their school serves, can be more anxious about managing their classrooms. Because a great many kids from poor neighborhoods are surrounded by violence, they develop a "defensive stance" and aggressive behavior as survival mechanisms. If urban schools don't adequately safeguard students and their property, students might ignore classroom rules because they feel vulnerable. They might reject the school's behavioral norms because they don't feel the rules protect them enough. "Children often violate school rules of conduct, sacrificing their prospect of academic success to safeguard themselves and their belonging because they do not trust authorities in schools to provide them with adequate protection" (Weiner, p. 68).

Teachers need to ensure that their classrooms are safe and orderly and that the property of the students is secure. If the environment is safe, students will be more inclined to follow rules and principles and refrain from engaging in power struggles to maintain their pride and guarantee their own safety.

Some students are more resilient and are capable of accepting change and recovering more quickly from problems and adversities. Gholar and Riggs (2004) describe resilient teachers and students who are able to demonstrate flexibility, optimism, endurance, and an openness to learn. They believe that conative intelligence (CI) builds upon "the winner within" to help students love learning and raise their performance in significant ways. They describe conative

Figure 7.6 Phases of a Power Struggle

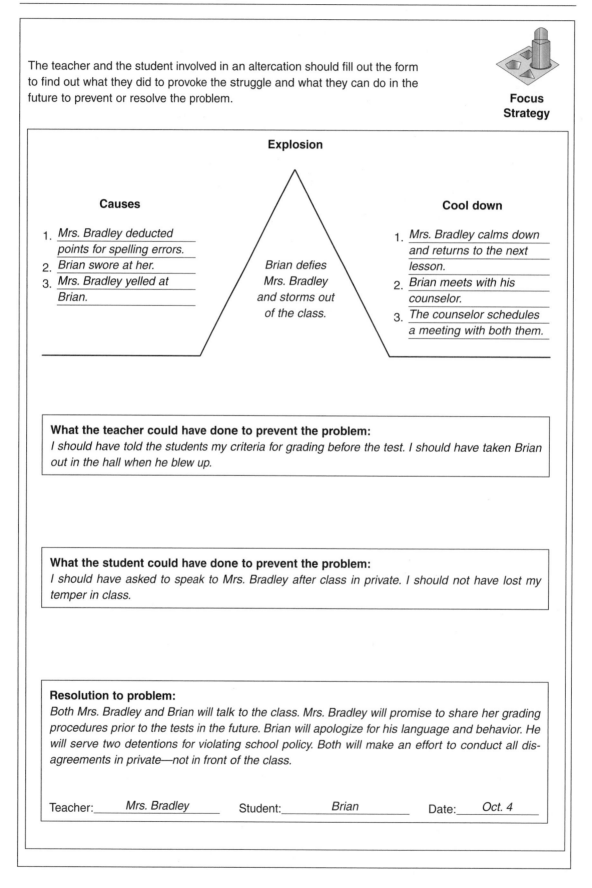

The teacher and the student involved in an altercation should fill out the form to find out what they did to provoke the struggle and what they can do in the future to prevent or resolve the problem.

Focus Strategy

Explosion

Causes

1. *Mrs. Bradley deducted points for spelling errors.*
2. *Brian swore at her.*
3. *Mrs. Bradley yelled at Brian.*

Brian defies Mrs. Bradley and storms out of the class.

Cool down

1. *Mrs. Bradley calms down and returns to the next lesson.*
2. *Brian meets with his counselor.*
3. *The counselor schedules a meeting with both them.*

What the teacher could have done to prevent the problem:
I should have told the students my criteria for grading before the test. I should have taken Brian out in the hall when he blew up.

What the student could have done to prevent the problem:
I should have asked to speak to Mrs. Bradley after class in private. I should not have lost my temper in class.

Resolution to problem:
Both Mrs. Bradley and Brian will talk to the class. Mrs. Bradley will promise to share her grading procedures prior to the tests in the future. Brian will apologize for his language and behavior. He will serve two detentions for violating school policy. Both will make an effort to conduct all disagreements in private—not in front of the class.

Teacher: _____*Mrs. Bradley*_____   Student: _____*Brian*_____   Date: _____*Oct. 4*_____

Figure 7.7 Phases of a Power Struggle Template

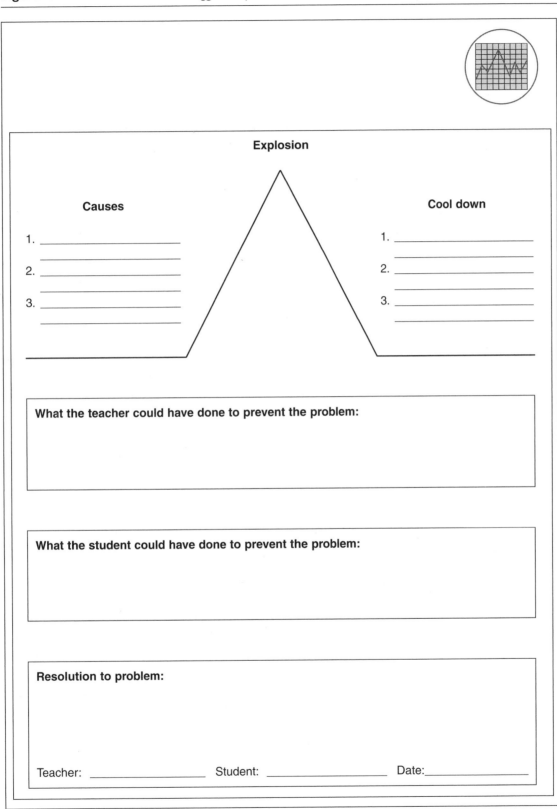

intelligence as "the ability to persist, pursue, strive, and commit to a goal; under-stand the role of persistence in high performance; and productively engage the energy of the will in active teaching and learning" (p. 18). When people utilize their conative intelligence, they strive to make wise choices, and they pursue per-sonal and academic goals. Students who don't have this inner confidence to suc-ceed might engage in power struggles with their peers, parents, and teachers to hide their feelings of insecurity or sense of powerlessness.

Teachers who are able to instill the power of positive thinking in students can change students' views of themselves and the world around them.

Other Strategies Teachers Can Use With Students Who Seek Power

- Keep cool and remain calm. The power-seeking student often tries to excite and anger the teacher and fellow students.
- Isolate the student from other group members or classmates. Don't allow a confrontation to erupt where people say and do things they later regret.
- Allow the student some time to cool down and get herself together. Let her go to a private area (office, media center, counselor, time-out corner) so she can compose herself.
- Defuse his anger by saying, "I see your point," or, "I know how you must feel," but then state what you think is necessary.
- Delay the issue by saying, "You can stay in your seat now, and I'll con-sider giving you a pass later."
- Conference with the student to find out if any personal or family problems are making her anxious or belligerent. Sometimes the blow-up is not caused by the minor incident that precipitated it; it is because of personal problems.
- Write a contract with the student to brainstorm alternative ideas he might try when he is upset and wants to take control of the class or the group.
- Try to give her a leadership position in one of the next class activities. She can then exercise her leadership role in a positive, rather than nega-tive, way.
- Reinforce anything the student does that is positive. Encourage his actions when he maintains his cool.
- Have the student keep a "Power Problem Journal" to record the specific things that upset her. The student will get time to process her feelings and reflect on her behavior. Self-analysis is a powerful tool in redirecting behavior.

Add some of your own solutions for helping students who seek power:

_____

_____

_____

_____

STUDENTS WHO SEEK REVENGE

Scenario

Coach Carden passes out the history test papers and proceeds to lecture the class.

"You must not care about passing this class and getting into college. These tests are pathetic! Did anyone here bother reading the chapter on the Civil War?" he asks sarcastically.

Rick stares at his 62 percent score and doesn't say a word. Then he suddenly crumbles his paper into a ball and tosses it toward the garbage can. It misses!

"Some basketball player you are," scoffs Coach Carden. "I'm glad I'm not your coach."

"I might not be a basketball player after I get my grade for this class. This sucks!" yells Rick.

"What did you say? You know I don't tolerate that kind of language in this class. See me after school today for an hour detention. We'll practice how to carry on a polite conversation."

"You can go to hell!" Rick shouts. "I have practice after school. You can't make me stay."

"Oh yeah, we'll see about that. You'll stay or you'll be suspended and miss a few games!" replies Coach Carden.

"That's not fair. You can't flunk the whole class and you can't make me stay in this sorry excuse for a class. I'm out of here."

Rick storms out of the room shouting, "We'll see what my parents and my coach say when they hear about this. My dad's a lawyer! I'll see you in court!"

Solving the Problem

Sometimes power seekers who never satisfy their need for power become revenge seekers to get back at the person or persons who thwarted their quest for power. Usually the revengeful student is trying to retaliate for something hurtful said by a parent, teacher, or peer or for some injustice or unfair deed. Albert (1989) says these students often sulk or scowl even when not lashing out. They put teachers on edge because teachers are never sure when these students will retaliate.

The most important thing teachers can do for students who are seeking revenge is to help them rebuild positive relationships with the teacher or the class. It may be difficult for a teacher to build a caring relationship with someone who has just announced to the whole class that the teacher "sucks," but it is important. The social skill of encouragement needs to be emphasized, and teachers should monitor group activities to make sure the revenge seeker is included. The student who seeks revenge needs to learn appropriate methods to express his hurt or anger appropriately by talking to the teacher or to peers to resolve the problem. Teachers themselves can try come of the tactics shown in Figure 7.8 with revenge seekers to encourage positive behavior and to reduce power struggles.

Revenge seekers need to have their desire to "get even" defused, or else their hidden agenda may torpedo the class. When this happens, the other students may become resentful and distrustful of the revenge seeker. As a result, the revenge seeker compounds her personal problems by alienating her peers in addition to the teacher whom she is out to get.

The revenge seeker's hidden agenda can snowball into a personality problem that serves to brand the student as a "bully," "incorrigible," or a "loner" for the rest of the year or even the rest of his schooling. Teachers need to take time

Figure 7.8   Tactics Teachers Can Use With Revenge Seekers

- Avoid sarcasm or put-downs.
- Do not confront the student in front of her peers.
- Don't seek revenge on revenge seekers.
- Listen carefully to his problems (probe for causes).
- Form a positive relationship with the student.
- Encourage the student when she behaves appropriately.
- Ask the student to keep a journal to process feelings and analyze the causes for his anger.
- Admit mistakes.
- Use frequent teacher-student conferences to monitor behavior.

from the textbook and curriculum to allow students to process their emotions. Conference with the student, call in a counselor or another teacher to talk to the student, have the student keep a diary or journal to record events that trigger an outburst, and analyze different responses.

If students are not happy, satisfied, and accepted in the classroom, they will continue to disrupt learning and interfere with group interactions until their personal needs are met—sometimes at a very extreme level. For example, the violence across American schools, especially in Columbine, Colorado, in 1999 and on the Virginia Tech Campus in 2007, can be linked to students who were enraged. When enraged students kill, they are often trying to extort revenge on those whom they perceived disrespected them. Sometimes, however, the violence is more random, and the enraged student seeks revenge on anyone in his path. There is a strong link between student revenge seekers and school violence.

The Divided Journal (see Figure 7.9) allows both teachers and students to reflect on what they may have said or done in anger and propose another way they could approach the problem if it occurs again. Sometimes these journals help teachers learn more about the inappropriateness of their own actions and how their behavior escalated a minor incident into a showdown. The ultimate revenge of a teacher is failing the student, but students should not suffer academically for their poor behavior. The problem needs to be addressed so it doesn't distract from learning.

The Divided Journal allows both teachers and students to reflect metacognitively on their actions. Given (2002) says that the Russian psychologist A. R. Luria described the use of "self-talk" to regulate one's behavior. Luria observed that prefrontal cortical damage often created impulsive behavior, explosive anger, and fear. He also found that students could be taught to use self-talk to curb their impulsive acts and function appropriately. The reflective system allows people to carry on dialogues in their heads, try out ideas, rethink interactions, and project the results of an action without actually doing it. Given says, "This allows us to cultivate thinking strategies and attitudes we can use to control genetic predispositions" (p. 121). In other words, students can self-monitor and manage their behavior through reflective learning. The journal is a metacognitive tool for students and teachers to *analyze* their thoughts and behavior and then act to attain their goals.

Figure 7.9   Divided Journal

The teacher and the student need to process what happened by describing the incident and reflecting on what they would do differently. They should discuss their reactions and try to arrive at a mutually beneficial compromise.

Focus Strategy

Student: _____Rick_____ Date: _____April 5_____

Description of What Happened

I was angry because I'd studied hard for the test and Coach was yelling about how we weren't going to get into college.

I freaked out and threw my test away. It upset him, but I was upset that I might get kicked off the basketball team. Basketball means everything to me.

Upon Reflection   Date: _____April 6_____

What I Would Do Differently

I realize that Coach was trying to motivate us to study harder. I should have talked to him after class about what I could do to bring up my grade. Then I would have been calmer and wouldn't have tried to save face with the class. I should never have threatened him with a lawsuit!

Teacher: _Coach Carden_ Date: _____April 5_____

Description of What Happened

I passed out the tests and talked to the class about their poor performance. Rick was upset and threw his test away.

I was upset because I had planned to review the test and discuss the right answers. He tried to get back at me in front of the class.

Upon Reflection   Date: _____April 6_____

What I Would Do Differently

I should not have passed out the test that way because kids saw each other's papers. I think Rick was embarrassed because one of the cheerleaders saw his 62 percent.

I shouldn't have made fun of him when he missed the trash with his wadded-up test. I hurt him, and he reacted the only way he could—to save face with his peers.

Figure 7.10 offers a Divided Journal template that teachers can use with their students. Reflection is a powerful tool to help adults, teenagers, and even young children process their feelings and analyze their actions in private.

Figure 7.10 Divided Journal Template

Student: _____ Date: _____	Upon Reflection Date: _____
Description of What Happened	**What I Would Do Differently**
Teacher: _____ Date: _____	Upon Reflection Date: _____
Description of What Happened	**What I Would Do Differently**

Other Strategies Teachers Can Use With Students Who Seek Revenge

- Use I-messages: "When I see you losing your temper, I feel upset because . . . "
- Ask for a conference with the student and ask to have a counselor present as an objective observer.
- Encourage students who have questions or concerns about assignments or grades to see you privately after class.
- Build in some downtime during class, while students are working, when you are available to discuss problems (especially for students who cannot come in after school).
- Fold over test papers and return them personally to students to preserve confidentiality.
- Don't take the hook. Teenagers are often not in control of their emotions, but teachers should try to be in control of their emotions.

Add some of your own solutions for helping students who seek revenge:

_____

_____

_____

_____

_____

STUDENTS WITH AGGRESSIVE BEHAVIORS

Scenario

Ms. Cox divides the class into cooperative groups and posts the directions for their projects on the board.

Domingo groans when he sees that Jimmy is in his group. "I don't want to work with him," Domingo says to Ms. Cox. "Get him out of my group!"

Ms. Cox walks over to Domingo and asks him, "What is wrong? You know we respect everyone in the class and we try to get along."

"He stole my lunch money," Domingo blurts out. "I don't want to be near that thief!"

"You can't prove that," Jimmy mumbles as he turns red.

I don't have to prove it," retorts Domingo. "I have three witnesses who saw you take it from my book bag."

Jimmy stands up menacingly and begins walking toward Domingo.

"Sit down," yells Ms. Cox as she runs toward the phone in the room.

Domingo turns to face Jimmy as the rest of the class begins to move their desks away from the impending fight.

Jimmy pulls a Swiss army knife from his pocket and flashes it in front of Domingo's nose. Domingo does not back down, and Jimmy inches closer.

One of the boys in the class holds out his foot and trips Jimmy.

Just as Jimmy begins to scuffle with the student who tripped him, the coach in the next room, who has heard the scuffle, runs into the classroom. He grabs Jimmy, Domingo, and the student who stuck his foot out and hauls them all down to the dean's office.

Solving the Problem

Students who display aggressive behavior are often trying to gain control over their lives. When students constantly utilize anger in an attempt to dominate other students or the group, they are incapable of finding a workable solution to their problems. Their inability to communicate causes them to try to overpower, intimidate, or hurt others. If students are taught to disagree with the idea and not the person, to negotiate, to discuss, and to compromise, aggressive behavior can be prevented. Anger can either be talked out or acted out. When students act out anger, aggression is the result.

A disinterested student rarely has a satisfying picture of school in his head; perhaps he has the picture of spending his days on the street "hanging out." But if his parents are able to force him to go to school, he may choose the angry behavior of disrupting to the extent that he is suspended. Now, out on suspension, he is satisfied. In school he was frustrated and he disrupted to get closer to the picture that he wants. On the street he is in control; in school he has almost no effective control at all. (Glasser, 1986, p. 53)

Jones and Jones (2001) recommend that teachers do not become emotional or display visible anger when dealing with a student who is demonstrating aggressive behavior. When a teacher begins turning red, speaking louder and faster, and getting upset, the student is so busy thinking about the teacher that he cannot think about his own mistake or make a new plan of behavior.

The Teacher Behavior Continuum

Wolfgang, Bennett, and Irvin (1999) contrast what they call the clear-cut recipe approach to responding to misbehavior with their approach of the Teacher Behavior Continuum (TBC). Rather than writing a student's name on the board and making checkmarks each time the student commits the same offense, they believe a teacher should use an orderly arrangement of teacher techniques that correlate to the degree of power that is needed under the circumstances.

Wolfgang et al. (1999) believe that the strategy employed by the teacher should vary according to each student and the teacher's knowledge as to which techniques are most effective. In some cases, just looking at or signaling the student could be all that is needed to make the student aware of her actions. At other times, depending on the seriousness of the infraction and the purpose of the act (power play, attention getting, revenge), a teacher may need to issue a command and articulate the explicit consequence for not following the command. Figure 7.11 outlines several strategies that teachers can use to make students aware of their actions.

Even though school violence is a critical issue, serious discipline problems such as assaults, destruction of property, and a clear defiance of the teacher's authority are rare events in most schools, occurring only about 5 percent of the time. Jones (as cited in Wolfgang et al., 1999) documents that

> 80 percent of all discipline problems involve off-task behavior of students talking to others when they should be working. The second most common form is goofing off or out-of-seat behaviors (15 percent), followed by such misbehaviors as note passing, playing with items smuggled into class, and tying shoelaces. (p. 37)

Figure 7.11 Teacher Behavior Continuum (TBC)

Step 1: Looking

In the first (minimum power) behavior on the TBC, the teacher uses a modality of looking, touch, or sound to signal the student to become aware of his or her own actions.

Step 2: Naming

In the second behavior on the TBC, the teacher uses words to describe the feelings, problem, or situation the student is facing regarding some episode (e.g., difficulty with another person or objects and materials).

Step 3: Questioning

In the third teacher behavior on the TBC, the student is called on to reflect on the situation and to think of new ideas to solve the situation; alternatively, questioning could be the teacher's offer to provide assistance.

Step 4: Commanding

In the fourth behavior on the TBC, the teacher makes a powerful direct statement, telling the student what to do. Promise a Consequence is a subbehavior under the larger category of Commanding. Once the teacher has told the student what to do and sees that the student is not complying, the teacher verbally gives a promise of consequence—a promise to follow up with a strong action (physical intervention) if the student does not quickly comply.

Step 5: Acting (Physical Intervention)

In this strongest and most intrusive behavior on the TBC, the teacher physically takes the student by the hand and restricts his or her body to stop an action that is occurring.

Reprinted with permission from Wolfgang et al. (1999). *Strategies for teaching self-discipline in the middle grades*, p. 15. Boston: Allyn & Bacon.

Jones adds that a serious discipline problem usually means taking five minutes or less to send the student to the office, whereas the minor disruption or the "nickel-and-dime" actions can eat up one-third or more of total class time. It is evident, therefore, that teachers need to develop strategies to keep students on task to raise academic achievement.

Of course, all the steps listed in the Teacher Behavior Continuum help diffuse the immediate aggressive situation, but the next steps involve meeting with the student and perhaps the counselor and/or the parents. The behavior needs to be analyzed as to what provoked it, and some form of behavioral interventions, checkpoints, or conferences need to be set up to monitor the student's ability to prevent future disturbances. In many cases, the aggressive outburst was merely a symptom of a more complex issue that needs to be articulated and addressed before the aggressive behavior stops.

Bullying

Roberts (2006) believes that the terms *bullying, teasing, taunting, victimization, hazing,* and *harassment* are similar incidents or situations that vary only in intensity along a continuum of behaviors. He says that taunting is a severe form of teasing in which the aggressor does not stop when asked. He believes that

> bullying, on the other hand, is often a combination of verbal and physical aggressions and aggravations directed from an **agent** (the bully) toward a **target** (the victim). Bullying often involves direct physical contact between the bully and the victim and should be considered a higher level of concern for interveners. (p. 14)

Both teasing and bullying can inflict long-term damage on the mental health of their victims, especially if they do not receive any assistance to offset the harassment.

Roberts (2006) describes six types of students who are at risk for victimization. In general, victims (1) are *social isolates* and *outcasts,* (2) have a *transient school history,* (3) exhibit *poor social skills,* (4) *desire to fit in* "at any cost," (5) are defenseless, and (6) are viewed by their peers as different (p. 31). Unfortunately, the advent of the Internet and MySpace.com have led to cyberbullying and "cybertaunting," where victims have been subjected to embarrassing pictures and words posted on Web sites or sent through e-mail, instant messaging, and cell phones.

Shore (2005) discusses how being taunted or attacked physically can be one of the most painful experiences of childhood and can leave lasting psychological scars. He says that

> victims of bullying may experience anxiety, low self-esteem, depression and in some cases even suicidal thoughts. They may come to view school, where most incidents of bullying take place, as an unsafe, anxiety-provoking environment and may be afraid of attending. Some may even refuse to go to school rather than face the ordeal of bullying." (p. 5)

In addition, bullying affects the students who witness the incidents, and it often causes a climate of fear and anxiety in the school. Obviously, students won't be able to concentrate on standards and student achievement when their basic need for safety is not being met. The teacher who has set a cooperative classroom climate, taught and revisited the social skills, uses his with-it-ness scrutiny of any impending problems can monitor potential "bullying" activity and, if not prevent it, at least address it immediately, before it destroys individual students and the atmosphere of the classroom.

Violent behavior problems cannot be handled by assigning a detention or writing students' names on the board. Teachers need to work with students to develop a long-term action plan. When a student uses a weapon or attempts to use a weapon, she is usually suspended or expelled, depending upon the school's rules. Other aggressive behaviors, however, include students' threatening others, using their fists, or using their books or a desk in a violent fashion. The teacher needs to react quickly to protect the other students, then work toward solving the long-term problem of the student's aggressive behavior when or if the student returns to class. Figure 7.12 shows a sample Action Plan for the scenario described, and Figure 7.13 offers a template that teachers can use to help their students.

Other Strategies Teachers Can Use With Students With Aggressive Behaviors

- After the student returns from suspension or expulsion, talk privately with him to find out why he behaves so aggressively with other students. Try to get to the cause of the problem by asking what personal issues may be causing the behavior. Perhaps a counselor needs to be involved if home problems involve abuse or parental problems.

- Call the student's parents and find out if she has displayed any aggressive tendencies at home or in other school situations, discuss possible solutions, and schedule follow-up conferences.

- Talk with the school counselor to see if there are any previous behavior problems on the student's record. See if a special education class or special counseling is warranted.

- Give the student the option of going to the time-out or satellite area to work on his own when the pressure builds. He should be responsible for all work, but he should do it individually, without assistance from the group.

- Set up a verbal or nonverbal signal that gives the student a warning that she is losing control. For example, one hand across another showing she has "crossed the line."

- Review the behaviors of the other students in the class to see if he is particularly aggravated by one of them and is, therefore, acting out because of a personality conflict.

- Build a personal relationship with the student by talking with her and discovering her special interests.

- Evaluate his academic status to see if he feels inadequate and is resorting to aggressive behavior to compensate for his inability to keep up with the rest of the group.

- Change the cooperative group frequently so she doesn't build up a long-standing feud.

Figure 7.12 Action Plan

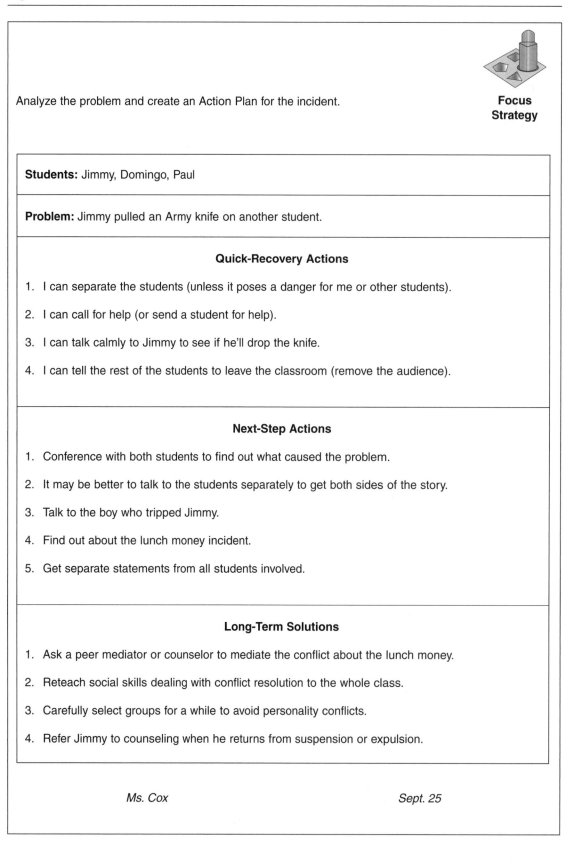

Analyze the problem and create an Action Plan for the incident.

Focus Strategy

Students: Jimmy, Domingo, Paul

Problem: Jimmy pulled an Army knife on another student.

Quick-Recovery Actions

1. I can separate the students (unless it poses a danger for me or other students).

2. I can call for help (or send a student for help).

3. I can talk calmly to Jimmy to see if he'll drop the knife.

4. I can tell the rest of the students to leave the classroom (remove the audience).

Next-Step Actions

1. Conference with both students to find out what caused the problem.

2. It may be better to talk to the students separately to get both sides of the story.

3. Talk to the boy who tripped Jimmy.

4. Find out about the lunch money incident.

5. Get separate statements from all students involved.

Long-Term Solutions

1. Ask a peer mediator or counselor to mediate the conflict about the lunch money.

2. Reteach social skills dealing with conflict resolution to the whole class.

3. Carefully select groups for a while to avoid personality conflicts.

4. Refer Jimmy to counseling when he returns from suspension or expulsion.

Ms. Cox   *Sept. 25*

Figure 7.13 Action Plan Template

Students:

Problem:

Quick-Recovery Actions

Next-Step Actions

Long-Term Solutions

- Have students keep a checklist to keep track of their own antisocial behaviors. Then conference with them at the end of the period, day, or week about how they did and what strategies could help them.
- Videotape or audiotape a class and play it back to the student to let him see how other people perceive his behavior.
- Have the student keep a journal or log where she writes about how she feels when she is upset or angry.
- Assign him a task in which he will succeed to increase his self-esteem.
- While reviewing social skills, role-play a simulated incident involving an aggressive situation and have a discussion about how students should handle the problem.

Add some of your own solutions for helping students with aggressive behaviors:

_____

_____

_____

_____

_____

STUDENTS WHO FEEL INADEQUATE

Scenario

Mr. Williams's world history class is studying Greek mythology. The students all have their books open as he calls on various students to read the myths.

"Jamie, will you please read the myth about Aphrodite and Cupid for the class?" Mr. Williams asks.

Jamie turns three shades of red and starts to read slowly and haltingly.

"Aph-ro-dite was very vain. She spent a lot of time primp-ing and gazing in a mirror. On Mount Olymp-us [pause] she lived in a gold palace with her . . .

"I can't pronounce the next word," Jamie mumbles under her breath. "Protégé," offers Mr. Williams.

"Can somebody else read," begs Jamie. "I don't feel well."

"Sure," Mr. Williams answers. "Lucas, will you please take over where Jamie left off?" Jamie puts her head down on the desk for the rest of the class.

Solving the Problem

Students often play the "I can't" game because they feel they cannot accomplish a task perfectly. Some "inadequate" students need to realize that it's okay to be imperfect. They can still cooperate with others, perform tasks reasonably well, and produce products that are acceptable.

Dinkmeyer and Losoncy (1980) say that inadequate students often say "I can't" when what they really mean is "I won't." "I can't" is a form of passive resistance, whereas "I won't" is a form of active resistance that usually provokes a power struggle or challenge to teachers. According to Dinkmeyer and Losoncy, "the 'I can't' phrase suggests helplessness and can serve the following purposes:

1. One believes others should serve him or her and puts others in service by proclaiming inadequacy.

2. One believes that he or she is an inadequate person and protects himself or herself from possible failure by 'copping out'— avoiding facing life's challenges.

3. One believes that he or she is unable, helpless, and should be excused from being expected to function. (pp. 55–56)

Often students who feel inadequate lack confidence in their ability and perceive life as unfair because while they may try very hard, but their efforts still lead to failure. These students become discouraged and develop negative self-concepts. In some cases, these students totally withdraw and give up completely (Dinkmeyer & Losoncy, 1980). Teachers often let these quiet and withdrawn students slip through the cracks because they are too busy managing the noisier students who are seeking attention or power. Unfortunately, the discouraged and inadequate block of students is much larger than most people realize, and these quiet students often become dropout statistics. In more cases than not, the roots of their difficulties can be traced to learning problems. Students who cannot read would rather refuse to read or appear uninterested rather than read in the class and embarrass themselves in front of their peers. Bellanca and Fogarty (2003) offer tactics to help inadequate students feel confident and in control (see Figure 7.14).

Figure 7.14 Tactics Teachers Can Use With Students Who Feel Inadequate

- Assign tasks that the student can successfully complete.
- Talk with the student to analyze why he or she feels inadequate.
- Pair the inadequate student with an empathetic student who can help.
- Lower the student's anxiety about mistakes.
- De-emphasize grades and emphasize a love of learning.
- Break larger tasks into small chunks (checklists).
- Remind students of past successes.
- Use team-building activities to build trust among group members.
- Arrange for homework buddies so the student gets additional help and support.
- Give positive feedback.

Some students who feel inadequate come to teachers with pessimistic expectations that have been ingrained in them since early childhood. Teachers will not always be able to lift the heavy weight from their shoulders after only one or two conferences. Persistence is the key to helping the student who feels inadequate feel successful, become a valuable member of the group, do well on whole-group activities, and succeed on individual tasks. These students try to avoid anything that could cause them to fail; therefore, the teacher's role is to structure activities that will make the student succeed, gain confidence, and develop a positive self-concept. Giving the students checklists and rubrics to guide their efforts often provides them with a road map to success and reduces their anxiety about not "knowing what the teacher wants."

One strategy teachers can use is to read between the lines to determine the real cause of a problem. A student could be acting out or withdrawing to cover a real problem that is causing him to feel insecure or inadequate. Sometimes a one-on-one private teacher-student conference can help teachers discover how best to help the student.

The key to effective problem solving in a conference is reflective listening. Teachers who use closed questions that call for a yes or no answer and who begin with the word *why* tend to cut off true communication.

Closed Questions

Closed questions sound accusatory, somewhat sarcastic, and negative. They antagonize students and put them on the defensive. The smart responses students sometimes give the teacher are in retaliation for the teacher's embarrassing them in front of their peers. Even if students say nothing or reply courteously, they have suffered humiliation, and their self-esteem has been lowered. It is doubtful that closed questions will motivate students to shape up. Some sample closed questions are given in Figure 7.15.

Open Questions

Open questions invite further conversation and many possible responses. They also help establish a rapport between teacher and student because they convey to the student a sense of caring and fairness (see Figure 7.16).

Figure 7.15 Sample Closed Questions

Question:	"Are you just going to sit there, or are you going to get busy?"
Answer:	"Yes, I'm going to sit here—what are you going to do about it?"
Question:	"Do you really think you're funny?"
Answer:	"Yes, I do think I'm funny!"
Question:	"Why don't you stop fooling around and get on task?"
Answer:	"Because I'm not quite finished fooling around yet."

Figure 7.16 Sample Open Questions

Question:	"So, you're saying that you're upset because you don't think you read well?"
Answer:	"I am not sure."
Question:	"Hmm. Would you like to explore some ways we can make you feel more confident when you read in front of the class?"
Answer:	"Yes, I would!"

As the teacher listens to the student talk about the problem, she may want to listen for and draw out the following "subtexts."

- Could it be that the student would like other students to notice her more?
- Could it be that other students tease her about reading out loud?
- Could it be that she has a language problem that embarrasses her?

Dreikurs recommends that during such a discussion, teachers look carefully at the student for what he calls a "recognition reflex," or an involuntary sign that the guess is correct. The reflex could be a shift in posture, a change in eye contact, or a nonverbal cue that indicates the underlying reason for the problem. Often, the student is not aware of what the real problem is, and it's the teacher's job to bring it to the surface (cited in Dinkmeyer et al., 1980, p. 114).

As shown in the focus strategy in Figure 7.17, teachers may want to include parents in the plan for solving the problem and bolstering the student's self-esteem. Figure 7.18 contains a Teacher-Student Conference template that teachers can use with their students.

Even though teachers are extremely busy and teach many students each day, the one-on-one conference accomplishes a great deal. First, the teacher devotes individual attention to the student. Second, the teacher focuses on the problem without the distractions of the rest of the class. Third, the teacher gets to know the student on a more personal basis. The interpersonal touch goes a long way in helping students gain confidence and overcome inadequacy.

Other Strategies Teachers Can Use With Students Who Feel Inadequate

- A student may increase his self-esteem by succeeding at an extracurricular activity.
- Work out a secret system with the inadequate student. Promise the student that you will only call on her if you are standing right next to her. That way the student does not have to worry about being called on at other times and can concentrate on the lesson.
- Give the inadequate student a great deal of wait time when you ask questions. Also, try to ask questions you know he can answer to build his confidence.

Figure 7.17   Teacher-Student Conference

After the teacher asks the student a series of open questions, both the teacher and the student fill out this form.

Focus Strategy

Student: _____*Jamie*_____   Teacher: _____*Mr. Williams*_____   Date: _____*Sept. 9*_____

Teacher's concern: _*I am concerned because you don't participate in class discussions and*_
*you always seem to get sick or have some other excuse whenever I call on you in class to read*
*or answer a question.*

Student's concern: _*I am really shy, and I don't like to talk in class because I'm afraid I might*_
*say something stupid and the other kids will laugh at me. I also hate to read out loud. I get really*
*nervous, and I don't understand one thing I read because I'm thinking about pronouncing*
*things wrong or not knowing the words.*

Possible options:

1. *Mr. Williams will not call on Jamie unless she has her hand raised.*
2. *Mr. Williams will not call on students to read in front of the whole class. He'll either put students in groups of 2 or 3 to read together or allow them to read silently.*
3. *Jamie will go to the reading teacher to get tested to see if she needs extra help.*

Parent involvement: *I will have Jamie read out loud to me every night to help her feel more comfortable with pronouncing words and reading out loud. I will also buy some audio tapes of stories for her to listen to as she reads.*

Parent's signature: _____*Mrs. Hansen*_____

Date of next conference: _____*Sept. 22*_____

Figure 7.18 Teacher-Student Conference Template

Student: _____   Teacher: _____   Date: _____

Teacher's concern: _____
_____
_____
_____
_____

Student's concern: _____
_____
_____
_____
_____

Possible options:

1. _____
_____

2. _____
_____

3. _____
_____

Parent involvement:

Parent's signature: _____

Date of next conference: _____

- Give specific encouragement for the student's accomplishment. In other words, don't just say "Great speech." Tell the student the speech was great because she used good eye contact, effective gestures, and appropriate humor.
- Make sure to allow enough time for each activity. Inadequate students often feel rushed, and they become frustrated when the teacher and the class are moving faster than they are.
- Leave some time between activities so students can make the transition. Inadequate students may also suffer from learning disabilities, and they have a difficult time changing their mind-set quickly from one task to another.
- Make sure all homework assignments are realistic. Do not give excessive amounts of homework because inadequate students get very frustrated when they cannot complete all the work. It takes them longer to complete assignments than other students.
- Do not give new material for homework because students might not understand the new concepts. The homework should be a review of concepts already studied.
- Provide checklists for rubrics for all major assignments so that students know the expectations for quality work.

Add some of your own solutions for helping students who feel inadequate:

_____

_____

_____

_____

_____

Working With Students Who Have Special Needs 8

Figure 8.0   Reauthorization of IDEA 2004

New ideas included in IDEA 2004:

- Districts are not required to use the IQ-Discrepancy Model.
- Districts must identify students with learning disabilities based on the child's response to scientific, research-based interventions (RTI).
- Districts may use other research-based procedures to determine whether a child has a learning disability.

THE HISTORY OF SPECIAL EDUCATION

In 1975, P.L. 94-42, originally referred to as the Education for All Handicapped Children Act, was enacted. The Act was later reauthorized and expanded as the Individuals with Disabilities Education Act (IDEA) in 1990 and reauthorized again in 1997. According to Vaughn et al. (2000), this legislation was designed to ensure that all children with disabilities receive an appropriate education through special education and related services. Some of the most common terms and their definitions include the following:

1. **Mainstreaming**—Places exceptional students in regular classes as soon as they are able to meet fundamentally the same requirements as typical students (Friend & Bursuck as cited in Sternberg & Williams, 2002).

2. **Full Inclusion**—Places students with disabilities entirely within the general education classroom for the entire school day (Mastropieri & Scruggs, 2000).

3. **Individual Education Program (IEP)**—A plan must be developed that specifies the goals and objectives set to improve each student's level of achievement and how these goals and objectives will be achieved to meet the special learning needs of each student with a disability (Sternberg & Williams).

4. **Least Restrictive Environment (LRE)**—The setting in which students are placed should be most like that of students with no disabilities and also meet each child's educational needs. Inherent in LRE is the idea of "continuum of services." The full range of services includes self-contained classrooms, resource rooms, and homebound and general education programs. (See Chapter 1 for more information.)

5. **Due Process**—Ensures that everyone with a stake in the student's education has a voice and will receive written notification, guidelines for appeal, and the right to an impartial hearing if IDEA guidelines are not followed to meet the needs of the student.

6. **Regular Education Initiative (REI)**—Promotes the placement of students with disabilities in the general education classroom for all or most of the day, where the regular education teacher and the special education teacher work cooperatively to meet the individual needs of all students in the general education classroom.

7. **Nondiscriminatory Evaluation**—An evaluation that does not discriminate on the basis of language, culture, or the student's background. This is particularly challenging in states such as California, Texas, and Florida, where more than 100 languages are represented.

Individuals With Disabilities Education Act (IDEA) 2004

The new Individuals with Disabilities Education (IDEA) regulations of 2004 include changes in methods to identify students with learning disabilities, early intervening services, highly qualified teachers, discipline, and meeting accessibility standards. Because of the new IDEA regulations, districts may use identification procedures other than IQ-Discrepancy Model to identify students with disabilities.

Also included in the new regulations are strengthened provisions to reduce disproportionate representatives of students in special education from diverse cultures. The new regulations also recommend teachers write stronger measurable IEP goals instead of short-term objectives and benchmarks that make them more relevant to student progress (see http://idea.ed.gov/ for Individuals with Disabilities Education Act Amendments of 2004). Under IDEA 2004, districts can initiate early intervening services (EIS) for students in Grades K–12 with an emphasis on these services for students in Grades K–3. These services are targeted at students who may require academic or behavioral support to succeed in general education classes, but who have not been identified as needing special education.

Response to Intervention (RTI)

Response to Intervention (RTI) was introduced in Chapter 1: Meeting the Educational Challenges of the Twenty-First Century.

Response to Intervention is, as simply put, a process of implementing high-quality, scientifically validated instructional practices based on learner needs, monitoring student progress, and adjusting instruction based on the student's response. When a student's response is dramatically inferior to that of his peers, the student may be determined to have a learning disability. (Fuchs as cited in Bender and Shores, 2007, p. 7)

The assumption is that a student may have a disabling condition if he fails to respond to effective instruction. The interventions must be based on scientifically based research. The term "scientifically based" is a term of significance in NCLB that has been integrated into IDEA to purposefully align the two Acts. Part B of IDEA 2004 emphasizes the use of research-based decision making as a cornerstone of effective educational practice. Every child's IEP must contain a statement related to the supplementary aids and services provided to the child and these services must now be based on peer-reviewed research to the extent practicable.

From the discussions available in the professional literature, Bender and Shores (2007) summarize some of the characteristics of the Three-Tier Pyramid of Interventions used by many for RTI:

Tier One: Core Instructional Curriculum where all the students in the class are involved and where as many as 80 percent of the students are experiencing educational difficulty. The students should receive instruction that alleviates the problem without further assistance.

Tier Two: Core Instruction and Supplemental Instructional Resources for individual students or groups of students who need additional assistance within the regular education class. This tier involves more intensive intervention and some assistance from other teachers or experts such as reading specialists. The educational difficulties of as many as 15 percent of the students who are having problems can be alleviated at this level of intervention.

Tier Three: Core Instructional and Intensive Resources for individual students who need intensive interventions and specialized resources. This could affect only 5 percent of the students at the final level of interventions and the team of educators at the school could determine that the students have learning disabilities.

Bender, W. N., & Shores, C. (2007). *Response to intervention: A practical guide for every teacher.* Thousand Oaks, CA: A Joint Publication from the Council for Exceptional Children and Corwin Press. Used with permission.

If students progress through each tier without making acceptable progress, they may then be considered for possible eligibility and placement in a special education program (Jankowski, as cited in Bender and Shores, 2007). Figure 8.1 shows strategies that could be used as interventions.

Research-Based Behavioral Management Strategies

Marzano, Marzano, and Pickering examined research-based strategies related to classroom management in their book *Classroom Management that Works: Research-Based Strategies for Every Teacher* (2003). They compiled a meta-analysis of four key management factors: (1) rules and procedures; (2) disciplinary interventions; (3) teacher-student relationships; and (4) mental set (a mindfulness of situational awareness such as "withitness" or the ability of the teacher to identify problem behavior or potential problem behavior quickly or to act on it immediately). They pose the question "Are effective classroom managers born, or can you become one if you are not one already? They conclude,

Fortunately, the answer to this question is that effective classroom managers are made. Good classroom managers are leaders who understand and use specific techniques. Awareness of and training in these techniques can change teacher behavior, which in turn changes student behavior and ultimately affects student achievement positively. Again, research evidence supports this assertion. (Marzano, Marzano, & Pickering, 2003, pp. 10–11).

Key Issues in Discipline in IDEA 2004

Bradley (2007, October) outlines the key issues in discipline in the IDEA 2004 Amendments in the *Legacy: IDEA 2004 Training Curriculum* prepared by The Office of Special Education Programs and the U.S. Department of Education in partnership with the National Dissemination Center for Children with Disabilities (NICHCY) www.nichcy.org or http://idea.ed.gov). Bradley discusses how the reauthorized IDEA 2004 includes discipline procedures as a means of addressing unacceptable behavior of children with disabilities in certain situations. The most prominent method to proactively address the needs of children who exhibit behavioral challenges is the individualized education program (IEP). For a child whose behavior impedes the child's learning or the learning of others, "the use of positive behavioral interventions and supports, and other strategies to address that behavior" must be consistent in the development of the child's IEP [§ 300.324 (a) (2) (i)]. Functional behavioral assessments (FBA) and behavioral intervention plans (BIP) are possible tools an IEP Team may consider when determining how to address problem behavior. Section §300.530 (Authority of School Personnel) sets out the general authority of school personnel in disciplinary situations relating to short-term or additional removals of the child who violates a code of student conduct

Figure 8.1   Strategies That Help All Students Learn

Classroom Environment	Management
1. Create an enriched environment (bulletin boards, posters) 2. Arrange furniture to support learning 3. Teach and practice social skills 4. Model social skills 5. Create a positive climate	1. Practice routines and procedures 2. Establish principles to guide behavior 3. Demonstrate self-control and stress-management techniques 4. Involve students in decision-making 5. Provide positive feedback
Instruction	Assessment
1. Set high expectations for all students 2. Encourage active discussion and participation 3. Address all the multiple intelligences 4. Give clear instructions 5. Use graphic organizers to help visual learners 6. Engage students in meaningful content	1. Correlate assessments to curriculum and standards 2. Provide corrective feedback in a positive manner 3. Create checklists and rubrics to help students meet criteria 4. Allow students some choice in how they are evaluated 5. Provide authentic assessments that evaluate application of knowledge

from his or her current placement to an appropriate interim alternative educational setting (IAES), another setting, or suspension, for not more than 10 consecutive school days in a school year. In most cases, the school administrators will work with the special education team to determine the appropriate course of action. The classroom teacher, however, will be responsible for applying a variety of research-based interventions to help the students control behavior problems before they are referred to administrators for discipline violations. The proactive teacher experiments with a wide variety of research-based interventions to attempt to address and solve the behavior problems in the classroom before requesting additional assistance from the school team.

STUDENTS WITH LEARNING CHALLENGES

Scenario

Benjamin cringes as Mr. Springer reviews the requirements for the middle school social studies project.

"You must prepare a photo essay about an assigned country in the Middle East and select photos that capture the human characteristics of the country to present to the class next week. You'll need to research your country," explains Mr. Springer.

"How long does it have to be?" Tony asks.

"What are we going to be graded on?" shouts Benjamin, close to hysterics. "We've never done a photo essay before. I don't know where to start!"

"Well, class, I've prepared some scoring guides to help you get ready for the project. We'll review the criteria and the scoring guides so that you'll know what has to be included," replies Mr. Springer.

Benjamin walks purposefully up to Mr. Springer and whispers that he needs to go see Ms. Rubin, his counselor.

"I need to get out of this class," he says. "I don't know if I can do this project, and I don't want get up in front of the whole class and present if I don't know what I am doing.

"Fine," agrees Mr. Springer. "Show Ms. Rubin and your parents the scoring guide so they can help you prepare. We're going to be videotaping each presentation and playing it back for you to self-evaluate. That way, you can do even better for the next time."

Benjamin returns to his desk and begins reviewing the checklist.

"There's no way I can do all this," he mumbles. "Just give me my F."

"Class, let's get out our checklists for the photo essay you will be sharing next week," Mr. Springer announces.

"Notice how we have included criteria such as photos, content, mechanics, and visuals."

"What kind of visual aid do you want?" asks Marcos.

"Ok, let's review how each criteria will be graded and show you some examples," Mr. Springer answers.

Solving the Problem

Students with learning challenges often experience frustration, anxiety, and tension when confronted with tasks that overwhelm them. Teachers who talk too fast, fire questions at students, don't give adequate wait time, make comments that embarrass students, and assign difficult, unstructured assignments may cause students to become anxious and even ill. The students frequently ask to see their special education teacher or a counselor to vent their frustration and fear.

Students who have learning difficulties sometimes have problems with processing language, visual perception, reading comprehension, and visual-motor coordination. They may be dyslexic; therefore, they cannot decode information as quickly as other students. They also have a difficult time listening and taking notes at the same time. Moreover, they are better able to understand a written passage if someone reads it to them or they listen to it on audiotape.

Students with learning challenges often have difficulty seeing connections among subject areas or seeing the "big idea" when they study a subject. By using a Performance Task, teachers present an authentic problem scenario to the students and provide whole-class instruction, small-group work, and individual work to involve the student.

The "The World Is Listening: Holy War or Struggle?" (Figure 8.2) is a middle school social studies unit that engages the students by asking them to solve a real-world problem.

The student will work in a group to complete one assignment, and the group uses the "Letter From a Child Checklist" (Figure 8.3) to help guide them through each step of the assignment. The checklist provides the "scaffolding" to help students complete each task. By knowing the expectations, students become more confident.

Figure 8.4 is a Student Group Work Checklist template that teachers can use to give directions to all students. The template helps teachers organize the components of the assignment prior to giving it to the students.

Figure 8.2   Middle School Social Studies Performance Task

THE WORLD IS LISTENING:
-Holy War or Struggle?-

Key Standard: Social Studies—Describe and locate physical and human characteristics of the Middle East.
Secondary Standards—Writing – Technology – Reading – Research

Problem Scenario:

The attacks of September 11, 2001, began a new era of American involvement in the Middle East. The United Nations Security Council needs your help in a region that has been plagued by conflict and violence for centuries. You have been commissioned as a student ambassador delegation by the five permanent members of the U.N. Security Council to help resolve conflicts in this region. As a special ambassador from your country, your expertise on the physical and human characteristics of this region will help bring about

---

(Continued)

Figure 8.2 (Continued)

peaceful resolutions. Your task is to inform the members of the Council of the unique issues/concerns of your country. This information will be used to formulate official policy for resolving conflict in the Middle East. Your job is very important! In order to inform the Council about your country, you must prepare one of the following projects or presentations about your country.

1. A PowerPoint presentation describing the physical features and natural resources of your country

2. A letter written from the perspective of a child living in the region to the U.N. Security Council (Arab, Jew, Berber, Bedouin, Kurd, Turk, Persian, Druze, Armenian)

3. A political/physical map that includes information on the ethnic and religious groups of your country

4. An interview presentation with a soldier who has served in the region

Be prepared to present your work to the U.N. Security Council on November 9.

Whole-Class Instruction:.

- Complete "Perceptions of the Middle East Chart" to assess students' prior knowledge and also what students want to learn.
- Listen to lectures by teacher, view United Streaming video on the Middle East, and take notes using graphic organizers.
- Introduce key vocabulary from the standards and textbook.
- Teach letter writing, interview techniques, analysis of political cartoon, and digital camera and scanner use.

Group Work: Students may select their group topic or presentation method.

Group 1	Group 2	Group 3	Group 4
Create PowerPoint presentation of physical features and natural resources of your country.	Write a letter from a child living in the region to U.N. Council.	Create political/ physical map that includes ethnic and religious groups in the country.	Present an interview conducted with a soldier who has served in the region.

Individual Work: Each student will complete the following:

1. Create a photo-essay demonstrating understanding of the human characteristics of the Middle East. What do photographs reveal about the human characteristics (language, religion, population distribution, quality of life) of a country?

2. Create a political cartoon that demonstrates the role that physical characteristics, natural resources, or human characteristics play in the conflict of the Middle East.

Methods of Assessment: List all the methods of assessment used in this unit:

1. Teacher-made tests
2. Checklists for PowerPoint, letter, interview, photo essay, and political cartoon
3. Checklists for all oral presentations
4. Rubrics for photo essay
5. Teacher observation

Created by Yvonne Stroud and Dr. Mary Elizabeth Kelly of Renfroe Middle School, City Schools of Decatur, Decatur, Georgia. Used with permission.

Figure 8.3   Group 2 Project: Letter From a Child Checklist

Standard: Social Studies—Describe and locate physical and human characteristics of the Middle East.

Grade 7—The student will describe the diverse cultural characteristics of the people who live in the Middle East, such as Arabs, Jews, Berbers, Druze, Bedouin, Kurds, Turks, Persians and, Armenians—including where they live and their religions, customs, and traditions.

The students will write a letter from the perspective of a child living in the Middle East to the U.N. Security Council.	Not Yet 0	Some Evidence 1
Introduction		
• Did you introduce yourself?		
• Did you tell your ethnic group and where you live?		
• Did you include your age, grade, and the name of your school if you attend?		
History/Location		
• Did you include historical information about your ethnic group?		
• Did you include population information about your ethnic group?		
• Did you include the absolute or relative location of your ethnic group?		
Religion		
• Did you include the name of your ethnic group's religion?		
• Did you include its history?		
• Did you include its major beliefs?		
Customs/Traditions		
• Did you include information about literary, artistic, or musical customs/traditions?		
• Did you include information about the role of education in your ethnic group?		
• Did you include information about family roles?		

The students will write a letter from the perspective of a child living in the Middle East to the U.N. Security Council.	Not Yet 0	Some Evidence 1
Conclusion		
• Did you begin with a transition word or phrase?		
• Did you repeat your reason for writing the letter?		
• Did you conclude with a powerful, personal sentence?		
Letter Format		
• Did your letter include the date at the top?		
• Did you have a salutation?		
• Did you have a body?		
• Did you include your signature at the end?		
Writing Structure		
• Does your letter contain two to three paragraphs?		
• Did you use transition words or phrases between topics or paragraphs?		
• Did each topic have two to three supporting details?		
Mechanics		
• Did you use correct spelling?		
• Did you use correct punctuation?		
• Did you use correct capitalization?		
• Did you use correct grammar?		

Created by Yvonne Stroud of Renfroe Middle School, City Schools of Decatur, Decatur, Georgia. Used with permission.

Figure 8.4   Student Group Work Checklist

Create a checklist for a group project in your performance task.

Criteria/Elements/Performance Indicators	Not Yet 0	Some Evidence 1
•		
•		
•		
•		
•		
•		
•		
•		
•		
•		
•		
•		
•		
•		
•		
•		
•		
•		

Scoring Guides

Students who have learning challenges in the traditional classroom setting focused on teacher-directed instruction may encounter additional problems when they work in cooperative groups focused on teamwork Teachers must structure cooperative group activities so that students with learning challenges not only understand the requirements but also can complete the task successfully. Moreover, following the group assignments, students are usually assigned a similar individual assignment to prove that each student can meet the standard on her own without the support of the group.

Students with learning challenges have trouble staying focused, listening, and understanding directions at times. If a teacher or a class develops a scoring guide, students with learning disabilities get clear expectations for their work and a blueprint for preparing assignments. Scoring guides also enable them to become more independent learners who can reflect on and self-assess their own work. The checklist shown in Figure 8.5 shows a road map to help each student complete her photo essay project for the social studies unit. Individual work requires specific instructions because the student is working independently.

Figure 8.6 is a Student Individual Checklist template that teachers can use to structure a multistep assignment.

Rubrics also help students improve the quality of their work. All students need to meet standards. Students with learning disabilities may be overwhelmed by the Rubric for Narrative Writing (Figure 8.7), but they know what they are expected to do. They may not score a "3" or a "4" on the assignment, but they know exactly how to improve. The specific feedback provided by the written rubric eliminates the need for the teacher to have to give oral feedback to each student on each criterion. Figure 8.8 is a Create a Rubric template that teachers can use to provide feedback using the key ideas, content, skills, and vocabulary of the state standards.

It is important that teachers spend time teaching the criteria included in the checklists or rubrics. Simply handing the student the scoring guide is not enough. The rubric serves as a guideline for what is required. It also provides scoring information. Students know in advance what they have to do to get a "3" for each criterion. The learning-challenged student may not get the "3," but at least the student knows why he didn't get it and what he needs to do the next time.

Other Strategies Teachers Can Use With Students With Learning Challenges

- Involve students in creating the rubric so they understand the criteria.
- Model each of the criterion in the rubric so students know what type of visual aid or eye contact would score a higher mark.
- Review with the entire class the social skill of encouragement so class members can help each other rehearse for the speech.
- Place the learning-challenged student with a hand-picked supportive group to help prepare the speech.
- Send the scoring guide to the resource teacher and the parents so they can help the student prepare.
- Allow students to present their projects in private to the teacher if they are too nervous to show them to the class.

(*Text continues on page 242*)

Figure 8.5 Photo Essay Checklists

Standard: Social Studies—Describe and locate physical and human characteristics of the Middle East.

The student will create a photo essay demonstrating understanding of the human characteristics of a Middle Eastern country.	Not Yet 0	Some Evidence 1
Photos or Drawings: Did you . . .		
• include at least two pictures/drawings for each characteristic?		
• identify the picture?		
• fully describe what you see in each picture?		
• include a title for each picture/drawing?		
• include a caption for each picture/drawing?		
• include a reference for each picture?		
Content: Did you/your . . .		
• include an introduction explaining the topic, why it was chosen, and what you hoped to learn?		
• use information that is specific to your topic?		
• pictures follow your theme?		
• photo essay convey a message?		
• include a conclusion explaining your experiences making the project and what you learned?		
• include bibliography of sources used?		
Mechanics: Did you . . .		
• use correct spelling?		
• use correct grammar?		
• use capital letters properly?		
• use correct punctuation?		
Visuals/Display: Did you . . .		
• include your name, date, and class period?		
• use correct size poster board (at least 24″ × 26″)		
• include a title for your photo essay?		
• make your presentation attractive and neat in appearance?		

Created by Yvonne Stroud of Renfroe Middle School, City Schools of Decatur, Georgia. Used with permission.

Figure 8.6 Student Individual Checklist for Individual Work

Create a checklist for the individual work in your performance task.

Criteria/Elements/Performance Indicators	Not Yet 0	Some Evidence 1
•		
•		
•		
•		
•		
•		
•		
•		
•		
•		
•		
•		
•		
•		
•		
•		
•		
•		

Figure 8.7 Rubric for Narrative Writing

Activity: Write a personal narrative about an exciting experience or event in your life. Self-assess your work using this rubric.

SCALE Performance Indicators:	1 Getting Started	2 In Progress	3 Meets Standards	4 Exceeds Standards
Engagement • Context	There is no evidence of context for story.	Context is evident but somewhat confusing.	Context establishes the scene for the story.	Context develops a clear framework for the story.
• Point of View (who is telling the story)	Vague idea of who is telling the story	Point of view that shifts from first to third person	One point of view maintained throughout most of story	One point of view maintained consistently
• Readers' Interest	Opening does not engage readers.	Opening attempts to hook the readers.	Opening captures the readers' attention.	Opening captivates the readers' attention.
Storyline • Plot (who, what, why)	Plot contains one element *(who, what, why)*.	Plot contains two elements *(who, what, why)*.	Plot contains all three elements *(who, what, why)*	Plot contains all three elements and is creatively developed.
• Setting (where or when)	Setting is not included or is unclear.	Setting describes *where (place)* **or** when *(time)*.	Setting describes **both** *where* and *when*.	Vivid adjectives describe both where and when.
• Conflicts	There is no evidence of conflict in the story.	Plot elements build to a conflict.	Plot elements (rising action) build to climax.	The conflict is resolved at the end of the story.
Organizing Structure • Chronological order • Cause and effect • Similarity & difference • Pose & answer question	No evidence of any organizing structure throughout the narrative	Use of a combination of organizing structures that confuse the readers in the narrative	Use of one appropriate organizing structure that is maintained throughout narrative	Use of one appropriate organizing structure that is maintained effectively and consistently
Sensory Details • Appeal to Senses	Use of rich details to describe how things *look*	Use of rich details about how things *look and sound*	Use of rich details about how things *look, sound, smell, and feel*	Paints vivid picture of how things *look, sound, smell, feel, act, and move*
• Figurative Language (similes and metaphors)	No evidence of *similes or metaphors*	Use of appropriate *similes or metaphors*	Use of appropriate *similes* **and** *metaphors*	Creative use of several *similes and metaphors*
• Figurative Language (personification, onomatopoeia, hyperbole)	No evidence of: • *personification* • *onomatopoeia* • *hyperbole*	Use of one: • *personification* • *onomatopoeia* • *hyperbole*	Use of two: • *personification* • *onomatopoeia* • *hyperbole*	Use of three: • *personification* • *onomatopoeia* • *hyperbole*

Figure 8.8 Create a Rubric Application

Goals/Standards: _____

Assignment: Select a group or individual checklist and convert it to a rubric.

SCALE	1	2	3	4
CRITERIA				
▭				
•				
•				
•				
▭				
•				
•				
•				
▭				
•				
•				
•				
▭				
•				
•				
•				

(Text continued from page 237)

- Encourage the learning-challenged student to select a topic that really interests him (racing, space travel, computers), so that he has a comfort level with the topic.
- Talk with the special education teacher about strategies to use with the student to complete the photo essay project and present it.
- Assign a peer tutor or "homework buddy" to help the student prepare and present the project.
- Allow the student to record or videotape her presentation in private and then present the tape to the class.

Add some of your own solutions for helping students with learning challenges:

_____

_____

_____

_____

_____

STUDENTS WITH BEHAVIOR PROBLEMS

Scenario

> *"Quit it!" yells Marci as she turns and hits Jeff in the arm. "Hit me again, and I'm going to tell Hopkins."*
>
> *"Brownnoser—'I'm going to tell Mr. Hopkins'—oh, I'm scared," sneers Baxter.*
>
> *Marci leaves her desk to get a dictionary. Baxter grabs Marci's homework off her desk and quickly draws a skull and crossbones on it.*
>
> *Marci returns to her desk and starts yelling, "I'm so sick of your juvenile behavior. You're such a jerk! I hate sitting behind you."*
>
> *Mr. Hopkins notices the altercation and walks toward their desks. Jeff pretends he is reading his book.*
>
> *"Jeff," Mr. Hopkins whispers, "I need you to come by after school. We need to talk."*
>
> *"Whatever," Jeff mumbles as Marci snickers under her breath.*

Solving the Problem

Often, students with behavior problems misbehave to cover up insecurity about a task. If a task is too complicated, difficult, or confusing, a student might resort to disruptive behavior when in reality, the student just doesn't know what to do. For some students, beginning an assignment can be overwhelming. As a result, they refuse to start working, or they misbehave to avoid the work (Friend & Bursuck, 1999). Teachers who immediately send the misbehaving student to the time-out area or to the office without trying to discover the real problem might be unintentionally encouraging the behavior. The student doesn't want to be in the specific situation in the first place, and if the teacher removes the student from the situation by sending him to time-out or to the office, the student never has to deal with the "real" problem. Teachers should observe the student to see when she becomes frustrated and perhaps simplify or chunk the complicated task that is causing the frustration. In addition, expressions of appreciation, encouragement, and compliments related to specific actions reinforce students' self-confidence.

A teacher-student conference is another tool to explore the student's real problem and arrive at a solution. Students with behavior challenges want to have choices. A teacher who listens empathetically to the student's problem and helps the student explore possible choices is modeling a problem-solving strategy. Teachers may need to ask good questions to find out if the student's behavior is related to an academic problem or a social problem.

Many disruptive students try to camouflage their weak academic skills by developing a tough persona; they would be humiliated if their peers found out they couldn't read or write. Too often, teachers react to the surface problem of misbehavior when the core problem is actually something else, such as feelings of inadequacy or frustration. One strategy that teachers can use to chronicle the behavior of a student and seek patterns or causes is the Modified Case Study. Sometimes the teacher-student conference does not provide enough information, and the teacher needs to talk to the parents, other teachers, counselor, or specialists to find out more about the student. Often, teachers will review the student's permanent records for incidents, test scores, or patterns of behavior that could be relevant. A sample of the case study is provided in Figure 8.9, and a Modified Case Study template is offered in Figure 8.10 for teachers to use.

Another strategy teachers can use is keeping a Behavior Log (see Figure 8.11) of the student's disruptive behavior, noting the time and date of the disruption as well as what the behavior was. Teachers use these logs to look for patterns and to brainstorm solutions to the disruptions. This log can be shared with the student and parents to show them what is occurring in the classroom and to get their input on finding solutions. A Behavior Log template that teachers can use with their students is provided in Figure 8.12.

Other Strategies Teachers Can Use With Students With Behavior Problems

- Use proximity to let the student feel your presence. If you stand nearby, you can observe activities, behaviors, or remarks that might lead to an outburst.
- Talk to special education teachers about strategies that can help the student curb her desire for attention and aggressiveness toward her peers.
- Allow the student to complete work in the time-out area so he can work alone until he calms down.
- Signal interference by agreeing on a nonverbal signal such as a gesture (finger to lips) or eye contact with the student.
- Pair the student with another student who is supportive and nurturing and would help tutor the student.
- Call the parents to see if personal or family problems could be making the student upset.

(*Text continues on page 248*)

Figure 8.9   Modified Case Study Template

The teacher of the student with chronic behavior problems documents patterns of behavior and gathers background information to use with the student, the parents, and the administrator in a conference.

Focus Strategy

Case Study

Date: _____January 13_____   School: _____Spring Elementary_____   Grade: _____5_____

Student: _____Jeff_____   Age: __11__   Teacher: _____Mr. Hopkins_____

Briefly describe the problem the student is having in class:

Jeff often loses his temper and does things that hurt other students. The other students resent his outbursts and do not want to work with him or sit next to him.

Log of specific behavior:

Date: December 6
Incident: Jeff asked Jimmy to borrow a crayon. When Jimmy told Jeff "no" because he was using the crayon, Jeff punched Jimmy.
Date: December 10
Incident: Jeff got frustrated when he couldn't answer his math problem, and he tore up his worksheet.
Date: December 15
Incident: Marci told Jeff she didn't want him in her group. Jeff knocked over his chair and ran out of the room crying.
Date: December 20
Incident: Jeff refused to work on his writing assignment. When I asked him to get to work, he put his head down on the desk.

Pertinent information from permanent files:

Jeff was referred for testing in special education in the third grade.
Jeff was held back in the fourth grade.
Jeff was assigned to the Resource Room for two periods a day.
Jeff's mother put him on Ritalin after he was diagnosed as ADHD.

Test scores:

ISAT _____142_____

Contact with parent:

12/7   Talked with mother about Jeff's fighting problem. The mother said he has been belligerent since his parents went through a divorce two years ago. She said she would talk to him, but he doesn't seem to listen to her.
12/16 Had conference with mother to discuss Jeff's poor grades. She promised to help him with his work.

Contact with counselor or administrator (ask about evaluations done by school psychologists or social worker):

12/17 Talked with school counselor. He said Jeff has a problem accepting being pulled out of his regular fifth-grade class and going to the Resource Room when the special ed teacher works with him in class. He feels embarrassed because all of his friends know he has a learning problem. He thinks the other kids know he is a special ed student, and he feels dumb.

Conference with student:

12/18 Jeff says he feels intimidated by his class members, especially Marci, because they are much smarter than he is. He says that is why he acts out and does wild things. We decided it would be best to change groups and put Jeff with another student who is more nurturing. That way he will feel more involved with the decisions, and he will get some one-on-one tutoring from the other student.

Follow-up meeting: _____January 23_____

Teacher: _____Mr. Hopkins_____   Student: _____Jeff_____   Parent: _____Mrs. Warner_____

Figure 8.10 Modified Case Study Template

Case Study

Date: _____ School: _____ Grade: _____

Student: _____ Age: _____ Teacher: _____

Briefly describe the problem the student is having in class:

Log of specific behavior:

Pertinent information from permanent files:

Test scores:

Contact with parent:

Contact with counselor or administrator (ask about evaluations done by school psychologists or social worker):

Conference with student:

Follow-up meeting: _____

Teacher: _____ Student: _____ Parent: _____

Figure 8.11   Behavior Log

Sometimes ADD and ADHD students are not aware of the disruptions they cause. Their hyperactivity causes them to interrupt the teacher and the class constantly. The Behavior Log helps students, teachers, and parents recognize and deal with the interruptions.

Focus Strategy

Student: *Jeff*   **Teacher:** *Mr. Hopkins*   **Date:** *March 23*

Time	Date	Interruption
2:25	1/24	Wadded up test paper and threw it out.
1:30	1/26	Pushed book off his desk.
3:00	1/29	Sharpened pencil five times.
1:45	2/2	Tapped pencil repeatedly.
12:30	2/7	Yelled out answer.
11:30	2/10	Called out to student across room
12:00	2/15	Opened and shut lunch-box loudly.

Patterns—Causes for Disruptions

Jeff appears to have more problems after lunch time. He also is more disruptive during the afternoon reading and social studies classes. He doesn't have nearly as many problems in the morning.

Recommendations

I think Jeff should be tested for reading. He may be causing disruptions because he feels inadequate. Also, since most of his problems occur after lunch, maybe he's eating too much sugar. I'll talk to the nutritionist.

Figure 8.12 Behavior Log Template

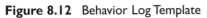

Student: **Teacher:**   **Date:**

Time	Date	Interruption

Patterns—Causes for Disruptions

Recommendations

(Text continued from page 243)

- Check the student's file to see if low academic abilities may be causing her to compensate for her inadequacies by using aggression.
- Keep a tally in the Behavior Log of the times of the day and the types of activities that seem to cause the most aggravation and frustration for the student.
- Review social skills of listening, sharing, encouragement, and taking turns with entire class or with the student who is having problems. Create T-charts to reinforce appropriate social behavior.

Add some of your own solutions for helping students with behavior problems:

_____

_____

_____

_____

_____

GIFTED STUDENTS

Scenario

As the students in Mr. Feinberg's biology class prepare for their lab assignment, Jennifer does not join in as her lab partners begin to set up their experiment.

"Come on, Jennifer," calls Frank. "Put on your safety goggles so we can begin."

"You don't know where to begin," Jennifer mumbles sarcastically. "I hate working in this group. I want to conduct my own experiment."

"Well, Feinberg is giving us a group grade on this lab," retorts Erin. "You'll just have to lower yourself to our level until we turn in our report."

"You guys better not lower my grade. I used to be in accelerated biology in my old school. We did this lab three months ago," Jennifer responds defiantly.

"Well, lower yourself to work with us. You are supposed to help the group—not insult us," gripes Greg.

"Okay, let's get this over with fast. I need to study for my Advanced Placement exam," Jennifer says.

Solving the Problem

In today's inclusive classrooms, the gifted and talented students are often taught in the regular education classes. They may still have special classes or pull-out programs referred to as GT classes (Gifted and Talented) or Enrichment classes, but not as many as in the past. Gifted education programs continue to generate a great deal of controversy. Some educators, parents, and politicians argue that this segment of gifted students does not receive the services they deserve; moreover, they are not being challenged in the regular education classroom. One recent study conducted by University of Chicago economists

Derek A. Neal and Diane Whitmore Schanzenback (as cited in Viadero, 2007) suggest that the No Child Left Behind Act may indeed be leaving behind students at the far ends of the academic ability spectrum—the least able students and those who are gifted. Their study lends some empirical support to the common perception "that schools are focusing on students in the middle— the so-called 'bubble kids'—in order to boost scores on the state exams used to determine whether schools are meeting their proficiency targets" (p. 7).

> Proponents of special programs for qualified students contend that by ignoring this valuable resource we not only fail to nurture the brain power our country will need to survive in a competitive international marketplace, but also fail to provide appropriate education for these students, regardless of their potential contribution to society. (Vaughn et al., 2000, p. 339)

Opponents of gifted programs argue that *all* children have exceptional gifts. They feel that all children should have the opportunity to have their special gifts recognized and developed. Many of the critics feel that it is undemocratic to provide special services for an elite subset of the student population who qualify for placement on the basis of an IQ test or special talents (Vaughn et al., 2000).

The focus on differentiated learning described in Chapter 2 and the work of Carol Tomlinson and others addresses these concerns about meeting the academic social and interest needs of all students in the inclusive classroom.

Characteristics of Giftedness

The 1988 definition of *giftedness* approved by the U.S. Congress (P.L. 100-297, Sect. 4103, "Definitions"), commonly used in designing state and local programs for the gifted, is the following:

> The term "gifted and talented students" means children and youth who give evidence of high performance capability in areas such as intellectual, creative, artistic, or leadership capacity, or in specific academic fields, and who require services or activities not ordinarily provided by the school in order to fully develop such capabilities. (as cited in Vaughn et al., 2000, p. 342)

Winebrenner (as cited in Vaughn et al., 2000, p. 345) states that the characteristics of gifted and talented students include the following:

- Advanced vocabulary for chronological age
- Outstanding memory; possess lots of information
- Curious: Ask endless questions
- Get totally absorbed in activities and thoughts
- Strongly motivated to do things of interest; may be unwilling to work on other activities
- Prefer complex and challenging tasks to "basic" work

- Catch on quickly, then resist doing work or work in a sloppy, careless manner
- Come up with better "ways" for doing things, then suggest them to peers, teachers, and other adults
- Sophisticated sense of humor; may be "class clown"
- Advanced sense of justice and fairness

The gifted student's curiosity sometimes interferes with a teacher's lesson, and the gifted student's high verbal ability leads to his dominating group work or whole-class discussions. Gifted students also become frustrated or bored easily when the teacher has to repeat directions or instructions for the benefit of other students or when others don't understand the concepts as quickly as they do. When gifted students focus on their own goals, they tend to ignore the goals of the teacher or the group, thus becoming labeled stubborn or self-absorbed.

Gifted students sometimes don't feel challenged when they are included in an inclusive classroom. They are very interested in global issues and other controversial topics that tend to bore many other students. Even though gifted students may possess advanced cognitive skills, they may lack affective skills that help them "read" the emotions of others. They may not realize that other students do not share their same enthusiasm for a topic and have "turned off" during their discussions or presentations.

The example of the Goal-Setting Model given in Figure 8.13 helps students focus on strengthening their interpersonal skills to correlate with their advanced academic skills. Figure 8.14 is a Goal-Setting Model template that teachers can use with their students. In most inclusive settings, students of all ability levels are included. The challenge for today's teacher is to achieve a "sense of flow" to meet the diverse needs of each student.

Other Strategies Teachers Can Use With Gifted Students

- Tier lessons so that they appeal to several ability levels.
- Allow gifted students to do extended enrichment activities in addition to their regular class work to challenge them.
- Make sure group roles rotate frequently and students adhere to the rules. Often gifted students attempt to take over the group to get their ideas implemented.
- Allow gifted students to research ideas or explore creative options beyond the basic lesson so they do not get bored with routine work.
- Don't make gifted students do "more of the same" activities if they finish their work early. Allow them to experiment with new ideas and extend their learning.
- Don't always make gifted or advanced students help other students who do not understand the assignment. Students do remember 95 percent of what they teach others, but they will become discouraged if they are always helping other students catch up rather than moving forward themselves.
- Give gifted students positive attention when they demonstrate appropriate social skills.
- Honor students' cooperative skills as much or more than you honor their academic skills.

Figure 8.13 Goal-Setting Model

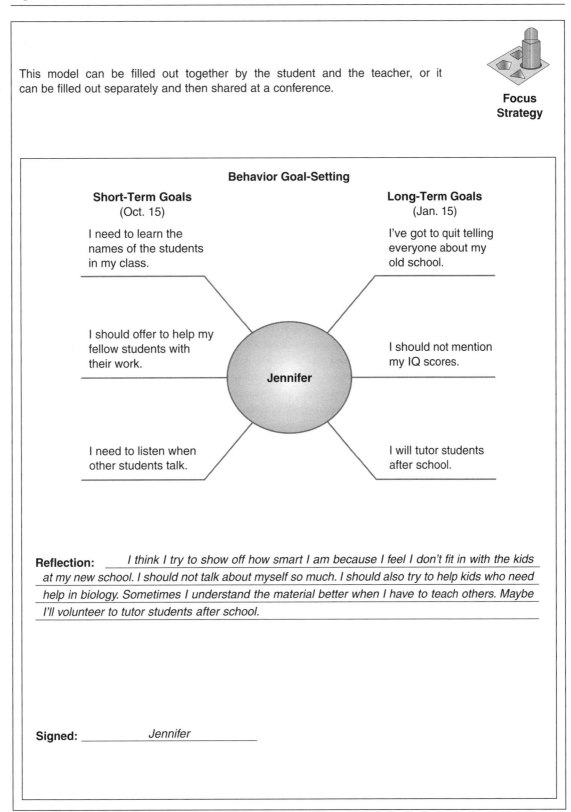

This model can be filled out together by the student and the teacher, or it can be filled out separately and then shared at a conference.

Focus Strategy

Behavior Goal-Setting

Short-Term Goals
(Oct. 15)

Long-Term Goals
(Jan. 15)

I need to learn the names of the students in my class.

I've got to quit telling everyone about my old school.

I should offer to help my fellow students with their work.

I should not mention my IQ scores.

Jennifer

I need to listen when other students talk.

I will tutor students after school.

Reflection: _I think I try to show off how smart I am because I feel I don't fit in with the kids at my new school. I should not talk about myself so much. I should also try to help kids who need help in biology. Sometimes I understand the material better when I have to teach others. Maybe I'll volunteer to tutor students after school._

Signed: _Jennifer_

Figure 8.14 Goal-Setting Model Template

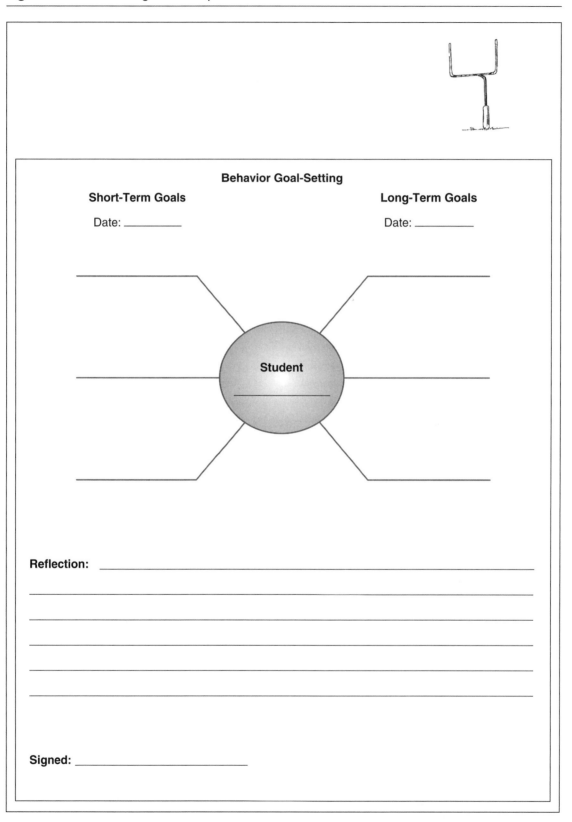

Behavior Goal-Setting

Short-Term Goals

Date: _____

Long-Term Goals

Date: _____

Student
_____

Reflection: _____

_____

_____

_____

_____

_____

Signed: _____

- Allow all students some choice in selecting projects so gifted students can pursue their passionate interests.
- Allow gifted students to present their projects in a different format (PowerPoint™, video, CD-ROM) to showcase their skills and keep them interested.
- Use portfolios to document student growth.
- Vary the content, process, and product to encourage differentiated learning.

Add some of your own solutions for helping gifted students:

_____

_____

_____

_____

_____

STUDENTS WITH LANGUAGE CHALLENGES

Solving the Problem

"José, welcome to our fifth-grade class," says Ms. Merrill. "We are happy to have you."
She addresses the class: "Boys and girls, I would like you to say hola to José. He just moved here from Mexico."

"Hola, José," yells the class in unison.

"Does anyone in here speak some Spanish?" asks Ms. Merrill.

"Rosa speaks some Spanish," Mark volunteers. "I've heard her talk to the bus driver."

"Rosa, would you mind partnering with José to help translate what we are doing?" Ms. Merrill asks. "He'll need some assistance when he's in our classroom."

"Yeah, I'll help some. But I don't want to be stuck with him all the time. I'll never get my work done, and I want to join different groups," replies Rosa.

"Okay," answers Ms. Merrill. "We'll work out a plan so you are not partnered with José all the time. Give me a few days to work it out."

Solving the Problem

After analyzing data from the 2000 census, demographer Harold Hodgkinson (2003) found that almost 9 million U.S. children between the ages of 5 and 17 speak a language other than English at home, and a full 2.6 million of them do not speak English well. (Hill & Flynn, 2006, p. xii)

There is a growing number of English language learners (ELLs) in middle and high schools. "Although more than 60 percent of ELLs in Grades 6–12 reside in California, Texas, New York, Florida, and Illinois, other states like Colorado, Nevada, Nebraska, Oregon, Georgia, and Indiana more than doubled their ELL population, and North Carolina experienced a 500 percent growth" (Perkins-Gough, 2007, p. 90).

ELLs once used to be taught by the English as a second language (ESL) staff, but now they are in every classroom. The classroom teacher may not have been trained in teaching ELL students, so helping the ELL students succeed and meet state standards on standardized tests is challenging. Adolescent ELLs must learn to speak, read, and write in English and understand the complex content introduced in secondary schools. Many students already mastered the content in their native language, so they will be able to perform well once they learn to speak English. Other immigrants, however, may have attended school intermittently or not at all and will have to learn not only how to speak English but also the content they never learned. "Only 4 percent of eighth-grade ELLs scored on the proficient or advanced levels on the reading portion of the 2005 National Assessment for Education Progress (NAEP); therefore, teachers face tremendous challenges helping these students achieve academic success and pass state tests required by NCLB legislation" (Perkins-Gough, 2007, p. 90).

One collaborative approach to meeting the needs of ELL students is to have regular education or mainstream teachers work together with ELL teachers. For example, the teacher can present a lesson on fractions, and the ELL teacher can make sure the ELL students understand the difference between the two English homonyms *whole* and *hole* (Pardini, 2006).

The ELL teacher could also work with small groups to preteach the lesson and try to anticipate problems. She could also help differentiate instruction by using guided reading activities or vocabulary lessons to help ELL students understand the words used in class. Pardini (2006) says that the ELL teacher can also help students make connections between what they already know and the new material and help clear up any embedded cultural assumptions that mainstream teachers might inadvertently make.

Cooperative learning groups provide powerful learning strategies for ELL students. Hill and Flynn (2006) discuss how small-group instruction allows more feedback and correction in the context of actual conversation. The setting is more informal, and ELL students are less likely to feel self-conscious about asking a question or making a mistake. The anxiety level of the ELL students is reduced, and students in a group tend to be more supportive.

Teachers should organize cooperative groups heterogeneously to include a mix of English-dominant students and ELLs. The English-dominant students model correct English.

> Students in mixed groups also need to negotiate meaning. As ELLs strive to convey information, English-dominant students can scaffold language development by helping them find the right word or verb tense. They can also ask ELLs questions to elicit further speech. (Hill & Flynn, 2006, p. 57)

IDEA 2004 Findings

Excerpts from *Findings* in IDEA 2004 include the following:

(11) (B) Studies have documented apparent discrepancies in the levels of referral and placement of limited-English-proficient children in special education.

(11) (C) Such discrepancies pose a special challenge for special education in the referral of, assessment of, and provision of services for, our Nation's children from non-English language backgrounds.

(12) (A) Greater efforts are needed to prevent the intensification of problems connected with mislabeling and high dropout rates among minority children with disabilities.

(12) (B) More minority children continue to be served in special education than would be expected from the percentage of minority children in the general school population.

Individuals with Disabilities Education Act (2004), Pub. L. No. 108-446, § 601 (c). (http://idea.ed.gov).

The concern is that many students from different cultures have been identified as needing special education because of their academic or behavioral difficulties. The challenge has been to differentiate between students who have real disabilities and those who have had inadequate or inappropriate instruction. When the response to interventions (RTI) model is implemented, Ortiz (2002) feels it is critical that the pre-referral intervention process ensures that the students' socio-cultural, linguistic, racial/ethnic, and other relevant background characteristics are addressed at all stages. If this does not occur, the intervention practices may not work and students will continue to be disproportionately assigned to special education.

Limited English Proficient (LEP) Students

Two-thirds of LEP students in U.S. public schools are Spanish speakers, the group most involved in native-language instruction programs. After 20 years of state-enforced Spanish-language instruction programs, the law now requires students to be given special help with English immediately on entering public schools. Porter (1999/2000) states that the goal is threefold: "early literacy development in English, subject matter instruction in English with a special curriculum, and early inclusion of LEP students in mainstream classrooms for maximum exposure to native speakers of English and for greater integration of diverse student populations" (p. 54).

The NCLB law requires that districts and schools be responsible for improving not only the academic achievements of students as a whole but also the achievements of each subgroup of students. Jennings and Rentner (2006) say that

states and school districts have consistently praised NCLB's requirement for the disaggregation of test data by subgroups of students, because it has shone light on poor performances of students who would have gone unnoticed if only general test data were considered. (p. 112)

Educators today are paying much more attention to the achievement gaps and the learning needs of specific groups of students. For the past three years, however, states and districts have repeatedly identified the law's testing and accountability provisions for students with disabilities and students who are learning English as problem areas. They have expressed frustration because the state tests may be inappropriate and serve no instructional purpose for disabled students with cognitive impairments.

Similarly, officials don't see the merit in administering an English/language arts test to students who speak little or no English. The U.S. Department of Education (ED) has made some administrative changes in those areas, but in the view of state officials and local educators, these modifications have not been enough. (Jennings & Rentner, 2006, p. 112)

Regardless of school or district policies, teachers today are faced with instructional, behavioral, and assessment challenges when limited-English proficient students are assigned to their classes. Cohen (1986) recommends creating mixed groups of students and asking a bilingual child in the group to serve as a "valuable bridge," translating what the English-speaking students are saying and offering special help to the non-English-speaking students. Cohen also believes that teachers should structure the learning by assigning rich tasks for group work that contain active involvement, relevancy, pictures, role-playing, manipulatives, and nonverbal cues so that all students can benefit from a multiple-intelligences approach to teaching and learning.

The bilingual student in a paired situation or in a supportive cooperative group can read out loud, paraphrase articles, summarize key points, and/or review important vocabulary terms to reinforce understanding. Teachers, however, should find ways to rotate the roles of bilingual students so they do not feel they are doing all the work and not learning themselves because of their tutoring responsibilities.

Teachers of bilingual students serving as peer tutors can use a Bilingual Lesson Log (see Figure 8.15) to help students practice their English skills. This log helps reinforce the learning of new content for limited-English-speaking students. A Bilingual Lesson Log template is offered in Figure 8.16 for teachers to use with students. If non- or limited-English-speaking students are going to feel comfortable in the classroom, communication should be established the first day the student enters.

Checklists help students self-assess their speaking and listening skills. Students can check each other, and the teacher can assess each student and provide feedback throughout the year. Figure 8.17 provides an example of a speaking skills checklist.

Other Strategies Teachers Can Use With Students With Language Challenges

- Place the student in a group with someone who has studied the non-English-speaking student's language in school.
- Find some reading materials or tapes in the student's language that are related to material the class is studying so that he feels like the teacher cares.

(*Text continues on page 260*)

Figure 8.15 Bilingual Lesson Log

Pair students who need help understanding English with one or two bilingual students who can share their notes regarding a recently studied topic. The group can work together to record key ideas in both English and the student's native language in the log.

Focus Strategy

Lesson: _____ *Friendly Letter* _____   **Date:** _____ *March 6* _____

Main Ideas—English	Main Ideas—Spanish

1. Five parts of friendly letter
   – Date
   – Inside address
   – Salutation
   – Body
   – Closing
	1. Cinco partes de una carta amistosa
	   – Fecha
	   – La dirección
	   – Saludos
	   – Cuerpo
	   – Despedida

2. Assignment: Write a friendly letter to your pen pal in Alaska.	2. Escribe una carta amistosa a sus compañeros de correspondencia en Alaska.
3. Tell them about our state.	3. Dígales sobre nuestro estado.
4. Due—Friday	4. Entregar viernes

Figure 8.16 Bilingual Lesson Log Template

Lesson: _____	Date: _____
Main Ideas—English	*Main Ideas—(native language)*

Figure 8.17   English Language Learners Speaking Skills

Name _____   Date _____

Grade _____   Teacher _____

Standard

- Respond appropriately
- Use correct subject/verb agreement
- Use correct word order
- Pronounce words correctly

Assignment—Interview a partner about your summer vacation.

Interviewee—Responses

	Not Yet 0	Yes 1
Content		
• Did I respond appropriately?		
• Did I describe my likes?		
• Did I describe my dislikes?		
Structure		
• Did I use correct word order?		
• Did I use correct subject/verb agreement?		
• Did I use the correct pronouns?		
• Did I use complete sentences?		
Fluency		
• Did I pronounce words clearly?		
• Did I use appropriate intonation?		
• Did I use simple sentences?		
• Did I use compound sentences?		
• Did I use complex sentences?		

Comments:

(Text continued from page 256)

- Plan a lesson or unit around multicultural activities so that the student has a chance to bring in costumes, games, and sports that represent her culture to share with the rest of the class.
- Place the student with one other student who wants to learn his language and provide the pair with a bilingual dictionary so that both students can practice learning a new language.
- Organize cooperative groups so that the non-English-speaking student gets easier roles, such as materials manager, encourager, or observer, until she builds her confidence.
- Arrange for afterschool tutoring for the non-English-speaking student.
- Establish pen pals from the student's country for the class. The LEP student can help edit letters in his native language to gain self-esteem.
- Learn some of the student's language and use it in class.
- Ask the LEP student to teach key words from her native language to the whole class.
- Make bilingual posters for group rules and consequences, social skills, and classroom procedures.
- Use a Word Wall to show key vocabulary words in both languages.

Add some of your own solutions for helping students with language challenges:

_____

_____

_____

_____

_____

STUDENTS WITH PHYSICAL CHALLENGES

Scenario

"We've got to rehearse our rap song," Lisa calls out. "We only have 20 minutes before we present it to the class."

"Let's go out in the hall and practice our dance steps to make sure we have the routine down pat," adds Patrick.

As the group members file out into the hall, Helen sits in her wheelchair staring at them. She starts to wheel herself toward the door, but then reconsiders and rolls back to her desk. She waits for the group to return and then watches while they present their rap song and dance to the class.

The song is a big hit, and the class breaks into wild applause as the group members finish the routine and return to her side.

"Wow, that was a lot of fun," says Lisa.

> *"We were the best group in the class,"* exclaims Patrick.
> *"How did you like it, Helen?"* asks Lisa.
> *"It was great,"* replies Helen. *"I only wish I could have gone up there with you."*
> *"Well, you could have come up with us to sing—why didn't you?"*
> *"I don't know why I didn't come up,"* answers Helen. *"Maybe it was because no one asked me!"*

SOLVING THE PROBLEM

Public education has become education for all since legislation passed in 1975. Along with the increased rights of individuals with disabilities from legislation come increased responsibilities for teachers. Nearly three-fourths of all students with disabilities currently receive all or most of their education in a general education classroom. Mastropieri and Scruggs (2000) say,

> Today, therefore, teachers must be especially aware of their responsibilities in providing appropriate instruction for students with disabilities. Although more responsibilities are placed on the general education teacher, you should not consider them a burden. On the contrary, classroom diversity—whether in the form of gender, race, ethnicity, or ability—is something to be valued in its own right. Diversity provides opportunities for students to understand, respect, and value others for their differences. (pp. 6–7)

Students with physical disabilities or health impairments are a small but diverse group. According to Vaughn et al. (2000), disabilities can range from asthma, a comparatively mild condition, to cerebral palsy, which may involve neurological impairment that affects mobility and other functional skills. "Most students with physical disabilities and health impairments may qualify for special education services under three Individuals with Disabilities Education Act (IDEA) categories: orthopedic impairment, other health impairment, and traumatic brain injury" (Vaughn et al., p. 263).

Orthopedic impairments include those caused by congenital problems (e.g., clubfoot), impairments caused by disease (e.g., tuberculosis), and other causes such as cerebral palsy, amputations, fractures, or burns that cause contractures (IDEA, Section 300.7 [7] as cited in Vaughn et al., 2000).

Orthopedic impairments or physical disabilities may also affect students' abilities to communicate, learn, and adjust. Section 504 of the Vocational Rehabilitation Act of 1973 defines a physical disability as an impairment that substantially limits a person's participation in one or more lifestyle activities. Other health impairments are defined as "having limited strength, vitality or alertness, due to chronic or acute health problems such as heart condition, tuberculosis, rheumatic fever, nephritis, asthma, sickle cell anemia, hemophilia, epilepsy, lead poisoning, leukemia, or diabetes, that adversely affects a child's educational performance" (IDEA, Section 300.7[8] as cited in Vaughn et al., 2000, p. 263). The new IDEA 2004 has added Tourette syndrome as a chronic or acute health problem under Other Health Impairment.

Cooperative Learning

Teachers have the responsibility of teaching social skills to special education students and the regular education students who work with them. "Proponents of inclusive education believe that all children profit from learning in heterogeneous settings; learning about human interconnectedness, caring, and responsibility is as important as learning math, reading, and writing" (Sapon-Shevin, 1991, p. 8).

Cooperative learning, therefore, provides an ideal structure for integrating these students into the regular education classroom. All students need to learn how to recognize and accept individual differences because diversity enriches learning. As society becomes more multicultural, teachers must recognize that all students differ. Students cannot be divided into *typical* and *handicapped*. Sapon-Shevin (1991) states, "Our students vary along many dimensions: race, class, gender, ethnicity, family background and make-up, religion, academic skills, motor skills, interests" (p. 10).

Students need to learn how to accept and value diversity and participate in cooperative groups that prepare them to live in inclusive, cooperative communities. Johnson and Johnson (cited in Tateyama-Sniezek, 1990) feel that "learning situations should be structured cooperatively, not competitively or individualistically, to maximize the achievement of handicapped students" (p. 436).

The challenge facing teachers involves structuring group activities so as to allow physically challenged students to achieve their academic goals while at the same time cultivating, nurturing, and reinforcing social skills that the research shows are necessary for their acceptance by regular education students. Careful attention must be paid to the types of tasks given to groups, the roles assigned to each member, and the method of evaluation used. Teachers need to be aware of what they can do to help challenged students succeed and to structure authentic assessments to measure the performance and development of these students.

An Atmosphere of Trust

Most important, an atmosphere of trust and caring must be established in the classroom, and an emphasis on social skills, cooperation, and understanding must permeate the learning environment if physically challenged students are to fit into the cooperative learning classroom.

If team members are truly bonded, they will be in tune with each other's feelings and emotions. Sometimes students are insensitive to the needs of physically challenged students. One strategy that increases students' awareness of the needs of physically challenged students is to ask them to write about how they like people to treat them and how they should treat others. This can be done through the use of a Thinking-At-Right-Angles Journal, as demonstrated in Figure 8.18. Figure 8.19 contains a Thinking-At-Right-Angles Journal template that teachers can use with their students.

This type of journal helps students of all ages process feelings. Despite periods when the teaching of values, ethics, and character education was banned from school curricula, parents and educators today realize that teaching students these skills is important. Teaching students to reflect on how they feel

Figure 8.18 Thinking-at-Right-Angles Journal

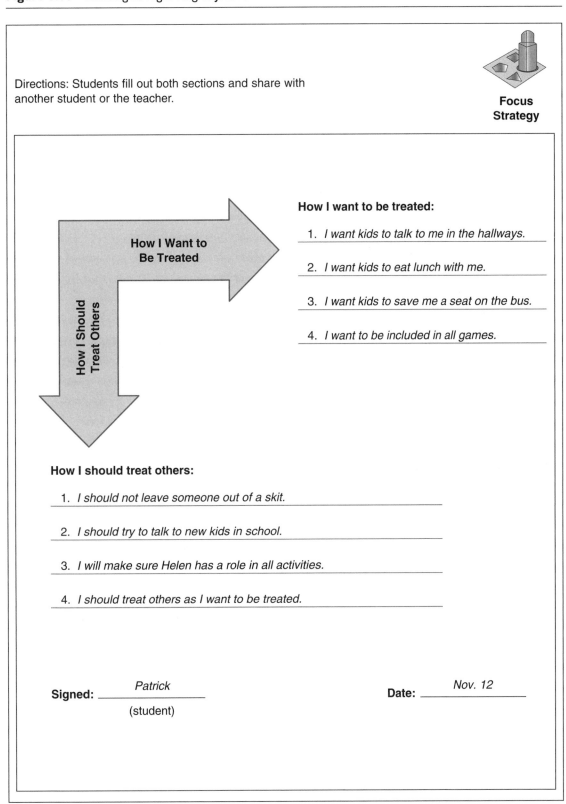

Directions: Students fill out both sections and share with another student or the teacher.

**Focus
Strategy**

**How I Want to
Be Treated**

**How I Should
Treat Others**

How I want to be treated:

1. *I want kids to talk to me in the hallways.*

2. *I want kids to eat lunch with me.*

3. *I want kids to save me a seat on the bus.*

4. *I want to be included in all games.*

How I should treat others:

1. *I should not leave someone out of a skit.*

2. *I should try to talk to new kids in school.*

3. *I will make sure Helen has a role in all activities.*

4. *I should treat others as I want to be treated.*

Signed: _____*Patrick*_____
(student)

Date: _____*Nov. 12*_____

Figure 8.19 Thinking-at-Right-Angles Journal Template

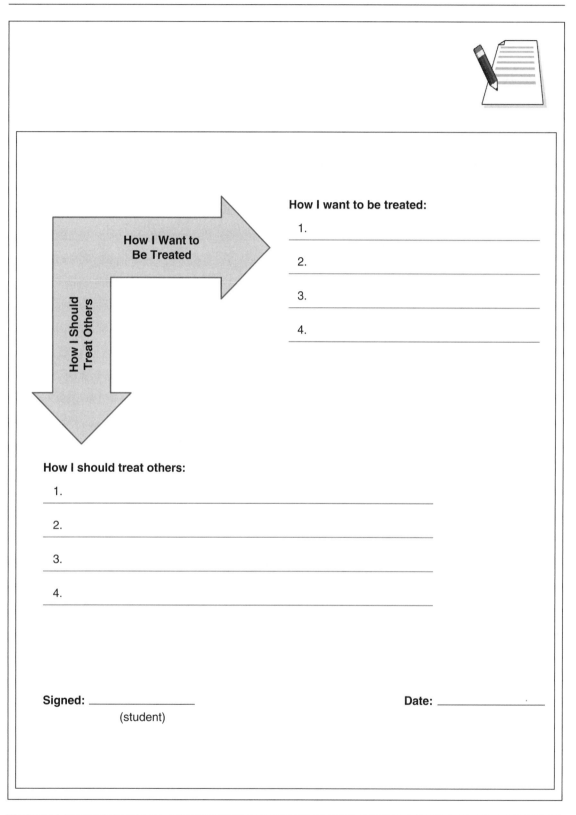

How I want to be treated:

1. _____

2. _____

3. _____

4. _____

How I should treat others:

1. _____

2. _____

3. _____

4. _____

Signed: _____   Date: _____
     (student)

when someone treats them unfairly or disrespectfully will help them avoid treating others that way. Even though these "people skills" are usually introduced to students in kindergarten, students of all grade levels need to revisit them. The skills of respecting each other, sharing, caring, taking turns, and being kind to one another are as important in the classroom as they are in the boardroom. It is evident that all students have special needs. Even though students might not be classified under the Individuals with Disabilities legislation, each student needs to feel accepted and valued.

Other Strategies Teachers Can Use With Students With Physical Challenges

- Become aware of what support services are available.
- Monitor groups more closely to make sure all students are included in group activities.
- Review the social skills of including everyone in all activities, giving encouragement, and helping each other.
- Make sure materials and equipment are accessible to students in wheelchairs.
- Raise a desk or secure a table so that students in wheelchairs are comfortable.
- Talk to group members privately and ask them to be aware of how they might feel if they were left out of a fun group activity because of a physical challenge.
- Talk to the student about ways she can assert herself more to make sure she contributes to the group effort.
- Assign the student to a nurturing group that will be sensitive to his needs as well as friendly and supportive.
- Have students in the class role-play situations that people who are blind, deaf, or physically challenged face each day so that they become more aware and sensitive to the needs of these students.
- Call on support service staff as collaborators.
- Educate classmates about how to facilitate students with disabilities without infringing on their independence.

Add some of your own solutions for helping students with physical challenges:

_____

_____

_____

_____

_____

Epilogue:
What to Do With
the Class That . . .

Conducting Class Meetings
to Address Problems

WHEN ALL THE STUDENTS MISBEHAVE

> *"Class, class,"* yells Mrs. Paul. *"Please get back in your seats so I can give you your assignment!"*
>
> *"Bruce took my pencil,"* Robin whines. *"Make him give it back!"*
>
> *"In your face,"* mumbles Bruce.
>
> *"Students, I have a fun lesson planned for today, but we can't start until you are all settled."*
>
> *"Dave is sitting in the wrong seat,"* Julie announces to the class. *"Make him move!"*
>
> *"John, quit sharpening your pencil and sit down!"* Mrs. Paul pleads. *"We really need to begin."*
>
> Suddenly Kim and Terry begin to giggle uncontrollably.
>
> *"Look at Ryan's haircut,"* they howl. *"It looks like his mother put a bowl over his head."*
>
> *"Okay, everyone. I think we need to put away our math books and call a class meeting. We have a lot to discuss."*

Sound familiar? Who has not experienced a class where "controlled chaos" is the order of the day?

In the traditional classroom, teachers might utilize the Obedience Model and punish the whole class by revoking a privilege (*"Okay, we won't be going on our field trip to the zoo on Friday."*) or by threatening (*"That's it—if I hear one more word, the whole class will have to diagram all 50 sentences tonight for homework!"*). Teachers also sometimes resort to subtle forms of punishment such as, *"Okay class, I see we are not mature enough to handle our activity today. Let's separate our desks, take out our ditto packets, and answer all the even problems. The packets must be turned in before you go home."*

A more effective way for teachers to handle whole-class disruptions is to hold a class meeting to discuss what the problems are, brainstorm solutions, redefine or reset rules as needed, set class goals, and build consensus. Class meetings are designed as a forum for the entire class to discuss general classroom procedures or classroom problems. According to Epanchin, Townsend, and Stoddard (1994), topics for the meeting can be brought up by students or the teacher. The primary focus of the class meeting is on group dynamics within the classroom—not on improving academic achievement. The outcome of the meeting could be to redesign a class procedure, rule, or consequence that doesn't seem to be working. However, "the real purpose of class meetings is to build a sense of community within the class" (p. 214). The scenario below demonstrates how a class meeting can be effective in solving problems.

Class Meeting

"Class, I've called this meeting so that we can discuss what just happened in our math class," Mrs. Paul begins.

"You mean, because we all were bad?" offers Robin.

"I mean when we were not treating each other with respect," replies Mrs. Paul. *"What do you think we can do about it?"*

"Well," Liz offers, *"We could review our social skills."*

"What do you mean?" asks Julie.

"Well, I think we could review put-downs," says John.

"You mean like 'in your face'?" Bruce asks.

"Yeah," replies John. *"We could practice getting into groups, taking turns, and giving each other encouragement."*

"We used to encourage all the time," Ryan adds.

"That's true," Julie answers.

"Okay, so what can we do?" asks Dave.

"I know," exclaims Terry. *"We can do another T-chart on what cooperation looks like and sounds like."*

"Good idea," says Michelle. *"And then we can role-play put-downs and how they make us feel."*

"Okay, that's fine," says Robin. *"But how are we going to keep track of who is still using put-downs and who is using put-ups?"*

"We can use checklists in our groups to keep track of put-downs," says Dave.

"What will we get if we go a whole day without slamming someone?" asks Bruce. *"A happy face?"*

"No," says Robin. *"We'll give each other a round of applause when the bell rings."*

"Let me summarize what you have all suggested and then we can have a class vote to decide on the ideas," offers Mrs. Paul.

"Terry, please write the following on the board:

1. Get into groups and complete T-charts on social skills we feel we need.

2. Try to follow one of the rules we voted on and respect each other.

3. Encourage each other by giving the group a round of applause at the end of the day if we all practice our targeted social skills.

> "Beth, will you please conduct the discussion on each of the three proposals?" asks Mrs. Paul.
>
> Beth begins, "Okay, all those in favor of proposal one will have a chance to discuss their views. And then anyone opposed will also be able to state their opposition or offer alternative proposals. Discussion for each proposal will be limited to five minutes. Remember to 'disagree with the idea—not the person.'"
>
> [Discussion for all three proposals lasts 15 minutes.]
>
> "Thank you, Beth. You did a good job conducting the discussion. I think we are now ready to take a reading using 'five-to-fist,'" says Mrs. Paul. [Class takes a reading.]
>
> "Well, class, I am pleased that we came to consensus and arrived at some procedures we can all live with. I am also anxious to see how your behavior checklists work. Usually I am the one who monitors your behavior, but now you have accepted the responsibility to monitor yourselves. I respect your desire to work together to solve your problems. Let's give ourselves a standing ovation for working so well together," Mrs. Paul announces.
>
> "And now let's review a T-chart on cooperation as a class before we brainstorm the social skills we all feel we need to review..."

The T-chart the class reviews is shown in Figure E.1.

Figure E.1   T-Chart: Cooperation

What does it sound like?	What does it look like?
"I like that idea."	Working together
"Do you need any help?"	Helping one another
"Thanks for helping me."	Smiling
"Way to go!"	Sharing
"I like working with you."	Eye to eye
"That's a great idea because . . . "	Knee to knee

Behavior Checklists

Students need to review the classroom procedures, rules, and consequences as well as the cooperative group rules and social skills on a periodic basis. It would be naive for teachers to assume that teaching the social skills once in September is enough to embed them firmly in students' minds until June.

As mentioned in the class meeting outlined above, groups can use checklists to monitor their social skills in the classroom. In the Group Observation Checklists shown in figures E.2 and E.3, one member of the group acts as the observer, recording the targeted social skills the other group members exhibit.

Figure E.2   Group Observation Checklist for Social Skills

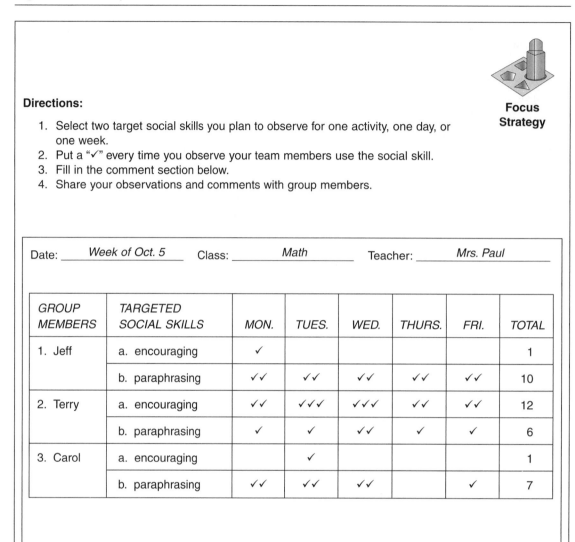

Directions:

Focus Strategy

1. Select two target social skills you plan to observe for one activity, one day, or one week.
2. Put a "✓" every time you observe your team members use the social skill.
3. Fill in the comment section below.
4. Share your observations and comments with group members.

Date: _Week of Oct. 5_   Class: _Math_   Teacher: _Mrs. Paul_

GROUP MEMBERS	TARGETED SOCIAL SKILLS	MON.	TUES.	WED.	THURS.	FRI.	TOTAL
1. Jeff	a. encouraging	✓					1
	b. paraphrasing	✓✓	✓✓	✓✓	✓✓	✓✓	10
2. Terry	a. encouraging	✓✓	✓✓✓	✓✓✓	✓✓	✓✓	12
	b. paraphrasing	✓	✓	✓✓	✓	✓	6
3. Carol	a. encouraging		✓				1
	b. paraphrasing	✓✓	✓✓	✓✓		✓	7

Comments About Members

1. Jeff: You are a good listener because you always report or paraphrase what people say. However, you hardly ever encourage. You tend to "put down" people rather than build them up.

2. Terry: You really keep the group going by both listening and energizing them. You're a group cheerleader.

3. Carol: You give few positive comments to anyone, although you do listen well.

Group Member Observer: _Pat_   Date: _Oct. 9_

Figure E.3   Group Observation Checklist for Social Skills Template

Date: _____   Class: _____   Teacher: _____

GROUP MEMBERS	TARGETED SOCIAL SKILLS	MON.	TUES.	WED.	THURS.	FRI.	TOTAL
1.	a.						
	b.						
2.	a.						
	b.						
3.	a.						
	b.						

Comments About Members

_____

_____

_____

_____

_____

_____

_____

_____

_____

Class Checklists

In addition to introducing the T-chart and student-initiated behavior checklists to the classroom, teachers might want to monitor appropriate classroom behavior with a Class Behavior Checklist (see Figure E.4) to get a feel for where the breakdown of rules is occurring. Several types of observation checklists can be used to monitor areas in which the whole class needs help or areas in which specific students are weak. The checklists also can be used as documentation for school referrals or parent conferences. A Class Behavior Checklist template is provided in Figure E.5.

Behavior checklists provide concrete documentation at a glance. Some teachers prefer to make a "check" whenever they witness the behavior. Any blanks on the checklists would, therefore, indicate a deficiency in the student's behavior.

Other teachers find it less time-consuming and more efficient to document only those students who are having problems. By focusing on the target behaviors and the students with problems, teachers address those specific behaviors immediately, early in the year, or whenever a series of violations occurs.

If teachers notice that many of the students are violating one or more of the rules or social skills, it is time to take class action by addressing the problem as a whole group rather than addressing the problem individually with every student who violates the rule.

Group Checklists

Behavior checklists also can be used by cooperative groups to monitor group behavior (see Figure E.6). Groups fill in the targeted behaviors in the columns and assess how they did individually and as a group after each activity, at the end of each day, or at the end of the week. One person in the group can ask the group members how they think they did on the checklist, or each member can rate himself.

By taking time to process their own behaviors, students in a group can reflect on the importance of practicing social skills and learn how to achieve academic goals by interacting effectively with others. A Group Behavior Checklist template that teachers can give to their students is offered in Figure E.7.

For teachers to help their students develop cooperation, self-discipline, and responsibility in the classroom, they have to empower them to self-regulate their own behavior. Sometimes, however, the teacher needs to monitor the behavior and offer gentle reminders to get the students back on track.

Figure E.4   Class Behavior Checklist

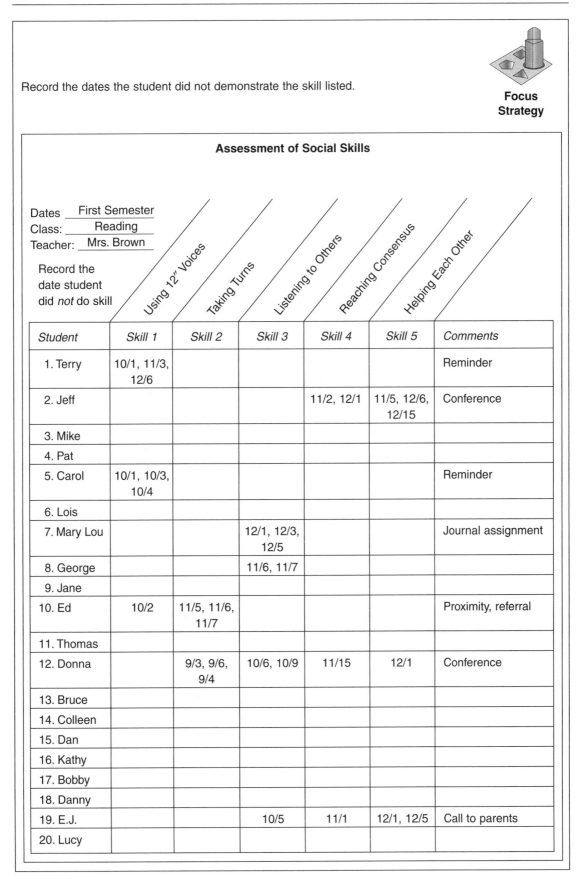

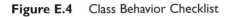
Focus
Strategy

Record the dates the student did not demonstrate the skill listed.

Assessment of Social Skills

Dates ___First Semester___
Class: ___Reading___
Teacher: ___Mrs. Brown___

Record the date student did *not* do skill

Skill 1 — Using 12" Voices
Skill 2 — Taking Turns
Skill 3 — Listening to Others
Skill 4 — Reaching Consensus
Skill 5 — Helping Each Other

Student	Skill 1	Skill 2	Skill 3	Skill 4	Skill 5	Comments
1. Terry	10/1, 11/3, 12/6					Reminder
2. Jeff				11/2, 12/1	11/5, 12/6, 12/15	Conference
3. Mike						
4. Pat						
5. Carol	10/1, 10/3, 10/4					Reminder
6. Lois						
7. Mary Lou			12/1, 12/3, 12/5			Journal assignment
8. George			11/6, 11/7			
9. Jane						
10. Ed	10/2	11/5, 11/6, 11/7				Proximity, referral
11. Thomas						
12. Donna		9/3, 9/6, 9/4	10/6, 10/9	11/15	12/1	Conference
13. Bruce						
14. Colleen						
15. Dan						
16. Kathy						
17. Bobby						
18. Danny						
19. E.J.			10/5	11/1	12/1, 12/5	Call to parents
20. Lucy						

Figure E.5   Class Behavior Checklist Template

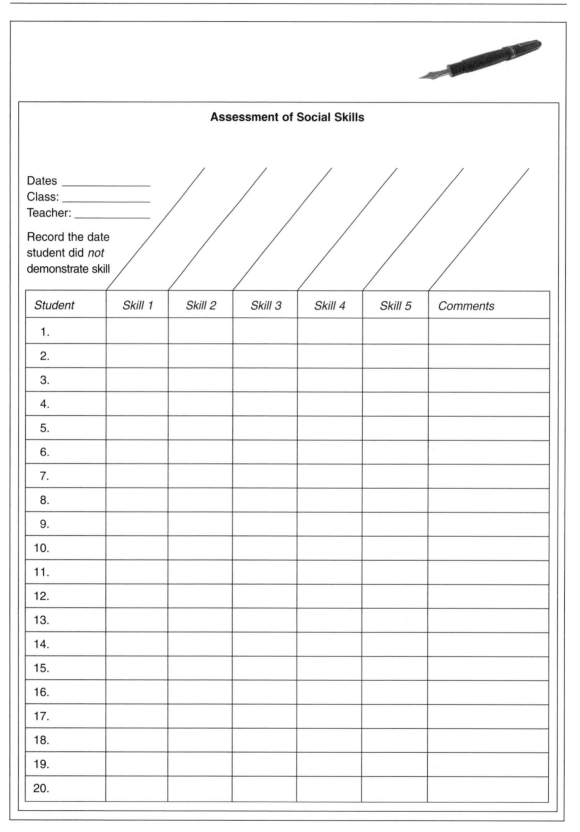

Assessment of Social Skills

Dates _____
Class: _____
Teacher: _____

Record the date
student did *not*
demonstrate skill

Student	Skill 1	Skill 2	Skill 3	Skill 4	Skill 5	Comments
1.						
2.						
3.						
4.						
5.						
6.						
7.						
8.						
9.						
10.						
11.						
12.						
13.						
14.						
15.						
16.						
17.						
18.						
19.						
20.						

Figure E.6   Group Behavior Checklist Template

Focus Strategy

Target social skill: _____ *Not interrupting others* _____

Check (✓) the number of times each person interrupts when another person is talking.

Group Members	M	T	W	T	F
Patsy	✓✓✓	✓✓✓	✓✓✓	✓✓	✓
Tom	✓✓	✓	✓		
Karen		✓	✓		
Joe	✓	✓			

Self-Evaluation (How did you do?): _____ *I think I might have a problem. I never realized how much I interrupted when other people were talking. I've got to control my outbursts. I will try to count to five before I talk so I am not cutting off other people.* _____

Group Evaluation (How did your group do?): _____ *Overall, my group did pretty well. Tom tends to interrupt too much, but Karen and Joe are good listeners. We are going to use a symbol like a plastic microphone to hand to people when they are speaking. Only one person can speak at a time.* _____

Signed: _____ *Patsy* _____   Date: _____ *9/27* _____

Figure E.7   Group Behavior Checklist Template

Target social skill: _____

Check (✓) the number of times each person interrupts when another person is talking.

Group Members	M	T	W	T	F

Self-Evaluation (How did you do?): _____

_____

_____

_____

_____

_____

Group Evaluation (How did your group do?): _____

_____

_____

_____

_____

_____

Signed: _____   Date: _____

Final Thoughts

Because of high-profile incidents of school violence in the last 20 years, many communities have allocated tremendous resources to protect their children in schools. More and more schools, even at the elementary levels, are installing metal detectors, searching students' lockers, and hiring police as hall guards. Students who write about violence in essays or stories, or who are heard talking about committing acts of revenge or violence, are immediately referred to school administrators or law enforcement. While some parents and educators feel that they can control student behavior and prevent possible violence through these external means, others feel that the message being sent to kids is "we don't trust you."

Toxic Schools

Hyman and Snook (2000) describe schools that rely solely on fear and intimidation tactics as *toxic*. "Toxic schools" are those where autocratic leadership focuses on punishment. Hyman and Snook state that the "intensifying and automatic use of punishment, as opposed to prevention of misbehavior and violence in schools, makes the schoolhouse toxic for many children" (p. 491). According to Hyman and Snook, too many poisonous practices by administrators and teachers are harming the emotional, academic, and physical health of children. In these authoritarian schools, the "Obedience Model" is used as a means to keep students in line. External controls, such as detentions, referrals, low grades, removal of privileges, suspensions, metal detectors, and searches of students and lockers, may act as deterrents when authority figures are supervising. However, the real question should be, How will a child act when no authority figures are present?

Democratic Schools

The alternative to toxic schools is what Hyman and Snook (2000) describe as "Democratic Schools." They state:

> In contrast to toxic schools, [Democratic] schools that encourage participatory democracy are characterized by a climate in which students and staff members understand the need to respect one another's rights. . . . They provide students with a sense of shared responsibility with the school staff for assuring the safety of all.
>
> Further, these schools will encourage students to participate in democracy when they become adults. (pp. 491–492)

Democratic schools, moreover, reinforce the "Responsibility Model," which encourages students to develop an internal locus of control. Students behave because it is the right thing to do and because they respect the rights of others—not because they are following orders or being watched! This idea is echoed by Johnson and Johnson (1995), who believe that educators cannot concentrate on the extrinsic manifestations of violence without also addressing the intrinsic needs of students that are not being met and that are causing them to "act out." Prevention requires a long-term commitment to a variety of programs to identify student needs.

Democratic Classrooms

Individual classrooms can also be labeled on a scale as either toxic or democratic or somewhere in the middle. Democratic teachers share in the decision-making process with students. They believe that involving students in the process of establishing expectations, addressing behavior problems, and participating in class meetings not only honors and respects the dignity of the students but also lays the foundation for a healthy classroom climate. Students in democratic classrooms tend to cooperate more with the teacher and each other. They tend to share responsibility, take more ownership for their behavior, feel empowered to make some choices in their learning, and empathize with others. Each student's emotional intelligence is valued as much as her academic intelligence. Students respect authority figures and their peers, and, most important, they respect themselves. They also feel good about themselves because their teachers, and hopefully their classmates, have provided them with the encouragement and support that is sometimes missing from their home life.

Internal Locus of Control

As students go through life, there will be times when the teacher is absent, the parents are out of town, or the boss is on vacation. Students who develop an internal locus of control through the Responsibility Model learn to respect themselves and others and will usually do the right thing, sometimes after some reflective soul-searching. Responsible students are better able to regulate their own behavior, self-evaluate their actions, and live up to their own expectations and the expectations of the people they love and respect. They are independent thinkers who will make mistakes but who are capable of facing the consequences of their actions.

As Glasser (1986) observes, the role of educators is not to coerce students into behaving but instead to teach and model interpersonal skills, ethics, and etiquette to empower students to make appropriate choices. Students who are capable of developing cooperation, self-discipline, and responsibility in the classroom will be better prepared to assume the responsibilities associated with being a good citizen in life. Hopefully, the theories, research, and strategies provided in this book will help educators develop their own philosophies, problem-solving strategies, and action plans when faced with the dilemma of *What to Do With the Kid Who. . . .*

References

Ainsworth, L., & Viegut, D. (2006). *Common formative assessments: How to connect standards-based instruction and assessment.* Thousand Oaks, CA: Corwin Press.

Albert, L. (1989). *A teacher's guide to cooperative discipline: How to manage your classroom and promote self-esteem.* Circle Pines, MN: American Guidance Service.

Armstrong, T. (1994). *Multiple intelligences in the classroom.* Alexandria, VA: Association for Supervision and Curriculum Development.

———. (1999). *ADD/ADHD alternatives in the classroom.* Alexandria, VA: Association for Supervision and Curriculum Development.

———. (2003). *The multiple intelligences of reading and writing: Making the words come alive.* Alexandria, VA: Association for Supervision and Curriculum Development.

———. (2006). *The best schools: How human development research should inform educational practice.* Alexandria, VA: Association for Supervision and Curriculum Development.

Baker, E. T., Wang, M. C., & Walberg, H. J. (1994/1995). Synthesis of research: The effects of inclusion on learning. *Educational Leadership 52*(4), 33–35.

Baker, J., & Zigmond, N. (1990). Are regular education classes equipped to accommodate students with learning disabilities? *Exceptional Children 56,* 515–526.

Barr, R. D., & Parrett, W. H. (2003). *Saving our students: Saving our schools: 50 proven strategies for revitalizing at-risk students and low-performing schools.* Thousand Oaks, CA: Corwin Press.

Bartlett, J. (1980). *Familiar Quotations* (15th ed.). Boston: Little, Brown & Company.

Barton, P. E., & Wenglinksy, H. (1998). Order in the classroom: Violence, discipline, and student achievement. Princeton, NJ: Policy Information Center Research Division, Educational Testing Service.

Begley, S. (1999, May 3). Why the young kill. *Newsweek, 133,* 32–35.

Bellanca, J. (1991). *Building a caring, cooperative classroom: A social skills primer.* Palatine, IL: IRI/Skylight Publishing, Inc.

Bellanca, J., & Fogarty, R. (2003). *Blueprint for achievement in the cooperative classroom* (3rd ed.). Thousand Oaks, CA: Corwin Press.

Belvel, P. S., & Jordan, M. M. (2003). *Rethinking classroom management: Strategies for preventive intervention and problem solving.* Thousand Oaks, CA: Corwin Press.

Bender, W. N., & Shores, C. (2007). *Response to intervention: A practical guide for every teacher.* A Joint Publication from the Council for Exceptional Children and Corwin Press. Thousand Oaks, CA: Corwin Press.

Benjamin, A. (2002). *Differentiated instruction: A guide for middle and high school teachers.* Larchmont, NY: Eye on Education.

Bradley, R. (2007, October). Key issues in discipline (Module 19). *Building the legacy: IDEA 2004 training curriculum.* Washington, DC: National Dissemination Center for Children with Disabilities. www.nichy.org/training/contents.asp IDEA 2004: Building the Legacy. http://idea.ed.gov

Brendtro, L., & Long, N. (1995). Breaking the cycle of conflict. In K. Burke (Ed.), *Managing the interactive classroom: A collection of articles* (pp. 111–121). Thousand Oaks, CA: Corwin Press. (Reprinted from *Educational Leadership, 52*(5), 52–56, 1995)

Bridgeland, J. M., Dilulio, J. J., Jr., & Morison, K. B. (2006, March). *The Silent Epidemic: Perspectives of high school dropouts.* Washington, DC: Civic Enterprises in association with Peter D. Hart Research Associates for the Bill and Melinda Gates Foundation.

Brophy, J. (2004). *Motivating students to learn* (2nd ed.). Mahwah, NJ: Lawrence Erlbam Associates.

Burke, K. (2006). *From standards to rubrics in six steps: Tools for assessing student learning, K–8.* Thousand Oaks, CA: Corwin Press.

Burke, K. (2005). *How to assess authentic learning* (4th ed.).Thousand Oaks, CA: Corwin Press.

Burke, K., Fogarty, R., & Belgrad, S. (2002). *The portfolio connection: Student work linked to standards* (2nd ed.). Thousand Oaks, CA: Corwin Press.

Campbell, L., & Campbell, B. (1999). *Multiple intelligences and student achievement: Success stories from six schools.* Alexandria, VA: Association for Supervision and Curriculum Development.

Carskadon, M. A. (1999). When worlds collide: Adolescent need for sleep versus societal demands. *Phi Delta Kappan, 80*(5), 348–353.

Charney, R. S. (2002). *Teaching children to care: Classroom management for ethical and academic growth, K–8* (Rev. ed.). Greenfield, MA: Northeast Foundation for Children.

Cohen, E. G. (1986). *Designing groupwork: Strategies for the heterogeneous classroom.* New York: Teachers College Press.

Collier, V. P. (1995). *Second language acquisition for school: Academic, cognitive, sociocultural and linguistic processes.* Paper presented at the Georgetown University Round Table on Language and Linguistics (GURT), Washington, DC.

Council for Exceptional Children Newsletter. http://www.cec.sped.org//

Csikzentmihalyi, M. (1990). *Flow: The psychology of optimal experience: Steps toward enhancing the quality of life.* New York: Harper Perennial.

Cummings, C. (2000). *Winning strategies for classroom management.* Alexandria, VA: Association for Supervision and Curriculum Development.

Curwin, R. L., & Mendler, A. N. (1988). *Discipline with dignity.* Alexandria, VA: Association for Supervision and Curriculum Development.

Darling-Hammond, L., & Falk, B. (1997). Using standards and assessments to support student learning. *Phi Delta Kappan, 79*(3), 190.

DeRoche, E. F., & Williams, M. M. (2001). *Character education: A primer for teachers.* Allen, TX: Argus Communications.

Diamond, M., & J. Hopson. (1998). *Magic trees of the mind: How to nurture your child's intelligence, creativity, and healthy emotions from birth through adolescence.* New York: Dutton.

Diffily, D., & Sassman, C. (2004). *Teaching effective classroom routines: Establish structure in the classroom to foster children's learning; From the first day of school and all through the year.* New York: Scholastic.

Digiulio, R. (2000). *Positive classroom management: A step-by-step guide to successfully running the show without destroying student dignity* (2nd ed.). Thousand Oaks, CA: Corwin Press.

Dinkmeyer, D., & Losoncy, L. E. (1980). *The encouragement book. Becoming a positive person.* New York: Prentice-Hall.

Dinkmeyer, D., McKay, G. D., & Dinkmeyer, D., Jr. (1980). *Systematic training for effective teaching.* Circle Pines, MN: American Guidance Service.

Duquette, C. (2001). *Students at risk: Solutions to classroom challenges.* Ontario, Canada: Pembroke Publishers.

Duke, D. L. (2002). *Creating safe schools for all children.* Boston: Allyn & Bacon.

Eisner, E. W. (1985). *The educational imagination: On the design and evaluation of school programs* (2nd ed.). New York: MacMillan.

Elias, M. S., Lantieri, L., Patti, J., Walberg, H. J., & Zins, J. E. (1999). Looking past Columbine: Violence is preventable. *Education Week, 18*(36), 45, 49.

Emmer, E. T., Evertson, C. M., Clements, B. S., & Worsham, M. E. (1997). *Classroom management for secondary teachers* (4th ed.). Boston: Allyn & Bacon.

Epanchin, B. C., Townsend, B., & Stoddard, K. (1994). *Constructive classroom management: Strategies for creating a positive learning environment.* Pacific Grove, CA: Brooks/Cole Publishing.

Etzioni, A. (1999). The truths we must face to curb youth violence. *Education Week, 18*(39), 72, 57.

Evertson, C. M., Emmer, E. T., Clements, B. S., & Worsham, M. E. (1997). *Classroom management for elementary teachers* (4th ed.). Boston: Allyn & Bacon.

Evertson, C. M., Emmer, E. T., & Worsham, M. E. (2000). *Classroom management for elementary teachers* (5th ed.). Boston: Allyn & Bacon.

Evertson, C., & Harris, A. (1991). *Components of effective classroom management: Materials selected from the NDN-approved classroom organization and management program (COMP).* Nashville, TN: Vanderbilt University.

Falvey, M. (1995). *Inclusive and heterogeneous schooling: Assessment, curriculum, and instruction.* Baltimore: Paul H. Brookes.

Fogarty, R. (2002). *Brain-compatible classrooms* (2nd ed.). Thousand Oaks, CA: Corwin Press.

Fogarty, R., & Stoehr, J. (1995). *Integrating curricula with multiple intelligences: Teams, themes, and threads.* Thousand Oaks, CA: Corwin Press.

Freiberg, H. J. (1998). Measuring school climate: Let me count the ways. *Educational Leadership, 56*(1), 22–26.

———— (Ed.). (1999). *Beyond behaviorism: Changing the classroom management paradigm.* Boston: Allyn & Bacon.

Friend, M., & Bursuck, W. D. (1999). *Including students with special needs: A practical guide for classroom teachers* (2nd ed.). Boston: Allyn & Bacon.

Gardner, H. (2006). *Multiple intelligences: New horizons.* New York: Basic Books.

Gardner, H. (1983, 1993). *Frames of mind: The theory of multiple intelligences; Tenth anniversary edition.* New York: Basic Books.

————. (1993) *Multiple intelligences: The theory in practice.* New York: Basic Books.

Gholar, C. R., & Riggs, E. G. (2004). *Connecting with students' will to succeed: The power of conation.* Thousand Oaks, CA: Corwin Press.

Given, B. K. (2002). *Teaching to the brain's natural learning systems.* Alexandria, VA: Association for Supervision and Curriculum Development.

Glasser, W. (1986). *Control theory in the classroom.* New York: Harper & Row.

————. (1990). *The quality school.* New York: Harper Perennial.

————. (1997). A new look at school failure and school success. *Phi Delta Kappan, 78*(8), 596–602.

Glatthorn, A. (1996). *The teacher's portfolio: Fostering and documenting professional development.* Rockport, MA: Proactive Publications.

Goleman, D. (1995). *Emotional intelligence.* New York: Bantam Books.

Gootman, M. E. (1997). *The caring teacher's guide to discipline: Helping young students learn self-control, responsibility, and respect.* Thousand Oaks, CA: Corwin Press.

————. (2001). *The caring teacher's guide to discipline: Helping young students learn self-control, responsibility, and respect* (2nd ed.). Thousand Oaks, CA: Corwin Press.

Gordon, T. (1974). *Teacher effectiveness training.* New York: Peter Wyden.

Gough, P. B. (1987). The key to improving schools: An interview with William Glasser. *Phi Delta Kappan, 68*(9), 656–662.

Gregory, G. H., & Chapman, C. (2002). *Differentiated instructional strategies: One size doesn't fit all.* Thousand Oaks, CA: Corwin Press.

Gronlund, N. E. (1998). *Assessment of student achievement* (6th ed.). Boston: Allyn & Bacon.

Guilfoyle, C. (2006). *NCLB: Is there life beyond testing?* Alexandria, VA. *Educational Leadership, 64*(3), 8–13.

Hansen, J. M., & Childs, J. (1998). Creating a school where people like to be. *Educational Leadership, 56*(1), 14–17.

Hill, J. D., & Flynn, K. M. (2006). *Classroom instruction that works with English language learners.* Alexandria, VA: Association for Supervision and Curriculum Development.

Holland, H. (2007). Can educators close the achievement gap? An interview with Richard Rothstein and Kati Haycock. *The Journal of Staff Development, 28*(1), 54–62.

Hyman, I. A., & Snook, P. A. (2000). Dangerous schools and what you can do about them. *Phi Delta Kappan, 81*(7), 489–501.

Individuals with Disabilities Education Act (2004), Pub. L. No. 108-446, § 601 (c). (http://idea.ed.gov).

Jenkins, P. (1989). *The joyful child: A sourcebook of activities and ideas for releasing children's natural joy.* Tucson, AZ: Harbinger House.

Jennings, J., & Rentner, D. S. (2006). Ten big effects of the No Child Left Behind Act on public school. *Phi Delta Kappan, 88*(2), 110–113.

Jensen, E. (1998a). How Julie's brain learns. *Educational Leadership, 56*(3), 41–45.

———. (1998b). *Teaching with the brain in mind.* Alexandria, VA: Association for Supervision and Curriculum Development.

Johnson, D. W., & Johnson, R. T. (1986). *Circles of learning: Cooperation in the classroom.* Alexandria, VA: Association of Supervision and Curriculum Development.

———. (1995). *Reducing school violence through conflict resolution.* Alexandria, VA: Association for Supervision and Curriculum Development.

Johnson, S. (2004). *Mind wide open: Your brain and the neuroscience of everyday life.* New York: Scribner.

Jones, V. F., & Jones, L. S. (1998). *Comprehensive classroom management: Creating communities of support and solving problems* (5th ed.). Boston: Allyn & Bacon.

———. (2001). *Comprehensive classroom management: Creating communities of support and solving problems* (6th ed.). Boston: Allyn & Bacon.

Kantrowitz, B., & Wingert, P. (1999, May 10). Beyond Littleton: How well do you know your kid? *Newsweek, 10,* 36–40.

Kauffman, J. M., Hallahan, D. P., Mostert, M. P., Trent, S. C., & Nuttycombe, D. G. (1993). *Managing classroom behavior: A reflective case-based approach.* Needham Heights, MA: Allyn & Bacon.

Kauffman, J. M., Mostert, M. P., Trent, S. C., & Hallahan, D. P. (1998). *Managing classroom behavior: A reflective case-based approach* (2nd ed.). Boston: Allyn & Bacon.

Kendall, J. S., & Marzano, R. J. (1997). *Content knowledge: A compendium of standards and benchmarks for K–12 education* (2nd ed.). Aurora, CO: Mid-continent Research for Education and Learning; Alexandria, VA: Association for Supervision and Curriculum Development.

Koenig, L. (2000). *Smart discipline for the classroom: Respect and cooperation restored* (3rd ed.). Thousand Oaks, CA: Corwin Press.

Kohn, A. (1991). Caring kids: The role of the schools. *Phi Delta Kappan, 72*(7), 496–506.

———. (1996). *Beyond discipline: From compliance to community.* Alexandria, VA: Association for Supervision and Curriculum Development.

———. (2006). Abusing research: The study of homework and other example. *Phi Delta Kappan, 88*(1), 9–22.

Kotulak, R. C. (1996). *Inside the brain.* Kansas City, MO: Andrews and McMeel.

Lantieri, L., & Patti, J. (1996). The road to peace in our schools. *Educational Leadership,* 54(1), 28–31.

Larrivee, B. (1999). *Authentic classroom management: Creating a community of learners.* Boston: Allyn & Bacon.

Lerner, J. W., Lowenthal, B., & Lerner, S. R. (1995). *Attention deficit disorders: Assessment and teaching.* Pacific Grove, CA: Brooks/Cole Publishing.

Levin, J., & Nolan, J. F. (1996). *Principles of classroom management: A professional decision-making model* (2nd ed.). Boston: Allyn & Bacon.

Lickona, T. (2004). *Character matters: How to help our children develop good judgment, integrity, and other essential virtues.* New York: Touchstone, Simon & Schuster.

Lindberg, J. A., Kelley, D. E., & Swick, A. M. (2005). *Common-sense classroom management for middle and high school teachers.* Thousand Oaks, CA: Corwin Press.

Marshall, M. (2004). Using a discipline system to promote learning: Part I; Creating the system. *Phi Delta Kappan, 85*(7), 498–502.

Marzano, R. J., Marzano, J. S., & Pickering, D. J. (2003). *Classroom management that works: Research-based strategies for every teacher.* Alexandria, VA: Association for Supervision and Curriculum Development.

Mastropieri, M. A., & Scruggs, T. E. (2000). *The inclusive classroom: Strategies for effective instruction.* Upper Saddle River, NJ: Merrill.

McCarthy, M., & Kuh, G. D. (2006). Are students ready for college? What student engagement data say. *Phi Delta Kappan, 87*(9), 664–669.

McIntosh R., Vaughn, R. S., Schumm, J. S., Haager, D., & Lee, O. (1993). Observations of students with learning disabilities in general education classrooms. *Exceptional Children, 60*(3), 249–261.

Mendler, A. N. (1997). *Power struggles: Successful techniques for educators.* Rochester, NY: Discipline Associates.

Merriam-Webster's Collegiate Dictionary (11th ed.). (2003). Springfield, MA: Merriam-Webster, Inc.

Miller, D. (1998). *Enhancing adolescent competence: Strategies for classroom management.* Belmont, CA: West Publishing.

Miller, P. (2006). GED battery no substitute for diploma. *Education Week, 25*(41S), 8.

National Center for Culturally Responsive Educational Systems (NCCRES) Newsletter. equinews@asu.edu.

Nitko, A. J. (2004). *Educational assessment of students* (4th ed.). Upper Saddle River, NJ: Pearson Merrill Prentice Hall.

O'Connor, K. (2002). *How to grade for learning.* Thousand Oaks, CA. Corwin Press.

Ogle, D. (1986). K-W-L: A teaching model that develops active reading of expository text. *The Reading Teacher, 39,* 564–571.

Olson, L. (2006). The down staircase. *Education Week, 25*(41S), 5–7.

O'Neil, J. (1994/1995). Can inclusion work? A conversation with Jim Kauffman and Mara pon-Shevin. *Educational Leadership, 52*(4), 7–11.

———. (1996). On emotional intelligence: A conversation with Daniel Goleman. *Educational Leadership, 54*(1), 6–11.

Pardini, P. (2006). In one voice: Mainstream and ELL teachers work side-by-side in the classroom, teaching language through content. *Journal of Staff Development, 27*(4), 20–25.

Perkins-Gough, D. (2007). Focus on adolescent English language learners. *Educational Leadership, 64*(6), 90–99.

Pool, C. R. (1997). Up with emotional health. *Phi Delta Kappan, 54*(8), 12–14.

Porter, R. P. (1999/2000). The benefits of English immersion. *Educational Leadership, 57*(4), 52–56.

Reeves, D. B. (2004). *Accountability for learning: How teachers and school leaders can take charge.* Alexandria, VA: Association for Supervision and Curriculum Development.

———. (2006). *The learning leader: How to focus school improvement for better results.* Alexandria, VA: Association for Supervision and Curriculum Development.

Reider, B. (2005). *Teach more and discipline less: Preventing problem behaviors in the K–6 classroom.* Thousand Oaks, CA: Corwin Press.

Rivera, D. P., & Smith, D. D. (1997). *Teaching students with learning and behavior problems* (3rd ed.). Needham Heights, MA: Allyn & Bacon.

Roberts, W. B., Jr. (2006). *Bullying from both sides: Strategic interventions for working with bullies and victims.* Thousand Oaks, CA: Corwin Press.

Robbins, P., & Alvy, H. (2004). *The new principal's fieldbook: Strategies for success.* Alexandria, VA: Association for Supervision and Curriculum Development.

Rosen, L. (2005). *School discipline: Best practices for administrators* (2nd. ed.). Thousand Oaks, CA: Corwin Press.

San Antonio, D. M. (2006). Broadening the world of early adolescents. *Educational Leadership, 63*(7), 8–13.

Sapon-Shevin, M. (1991). Cooperative learning in inclusive classrooms: Learning to become a community. *Cooperative Learning, 12*(1), 8–9.

Schaps, E. (2003). Creating a community. *Educational Leadership, 60*(6), 31–33.

Scherer, M. (1998). A conversation with Herb Kohl. *Educational Leadership, 56*(1), 8–13.

———. (2006). Perspectives: The NCLB issue. *Educational Leadership, 64*(3), 8.

Sharon, S., & Sharon, Y. (1996). *Small-group teaching.* Englewood Cliffs, NJ: Educational Technology Publications.

Shore, K. (2005). *The ABCs of bully prevention: A comprehensive schoolwide approach.* Port Chester, NY: DUDE Publishing.

Short, P. M., Short, R. J., & Blanton, C. (1994). *Rethinking student discipline: Alternatives that work.* Thousand Oaks, CA: Corwin Press.

Sigford, J. L. (2006). *The effective school leader's guide to management.* Thousand Oaks, CA: Corwin Press.

Slavin, R. E. (1983). *Cooperative learning.* New York: Longman.

Smelter, R. W., Rasch, B. W., Fleming, J., Nazos, P., & Baranowski, S. (1996). Is attention deficit disorder becoming a desired diagnosis? *Phi Delta Kappan, 77*(6), 429–432.

Solomon, P. G. (2002). *The assessment bridge: Positive ways to link tests to learning standards and curriculum improvement.* Thousand Oaks, CA: Corwin Press.

Sousa, D. A. (2001). *How the brain learns* (2nd ed.). Thousand Oaks, CA: Corwin Press.

Spear-Swerling, L., & Sternberg, R. J. (1998). Curing our "epidemic" of learning disabilities. *Phi Delta Kappan, 81*(5), 397–401.

Stainback, S., & Stainback, W. (Eds.). (1992). *Curriculum considerations in inclusive classrooms: Facilitating learning for all students.* Baltimore, MD: Paul H. Brookes.

Sternberg, R. J., & Williams, W. M. (2002). *Educational psychology.* Boston: Allyn & Bacon.

Stiggins, R. J., Arter, J. A., Chappuis, J., & Chappuis, S. (2004). *Classroom assessment for student learning: Doing it right—using it well.* Portland, OR: Assessment Training Institute.

Sylwester, R. (1998). The neurobiology of self-esteem and aggression. In R. Sylwester, *Student brains, school issues: A collection of articles* (pp. 41–48). Thousand Oaks, CA: Corwin Press.

Tateyama-Sniezek, K. (1990). Cooperative learning: Does it improve the academic achievement of students with handicaps? *Exceptional Children, 56*(5), 426–437.

Thompson, A. M. (1996). Attention deficit hyperactivity disorder: A parent's perspective. *Phi Delta Kappan, 77*(6), 433–436.

Thousand, J. S., Villa, R. A., & Nevin, A. I. (Eds.). (1994). *Creativity and collaborative learning: A practical guide to empowering students and teachers.* Baltimore, MD: Paul H. Brookes.

Tileston, D. W. (2004). *What every teacher should know about classroom management and discipline.* Thousand Oaks, CA: Corwin Press.

Tomlinson, C. A., & Eidson, C. C. (2003). *Differentiation in practice: A resource guide for differentiating curriculum, grades 5–9.* Alexandria, VA: Association for Supervision and Curriculum Development.

Turnbull, R., & Cilley, M. (1999). *Explanations and implications of the 1997 amendents to IDEA.* Upper Saddle River, NJ: Merrill/Prentice Hall.

U.S. Department of Education. (1999). A joint report by the office of Educational Research and Improvement and the Bureau of Justice. Washington, DC: Author.

Vaughn, S., Bos, C. S., & Schumm, J. S. (2000). *Teaching exceptional, diverse and at-risk students in the general education classroom* (2nd ed.). Boston: Allyn & Bacon.

Viadero, D. (2007). Study: Low, high fliers gain less under NCLB. *Education Week, 26*(44), 7.

Villa, R. A., & Thousand, J. S. (Eds.). (1995). *Creating an inclusive school.* Alexandria, VA: Association for Supervision and Curriculum Development.

Vitto, J. M. (2003). *Relationship-driven classroom management: Strategies that promote student motivation.* Thousand Oaks, CA: Corwin Press.

Wagner, T. (1999). Reflections on Columbine: Standards for the heart? *Education Week, 18*(35), 48, 33.

Walker, H. M., Colvin, G., & Ramsey, E. (1995). *Antisocial behavior in school: Strategies and best practices.* Pacific Grove, CA: Brooks/Cole Publishing.

Wang, M., Reynolds, M., & Walberg, H. J. (1994/1995). Serving students at the margins. *Educational Leadership, 52*(4), 12–17.

Weiner, L. (1999). *Urban teaching: The essentials.* New York: Teachers College Press.

Wolfe, P. (2001). *Brain matters: Translating research into classroom practice.* Alexandria, VA: Association for Supervision and Curriculum Development.

Wolfe, P., & Brandt, R. (1998). What we know from brain research. *Educational Leadership, 56*(3), 8–13.

Wolfgang, C. H. (1999). *Solving discipline problems: Methods and models for today's teachers* (4th ed.). Boston: Allyn & Bacon.

Wolfgang, C. H., Bennett, B. J., & Irvin, J. L. (1999). *Strategies for teaching self-discipline in the middle grades.* Boston: Allyn & Bacon.

Wong, H. K., & Wong, R. T. (1998). *The first days of school.* Mountain View, CA: Harry K. Wong.

Wright, W. E. (2006). A catch-22 for language learners. *Educational Leadership, 64*(3), 22–27.

Index

Absenteeism, 152–153,
154–155 (figure)
Achievement gap, 6, 256
Active learning, 57, 62, 208
Adequate yearly progress (AYP), 19
Adolescents. *See* Contemporary youth;
Social skills instruction
African American students, 8, 20, 21
After-school programs, 7
Aggressive behaviors, 213–214, 217
action plan for, 217, 218–219 (figures)
bullying, 216–217
psychological outcomes of, 216, 217
teacher behavior continuum and,
214–216, 215 (figure)
witnesses to, 217
See also Disruptive behavior
Agree/disagree chart activity,
133, 134–137 (figures)
Ainsworth, L., 37
Albert, L., 148, 198, 203, 205, 209
Alienation, 27–28, 209
American Council on Education
(ACE), 22
American Federation of Teachers, 25
American Indian students, 21
American Medical Association, 14
American Psychiatric Association, 14
American Psychological
Association, 23
Anger management, 93–94, 151
See also Aggressive behaviors;
Violence in schools
Anorexia nervosa, 54
Antecedents, 196–197
Apathy, 34, 180–181,
182–183 (figures)
Armstrong, T., 16, 62, 93
Arter, J. A., 45
Asian students, 21
Assertive Discipline program, 63

Assessment:
assessment of learning vs. for learning, 45
Balanced assessment model,
46, 46 (figure)
deep understanding and, 6
functional behavioral
assessments, 230
individual education plans and, 9
individualized education
effectiveness, 10
multiple measures, 6
nondiscriminatory evaluation, 228
progress monitoring, 10
standards-based vs.
norm-based evaluation, 47
See also Authentic assessment;
High-stakes testing; Performance
assessment; Response to
intervention (RTI) approaches;
Standardized tests
At-risk students, 25, 26–29, 195–196
See also Contemporary youth;
Disruptive behavior;
Violence in schools
Attention deficit disorder/attention
deficit hyperactivity disorder
(ADD/ADHD), 13
characteristics of,
13–14, 14 (figure)
controversy over, 16–17
diagnostic criteria for,
14, 15 (figure)
fast-paced media and, 14
intervention strategies for, 14, 16
teaching strategies for,
17–18, 18 (figure)
traditional classroom structure
and, 16–17
See also Educational challenges
Attention-seeking behaviors,
198–202, 200–201 (figures)

Authentic assessment, 32, 44
portfolios, 46
See also Assessment; Performance
assessment
Authoritarian leadership. *See* Obedience
model of discipline

Baker, E. T., 8
Baker, J., 9
Baranowski, S., 17
Barr, R. D., 7, 22, 23, 25, 29, 195
Bartlett, J., 152
Barton, P. E., 25
Basic interaction. *See* Interaction skills
Before-school programs, 7
Begley, S., 28
Behavioral intervention
plans (BIP), 230
Behaviorally disordered. *See* Disruptive
behavior; Emotionally/behaviorally
disordered; Risk behaviors;
Special education
Behavior checklists:
cooperative social skills,
119, 121–123 (figures)
positive classroom climate, 75, 76
(figure), 78, 82 (figure)
social skills instruction,
96, 96 (figure)
special education students,
243, 246–247 (figures)
See also Behavior management
strategies; Class meetings;
Disruptive behavior
Behaviorism, 32, 63
Behavior management strategies,
14, 16–17, 25, 32
minor misbehaviors, 173, 174 (figure)
research-based behavioral
management, 229–230
See also Class meetings; Classroom
management; Classroom rules;
Disruptive behavior; Positive
classroom climate; Responsibility
development
Behavior modification. *See* Behaviorism;
Behavior management strategies
Belgrad, S., 123
Bellanca, J., 57, 58, 94, 99, 139, 142,
167, 199, 204, 221
Belvel, P. S., 69, 70
Bender, W. N., 10, 11, 12, 229
Benjamin, A., 44
Bennett, B. J., 149, 150, 214, 215
Bill and Melinda Gates Foundation, 20

Black students, 8, 20, 21
Blaming the victim, 27
Blanton, C., 196
Block scheduling, 32, 35, 37
Bonding activities, 17, 124
create a business activity,
125–127, 127 (figure)
creative energizers activity,
127–128, 129–130 (figures)
true-false quiz activity, 124–125
Venn/triple Venn diagrams,
125, 125–126 (figures)
See also Cooperative learning; Social
skills instruction; Team-building
skills; Trust
Bos, C. S., 227, 249, 261
Brain-compatible learning, 32–33
chunking direct instruction, 35–36
classroom management and, 37–38
metacognition, 36–37
positive feedback, 37
readiness factor, 33–34
sleep patterns, 34–35
See also Cooperative learning; Multiple
intelligences (MI);
Teaching/learning theories
Brain dysfunction, 28, 33–34
Brandt, R., 33
Brendtro, L., 17
Bridgeland, J. M., 21, 22
Brophy, J., 56
Bubble students, 249
Bulimia nervosa, 54
Bullying, 3, 25, 62, 209,
216–217, 218–219 (figures)
Burke, K., 42, 43, 46, 52, 72, 76, 80,
81, 82, 84, 88, 90, 97, 101, 102,
110, 112, 113, 121, 122, 123,
130, 134, 135, 137, 143, 144,
155, 160, 164, 168, 179, 183,
186, 191, 201, 207, 212, 219,
236, 239, 241, 245, 247, 252,
258, 259, 264, 271, 274, 276
Business creation activity, 125–127,
127 (figure)

Cameron, S., 22
Campbell, B., 39
Campbell, L., 39
Caring climate. *See* Cooperative learning;
Empathy; Physically disabled
students; Positive classroom climate
Carskadon, M. A., 34
Case study strategy,
243, 244–245 (figure)

Cause-and-effect model,
    184, 185–186 (figures)
Centers for Disease Control and
    Prevention, 28
Challenges in education. *See* Disruptive
    behavior; Educational challenges;
    English language learners
    (ELLs); Special education;
    Violence in schools
Chapman, C., 44, 45
Chappuis, J., 45
Chappuis, S., 45
Charney, R. S., 63
Checklists. *See* Behavior checklists;
    Class meetings; Criterion-based
    checklists
Choice theory, 1, 162
Chunking direct instruction, 35–36, 38
Circle of friends activity,
    104, 104 (figure)
Citizenship behaviors, 57, 172, 278
Class meetings, 267–269, 269 (figures)
    behavior checklists,
        269, 270–271 (figures)
    class checklists, 272,
        273–274 (figures)
    classroom rules and, 75
    group checklists, 272,
        275–276 (figures)
    See Positive classroom climate
Classroom management, 3, 12
    behaviorism and, 32, 63
    behavior management strategies, 14,
        16–17, 25
    brain-compatible learning and, 37–38
    bullying, 3, 25
    components of, 38, 38 (figure)
    cooperative learning and, 59
    disruptive behaviors and, 12–13
    emotional intelligence and, 56–57
    grading issues, 3
    meaningful/motivating instruction
        and, 12
    multiple intelligences and, 41
    organizational training techniques
        and, 16
    performance assessments and,
        51, 53, 53 (figure)
    positive classroom climate and,
        63, 64 (figure)
    power dynamics and,
        64–65, 64 (figure)
    proactive strategies for, 13
    time management and, 16
    violence-prone youth and, 25

See also Classroom rules; Disruptive
    behavior; Positive classroom
    climate; Social skills instruction;
    Teaching/learning theories
Classroom rules, 12, 16, 17,
    61 (figure), 73
    basic understandings in, 75
    behavior as attitude vs. skill, 83
    behavior checklists, 75,
        76 (figure), 78, 82 (figure)
    consequences and, 77–78,
        79–81 (figures)
    development of, 83, 84 (figure)
    guidelines for, 74–75
    student self-assessment checklist,
        75, 76 (figure)
    terminology of, 73–74
    See also Class meetings; Disruptive
        behavior; Positive classroom
        climate; Social skills instruction
Clements, B. S., 103
Climate. *See* Enriched climate;
    Positive classroom climate
Coercive interaction,
    1, 197, 197 (figure)
Cognitive intelligence (CI), 205, 208
Cognitive learning theory, 63
Cohen, E. G., 256
Collaborative learning, 33
    See also Cooperative learning
Collier, V. P., 17
Columbine High School, 27, 210
Colvin, G., 171
Communication skills,
    7, 17, 20, 25, 91 (figure), 94
    aggressive behaviors and, 214
    hidden curriculum and, 93
    listening skill practice,
        106–109, 107–110 (figures)
    round robin listening circle,
        108–109, 110 (figure)
    social skills and, 105, 106 (figure)
    See also Social skills instruction
Competitive school culture, 58, 262
Conferences. *See* Teacher-student
    conferences
Conflict resolution,
    57, 91 (figure), 94, 131
    agree/disagree chart activity,
        133, 134–137 (figures)
    conflict resolution activity,
        140–142, 142 (figure)
    consensus chart activity,
        138, 138–139 (figures)
    gifted students and, 131

human graph activity,
140, 141 (figure)
social skills related to,
131–132, 132 (figure), 194
solutions T-chart, 95, 96 (figure)
See also Social skills instruction
Conscientious/loner students,
175, 177–180, 178–179 (figures)
Consensus chart activity,
138, 138–139 (figures)
Consequences, 77–78, 79–81 (figures)
See also Classroom rules;
Punishments; Rewards
Contemporary youth:
angst among, 26
brain dysfunction and, 28
depression/loneliness and, 26–27
rejection/alienation and, 27–28
risk behaviors and, 28–29
violence-prone youth, 25, 26
See also Educational challenges;
Teaching/ learning theories;
Violence in schools
Contentious students,
187–189, 190–191 (figures)
Continuum of services, 228
Cooperative learning, 3, 32, 57–58
base grouping and, 116
behavior checklists for,
119, 121–123 (figures)
bonding activities, 124–128, 125–127
(figures), 129–130 (figures)
caring classrooms,
establishment of, 58
classroom management and, 59, 73
English language learners and, 254
facilitation of,
114–119, 115–116 (figures)
group activity template,
144 (figure), 145
group work and, 58, 114
I-messages and, 150
off-task behaviors and, 162
physically disabled students and, 262
power-seeking behaviors and, 204
problems/solutions
brainstorming, 118–119,
118–120 (figures)
roles in, 116, 117 (figures)
social skills for, 116, 116 (figure)
student self-assessment of,
96, 97 (figure)
See also Positive classroom climate;
Social skills instruction;
Team-building skills

Creative energizers activity, 127–128,
129–130 (figures)
Creativity, 58
Criminal activity, 21, 23, 24–25, 54
Criterion-based checklists,
47–48, 48–50 (figures)
Csikzentmihalyi, M., 12, 55
Cummings, C., 14, 16, 151
Curwin, R. L., 74, 77, 194, 203

Darling-Hammond, L., 47
Decision-making model, 162, 163–164
(figures), 181, 182–183 (figures)
Deep understanding, 6, 35, 37, 62
Democratic learning communities,
64, 277–278
Depression, 26–27
DeRoche, E. F., 92, 194
Developmentally/cognitively
disordered (DCD), 8
Diamond, M., 33
Differentiated learning,
6, 32, 44, 45 (figure), 254
Diffily, D., 67
DiGiulio, R., 74, 148, 149, 174
Dilulio, J. J., Jr., 21, 22
Dinkmeyer, D., 181, 198
Dinkmeyer, D., Jr., 198, 221, 223
Direct instruction, 35–36, 38, 92
Disabled students. *See* Inclusion
strategies; Physically disabled
students; Special education
Disagreement. *See* Conflict resolution
Discipline:
discipline procedures/practices,
improvement in, 24–25
empathy/structure and, 63
interim alternative educational
settings, 230
obedience model of, 1
positive learning and, 63
self-discipline, 3
special education and, 230–231
standards and, 151–152
See also Classroom management;
Disruptive behavior; Positive
classroom climate;
Teaching/learning theories;
Violence in schools
Discrepancy documentation, 8, 10
Disruptive behavior, 194
aggressive behaviors,
213–220, 218–219 (figures)
antecedents, identification of,
196–197

at-risk students and, 195, 196
attention-seeking behaviors, 198–202
conflict resolution skills and, 194
divided journals and,
    210–211, 211–212 (figures)
80–15–5 model and, 194
encouragement/caring
    relationships and, 209
inadequacy beliefs,
    220–226, 221–223 (figures)
minor misbehaviors, 173, 174 (figure)
newspaper model and,
    199, 200–201 (figures)
poverty, pressures of, 195–196, 205
power-seeking behaviors,
    202–208, 204 (figure)
power struggles and, 193 (figures),
    197, 203–205, 204 (figure),
    206–207 (figures), 209
revenge-seeking behaviors,
    209–213, 210 (figure)
ripple effect of, 194–195
school structures and, 199
teacher behavior continuum and,
    214–216, 215 (figure)
teacher-student conferences and,
    210, 213, 223, 224–225 (figures)
urban classrooms and, 205, 208
win-win outcomes and, 197
See also Class meetings; Classroom
    management; Classroom rules
Distractibility, 16
Distressed communities, 7, 21, 23, 24
Divided journal, 210–211, 211–212
    (figures)
Dominating students,
    184–187, 185–186 (figures)
Dropouts. *See* High school dropouts
Drugs. *See* Illegal drugs; Medications
Due process procedures, 11, 228
Duke, D. L., 26

Early childhood procedures,
    67, 68 (figure)
Early intervention services (EIS), 228
Early literacy development, 255
Economic Policy Institute, 196
Educate America Act. *See* Goals 2000:
    Educate America Act
Educational challenges, 6
    agree/disagree chart analysis,
        5 (figure)
    attention deficit disorders, 13–18,
        14–15 (figures), 18 (figure)
    classroom management, 12–13

contemporary youth, 26–29
    English language learners and,
        18–20, 20 (figure)
    high school dropouts, 20–23
    inclusion strategies and, 7–13
    poverty-level students and, 7
    violence in schools, 23–25
    See also No Child Left Behind (NCLB)
        Act of 2001; Special education
Education for All Handicapped
    Children Act of 1975, 227
Educational Testing Service, 24
Education Trust, 7, 196
Eidson, C. C., 44
80–15–5 model, 194
Eisner, E. W., 31
Elementary classroom procedures,
    67–68, 68 (figures)
Elementary and Secondary Education
    Act (ESEA), 6
Elias, M. S., 23
Emmer, E. T., 67, 68, 103
Emotion-based learning, 33, 44, 53
Emotional intelligence (EI), 32, 53
    classroom management and, 56–57
    components of, 53–54, 94
    marshmallow study and, 54–55
    social skill mastery and, 94
    state of flow and, 55–56, 55 (figure)
    See also Cooperative learning;
        Teaching/learning theories
Emotional skill development, 14
    See also Emotional intelligence (EI)
Emotionally/behaviorally disordered
    (E/BD), 8, 93
Emotionally disordered (ED), 8, 93
Empathy, 53, 54, 57, 63, 278
Empowerment, 203, 208, 278
Encouragement, 209
Energizers activity, 127–128,
    129–130 (figures)
Engaged learning, 2, 12–13, 17, 44
English language learners (ELLs),
    3, 18–19
    bridge role and, 256
    cooperative learning and, 254
    early literacy development and, 255
    English as a second language staff
        and, 19, 254
    hidden curriculum and, 93
    immigrant students, 19
    Individuals with Disabilities Education
        Act and, 255
    limited English proficient students,
        19–20, 20 (figure), 255–256

peer tutors and, 256
response to intervention
    model and, 255
standardized testing and, 256
teaching strategies for,
    253–260, 257–259 (figures)
    See also Educational challenges;
        Special education
English as a second language (ESL), 19
Enriched climate, 1, 14, 33, 34, 38
Enrichment classes. *See* Gifted and
    talented (GT) students
Entended-time scheduling, 35
Environment. *See* Enriched climate;
    Positive classroom climate
Epanchin, B. C., 268
Etzioni, A., 26
Evertson, C. M., 67, 68, 74, 103
Expectations, 13, 17, 29, 46–47,
    57, 93, 148, 196, 222

Facilitation role, 3
Factory model curriculum, 32
Falk, B., 47
Falvey, M., 8
Family involvement, 26, 27
    attention-seeking behaviors and,
        199, 203
    brain development and, 28
    childhood traumas, 25, 33–34, 196
    mental stimulation and, 34
    See also Teacher-student conferences
Feedback, 37, 38, 47, 56, 151, 161
Fight-or-flight response, 27, 28, 93, 150
Fishbowl activity, 106–108,
    107–108 (figures)
Fleming, J., 17
Flow, 55–56, 55 (figure)
Flynn, K. M., 18, 19, 253, 254
Fogarty, R., 36, 37, 39, 53, 57, 94, 123,
    139, 142, 167, 199, 204, 221
Freiberg, H. J., 62, 63
Freshman Academies, 199
Full-day kindergarten, 7
Full inclusion. *See* Inclusion strategies;
    Special education
Functional behavioral assessments
    (FBA), 230

Gang activity, 24
Gardner, H., 38–43, 172
Gates Foundation, 20
General education. *See* Inclusion
    strategies; Regular education
    initiative (REI)

General Educational Development
    Certificate (GED), 3, 22–23
Getting tough approach, 1
Gholar, C. R., 205
Gifted and talented (GT) students,
    131, 248–253, 251–252 (figures)
Given, B. K., 210
Glasser, W., 1, 78, 128, 148,
    162, 203, 214, 278
Glatthorn, A., 31
Goal-setting model,
    250, 251–252 (figures)
Goals 2000: Educate America Act, 23
Goleman, D., 54, 55, 57, 94
Gootman, M. E., 77, 174, 175, 176
Gordon, T., 150
Gough, P. B., 203
Grading issues,
    3, 51, 53, 157, 165, 203
Gregory, G. H., 44, 45
Gronlund, N. E., 44
Group work, 58, 94, 222
    See also Cooperative learning;
        Social skills instruction;
        Team-building skills
Guided practice time, 35, 95–96
Guilfoyle, C., 6
Gun control, 23, 24
Gun-Free Schools Act of 1994, 23

Haager, D., 9
Hallahan, D. P., 149, 197
Harris, A., 74
Hazing. *See* Bullying
Heckman, J. J., 22
Higher-order thinking, 6, 57
High school dropouts, 3, 20–21
    factors in dropping out, 21–22
    General Educational Development
        Certificate and, 22–23
    high school dropouts, 20–23
    inadequacy beliefs and, 221
    low graduation rates, consequences
        of, 21–22
    See also Educational challenges;
        Freshman Academies;
        School-within-a-school structure
High-stakes testing, 1, 6, 47, 194
    See also Standardized tests
Hill, J. D., 18, 19, 253, 254
Hispanic students, 21
Hodgkinson, H., 253
Holland, H., 196
Homework, 157–158
Hopson, J., 33

Human graph activity, 140, 141 (figure)
Hyman, I. A., 277
Hyperactivity. *See* Attention deficit disorder/attention deficit hyperactivity disorder (ADD/ADHD)

I-messages, 149–151, 149–150 (figures), 213
Illegal drugs, 21, 26, 93
Immigrant students, 19, 20, 254
Impoverished students, 7
Impulsivity, 13, 14, 16, 28, 33, 34, 54–55, 93, 151, 210
Inadequacy beliefs, 220–226, 221 (figure)
  dropouts and, 221
  learning problems and, 221
  persistence and, 222
  pessimistic expectations and, 222
  teacher guidance and, 222
  teacher-student conferences and, 222–223, 222–225 (figures)
  See also Disruptive behavior
Inclusion strategies, 7–8, 227
  academic/social outcomes and, 9–10
  classroom management and, 12–13
  gifted students and, 250
  labeling learners and, 8
  least restrictive environments, 8–9
  physically disabled students and, 262
  regular education initiative, 9–10
  response to intervention approaches, 10–12
  See also Educational challenges
Independent learning, 35
Individual accountability, 166
Individual education plan (IEP), 9, 227, 230
Individualized instruction, 10
Individuals with Disabilities Education Act (IDEA) of 1990, 227, 261
Individuals with Disabilities Education Act (IDEA) reauthorization of 2004, 3, 10, 12, 227 (figure), 228, 229, 230–231, 255
Industrial Revolution, 32
Information age, 1
Information processing, 2, 35
Instruction:
  attention deficit disorders and, 17–18, 18 (figure)
  behavior management strategies and, 14, 16–17, 25, 41
  differentiated learning and, 6, 32, 44, 45 (figure)
  limited English proficient students, 19–20, 20 (figure)
  meaningful/motivating instruction, 12–13, 18
  standardized curriculum, 32
  technology in, 18
  See also Social skills instruction; Student achievement; Teachers; Teaching/learning theories
Integration, 9
Interaction skills, 91 (figure), 103, 104 (figure)
  circle of friends activity, 104, 104 (figure)
  show and tell activity, 105
  See also Bonding activities; Cooperative learning; Interpersonal skill development; Social skills instruction; Team-building skills
Interim alternative educational setting (IAES), 230
Internal locus of control, 278
Internet resources:
  access to, 1, 26
  violence and, 26
Interpersonal skill development, 171–172, 171 (figure)
  apathetic students and, 180–183
  cause-and-effect model and, 184, 185–186 (figures)
  contentious students, 187–191
  decision-making model and, 181, 182–183 (figures)
  dominating students and, 184–187
  goal-setting model and, 250, 251–252 (figures)
  loner/conscientious students and, 175, 177–180
  minor misbehaviors, 173, 174 (figure)
  overlapping/multitasking and, 173
  prosocial behaviors, 174–175, 176 (figure)
  social contract strategy, 177, 178–179 (figures), 189, 190–191 (figures)
  with-it-ness and, 172–173
  See also Interaction skills; Social skills instruction
Intervention. *See* Response to intervention (RTI) approaches
IQ, 8, 10, 54
IQ/Achievement Discrepancy Operation, 8, 10, 228
IQ tests, 8
Irvin, J. L., 149, 150, 214, 215
Isolation, 27, 93

Jenkins, P., 184
Jennings, J., 255
Jensen, E., 32
Johnson, D. W., 57, 278
Johnson, R. T., 57, 278
Jones, L. S., 73, 83, 204, 214
Jones, V. F., 73, 83, 204, 214
Jordan, M. M., 69, 70

Kantrowitz, B., 26
Kauffman, J. M., 149, 197
Kelley, D. E., 62, 69
Kelly, M. E., 233
King, L., 79, 136
Klein, K., 48, 50
Koenig, L., 173, 174
Kohn, A., 1, 62, 74, 157
Kotulak, R. C., 33
Kuh, G. D., 161
K-W-L (know/want to know/learned)
    matrix, 114, 115 (figure)

Labeling process, 8, 10,
    27, 93, 196, 249
Lantieri, L., 23
Larrivee, B., 64
Leadership skills, 57, 58, 94, 204
Learning:
    choice theory and, 1
    classification of disorders, 8
    coercion and, 1
    connections and, 2
    differentiated learning, 6
    disruptive behaviors and, 12–13
    higher-order problem-solving
        skills, 6, 57
    information processing and, 2
    rehearsal and, 34
    social/collaborative learning, 33
    See also Cooperative learning;
        Educational challenges;
        Engaged learning;
        Positive classroom climate;
        Student achievement;
        Teaching/learning theories
Learning communities, 64, 199
Learning disabled (LD) students,
    8, 10, 14, 93, 227, 228
Learning styles, 44
Least restrictive environment
    (LRE), 8–9, 228
Lee, O., 9
Levin, J., 194, 195
Lickona, T., 74
Life experiences, 7

Limited English proficient (LEP) students,
    19–20, 20 (figure), 255–256
Lindberg, J. A., 62, 69
Listening skills, 106–109, 107–110 (figures)
Loneliness, 26–27, 93
Loner students, 175, 177–180,
    178–179 (figures), 209
Long, N., 27
Losoncy, L. E., 181, 221, 223
Luria, A. R., 210

Mailgram strategy, 166, 167–168
    (figures)
Mainstreaming, 9, 227, 255
Management. See Behavior
    management strategies;
    Classroom management; Discipline
Marshmallow study, 54–55
Marzano, J. S., 14, 57, 85, 229, 230
Marzano, R. J., 14, 57, 85, 229, 230
Maslow, A., 62
Mastropieri, M. A., 227, 261
McCarthy, M., 161
McIntosh, R., 9
McKay, G. D., 198
Meaningful instruction,
    12–13, 18, 35–36, 37, 44, 58
Media effects, 14, 23–24, 26
Medications, 14, 16, 17
Memory, 33, 35, 58
Mendler, A. N., 74, 77, 194, 203
Mentally retarded (MR) students, 8, 93
Metacognition, 36–37, 38, 210
Miller, D., 93, 103
Miller, P., 22, 23
Misbehavior, 173, 174 (figure)
    See also Class meetings;
        Disruptive behavior
Mischel, W., 54
Modeling desired behaviors,
    17, 57, 94, 148
Moral development, 74
Morison, K. B., 21, 22
Mostert, M. P., 149, 197
Motivating instruction, 12–13, 58
Motivation, 53, 54, 57
Multicultural student body,
    18–19, 93, 94, 228
    See also English language
        learners (ELLs)
Multiple intelligences (MI),
    32, 38–41, 40 (figure), 172
    classroom management and, 41
    differentiated learning and, 44, 45
        (figure)

Greek mythology unit example,
41, 43 (figure)
learning experiences grid,
41, 42 (figure)
See also Brain-compatible learning;
Interpersonal skill development;
Teaching/learning theories

National Academy of Sciences, 7, 8
National Assessment for Education
Progress (NAEP), 254
National Center for Education
Statistics, 19, 24
National Centers for Disease Control, 14
National Dissemination Center for
Children with Disabilities
(NICHCY), 230
National School Safety Center, 24
Native American students, 21
Nature vs. nurture debate, 28
Nazos, P., 17
Nevin, A. I., 9
Newspaper model, 199, 200–201
(figures)
No Child Left Behind (NCLB) Act of
2001, 3, 6, 10, 19, 24, 44, 45, 195,
229, 249, 254, 255
Nolan, J. F., 194, 195
Nutrition supports, 7
Nuttycombe, D. G., 197

Obedience model of discipline, 1, 32, 62,
63, 64, 64 (figure), 277
Office of Juvenile Justice and
Delinquency Prevention, 24
Off-task behaviors, 161–162, 163–164
(figures)
Olson, L., 21
O'Neil, J., 54
Open learning environment, 63
Operant conditioning, 63
Oppositional defiant disorder (ODD), 8
Organizational training techniques, 16
Other health impairment (OHI), 8
Overlapping/multitasking, 173

Pardini, P., 254
Parents. *See* Family involvement
Parrett, W. H., 7, 22, 23, 25, 29, 195
Patti, J., 23
Peer harassment, 3, 25, 27, 93
Peer influence, 27
Peer tutors, 256
People skills. *See* Interpersonal skill
development

Performance assessment, 44–45
balanced assessment model, 46, 46
(figure)
classroom management and, 51, 53,
53 (figure)
criterion-based checklists, 47–48,
48–50 (figures)
rubrics for, 51, 52 (figure)
standards framework and, 46–47
See also Assessment;
Teaching/learning theories
Persistence, 205, 208, 222
Physically disabled students, 260–261
cooperative learning and, 262
trust/caring and, 262, 263–264
(figures), 265
See also Inclusion strategies; Special
education
Pickering, D. J., 14, 57, 85, 229, 230
Point/counterpoint strategy,
158, 159–160 (figures)
Pool, C. R., 55
Porter, R. P., 255
Portfolio assessment, 46
Positive classroom climate, 3, 62–63
activity procedures, 67, 70 (figure)
agree/disagree chart analysis, 89, 90
(figure)
anger management strategies and, 94
attention deficit disorders and, 17–18,
18 (figure)
brain-compatible learning strategies
and, 37–38
classroom management and, 63, 64
(figure), 67
classroom procedures, 65–69, 71–72
(figure)
classroom rules/consequences, 73–83,
79–82 (figures), 84 (figure)
creation of positive climate, 83–89
democratic classrooms, 278
discipline and, 63
early childhood procedures, 67, 68
(figure)
elementary classroom procedures, 68,
68 (figure)
expectations, explicit teaching of, 67
hidden curriculum and, 92–93
immigrant students and, 20
negative teacher behaviors and, 83,
85–86, 86–88 (figures)
physical room arrangement, 65–66,
66 (figure)
positive staff-student relationships, 29
power dynamics in, 64–65, 64 (figure)

principal role in, 89
proactive teacher responses and,
    86–87, 89
rule-setting and, 61 (figure)
secondary classroom procedures,
    68–69, 69 (figure)
traditional classroom structure
    and, 16–17
violence in schools and, 23, 25
See also Cooperative learning;
    Enriched climate
Positive feedback, 37, 38, 151
Positive peer relationships, 58
Pour-and-store approach, 1–2
Poverty-level students,
    3, 6, 7, 20, 23, 195–196, 205
Power dynamics, 64–65, 64 (figure),
    193 (figure), 203
See also Disruptive behavior;
    Power-*See*king behaviors
Power-seeking behaviors, 202–204
    conative intelligence and, 205, 208
    cooperative group work and, 204
    leadership roles and, 204
    power struggles and, 193 (figures),
        197, 203–204, 204 (figure)
    power struggles, phases in, 204–205,
        204 (figure), 206–207
        (figures), 209
    student self-determination and, 203
    urban classrooms and, 205, 208
    See also Disruptive behavior;
        Power dynamics
Practice time, 35, 38
Preschool programs, 7, 14
Primary classroom procedures,
    67–68, 68 (figures)
Principal role, 89
Prior knowledge, 33, 35, 44
Proactive approach, 86–87, 89,
    144 (figure), 145, 205
Problem-solving RTI model, 10, 11
    classroom intervention
        stage, 11
    problem-solving team
        intervention stage, 11
    special education referral/due process
        procedure initiation stage, 11
    See also Response to intervention
        (RTI) approaches
Problem-solving skills, 6, 35, 174–175
Procedures. *See* Classroom management;
    Positive classroom climate
Proficiency requirements, 6, 19
Project Zero, 38

Prosocial skills, 92, 148, 149 (figure),
    174–175, 176 (figure)
Pull out programs, 9
Punishments, 32, 63, 77, 78
Put-downs, 58

Quality school concept, 128

Race, 8, 20, 21, 58
Ramsey, E., 171
Rasch, B. W., 17
Readiness models, 9, 33–34
Reauthorization of the Individuals with
    Disabilities Education Act (IDEA) of
    2004, 3, 10, 12, 227 (figure), 228,
    229, 230–231, 255
Recognition reflex, 223
Reeves, D. B., 47, 157
Referral procedure, 11
Reflection, 36–37, 38
    chapters 1–4 reflection,
        142, 143 (figure)
    communication skills, 98,
        98 (figure), 102 (figure),
        109, 111–114 (figures)
    reflective listening, 222
    self-talk strategy and, 210
Regular education initiative (REI),
    9–10, 228
Reider, B., 58
Rejection, 27–28
Rentner, D. S., 255
Research-based behavioral management
    strategies, 229–230, 231
Research-based instruction,
    10, 11–12, 32, 227, 229
    See also Teaching/learning theories
Resilience, 205, 208
Respect. *See* Positive classroom climate
Response to Intervention (RTI)
    approaches, 3, 10–11, 227 (figure)
    English language learners and, 255
    problem-solving model of, 10, 11
    special education services and,
        228–229
    standard protocol model of, 11–12
    three-tier pyramid of
        interventions, 11, 229
    See also Inclusion strategies
Responsibility development,
    3, 74, 128, 148
    absenteeism and,
        152–153, 154–155 (figures)
    decision-making model and,
        162, 163–164 (figures)

I-messages and, 149–151, 149–150 (figures)
incomplete/neglected student work, 156–160
individual accountability and, 166
internal locus of control and, 278
mailgram strategy, 166, 167–168 (figure)
non-contributing students and, 165–169
off-task behaviors and, 161–164
point/counterpoint strategy, 158, 159–160 (figures)
prosocial behaviors, instructional interventions for, 148, 149 (figure)
responsible students, characteristics of, 147 (figure)
standards-discipline link and, 151–152
teacher behavior and, 148–149
Responsibility model of discipline, 63, 64 (figure), 151, 278
Revenge-seeking behaviors, 27, 197, 209–213, 210–212 (figures)
Rewards, 32, 63, 78
Reynolds, M., 8
Riggs, E. G., 205
Right angles. *See* Thinking-at-right-angles journal
Ripple effect of disruptions, 194–195
Risk behaviors, 28–29
Rivera, D. P., 12, 13
Roberts, W. B., Jr., 216
Role-playing activity, 106–108, 107–108 (figures)
Rosen, L., 24
Round robin listening circle, 108–109, 110 (figure)
Rules. *See* Class meetings; Classroom rules; Positive classroom climate

Safety, 3, 23, 24, 27
learning process and, 33
unsafe climate, 62
See also Positive classroom climate; Violence in schools
San Antonio, D. M., 94
Sapon-Shevin, M., 262
Sassman, C., 67
Scaffolding, 47, 254
Schaps, E., 62
Scherer, M., 6, 83, 84
Schneider, B., 26
School violence. *See* Violence in schools

School-within-a-school structure, 199
Schumm, J. S., 9, 227, 249, 261
Scoring rubric, 51, 52 (figure)
Scruggs, T. E., 227.261
Secondary classroom procedures, 68–69 (figure)
Self-awareness, 53, 54, 56
Self-concept, 58, 151, 221, 222
Self-determination, 1, 63, 128, 203, 214
Self-discipline, 3, 63, 278
Self-regulation, 53, 54, 56, 64, 151, 278
Self-talk, 210
Shared power, 64–65, 64 (figure)
Sharon, S., 57
Sharon, Y., 57
Shore, K., 216
Shores, C., 10, 11, 12, 229
Short, P. M., 196
Short, R. J., 196
Show and tell activity, 105
Sigford, J. L., 9, 19, 20
Silent Epidemic Report, 20–22
Skill-deficit model, 92
Skillstreaming, 92
Skinner, B. F., 32, 63
Slavin, R. E., 57
Sleep patterns, 34–35
Smelter, R. W., 17
Smith, D. D., 12, 13
Snook, P. A., 277
Social contract strategy, 177, 178–179 (figures), 189, 190–191 (figures)
Social learning, 33, 37
Social problems, 1, 13
Social resources, 195
Social skills, 10, 14, 16, 25, 38, 54, 57, 62
See also Interpersonal skill development; Social skills instruction
Social skills instruction, 91 (figure), 92
adolescent behaviors and, 93–94
agree-disagree chart activity, 133, 134–137 (figures)
anger management and, 93–94
basic interaction skills, 103–105, 104 (figure)
behavior checklists, 96, 96 (figure), 119, 121–123 (figures)
bonding activities, 124–128, 125–127 (figures), 129–130 (figures)
business creation activity, 125–127, 127 (figure)

circle of friends activity,
104, 104 (figure)
communication/listening skills,
105–111, 106 (figure)
conflict resolution,
131–142, 132 (figure)
conflict resolution activity,
140–142, 142 (figure)
consensus chart activity,
138, 138–139 (figures)
creative energizers activity, 127–128,
129–130 (figures)
discussion format, 96, 98
fishbowl technique,
106–108, 107–108 (figures)
guided practice, 95–96
hidden curriculum and, 92–93
human graph activity,
140, 141 (figure)
initiation of, 94
K-W-L matrix, 114, 115 (figure)
lesson plan development,
94–99, 100–101 (figure)
problems/solutions brainstorming,
118–119, 118–120 (figures)
progress, recognition/celebration
of, 98, 128
reflection process, 98, 98 (figure), 102
(figure), 109, 111–114 (figures)
role assignment in groups,
116, 117 (figures)
role-playing activity,
106–108, 107–108 (figures)
round robin listening circle,
108–109, 110 (figure)
show and tell activity, 105
skill-deficient model and, 92
student self-assessment, 96, 97
(figure), 114 (figure)
T-chart device, 95, 95 (figure),
107–108 (figures)
team building, 111–130, 116 (figure)
template for cooperative group
activities, 144 (figure), 145
transfer of skills, 99
true-false quiz activity, 124–125
Venn/triple Venn diagrams activity,
125, 125–126 (figures)
web graphic organizer, 108, 109
(figure), 118 (figure), 120 (figure)
Solomon, P. G., 51
Sousa, D. A., 33
Spear-Swerling, L., 8, 10
Special education, 227
academic outcomes and, 9–10

attention deficit disorders and, 13–18,
14–15 (figures), 18(figure)
behavior logs, 243, 246–247 (figures)
behavior problems and, 242–248
case study strategy,
243, 244–245 (figures)
continuum of services and, 228
discipline strategies for, 230–231
disruptive behaviors and, 12
early intervention services, 228
gifted and talented students and,
248–253
goal-setting model and,
250, 251–252 (figures)
history of, 227–231, 230 (figure)
identification process for, 8, 10, 228
individual education plans,
9, 227, 230
labeling learners and, 8, 249
learning challenged students,
231–242
nondiscriminatory evaluation, 228
over-identification and, 10
physically disabled students, 260–265
pull out programs, 9
race and, 8
referral for, 11
research-based behavioral
management strategies and,
229–230
response to intervention and,
228–229
rubrics/standards,
237, 240–241 (figures)
scoring guides,
232, 237, 238–239 (figures)
social outcomes and, 9–10
thinking-at-right-angles journal,
262, 263–264 (figures)
whole-class/small-group/individual
work, 232, 232–236
(figures), 237, 242
See also English language learners
(ELLs); Inclusion strategies;
Learning disabled (LD) students
Stainback, S., 8
Stainback, W., 9
Standardized tests, 1, 6, 44, 45
assessment of learning, 45
cognitively disabled students and, 256
education effectiveness
evaluation and, 10
English language learners
and, 19, 256
impulsivity and, 55

IQ tests, 8
    teaching to the tests, 6
    violence-prone youth and, 25
    whole-child focus and, 57
Standard protocol RTI model, 11–12
    See also Response to intervention (RTI)
        approaches
Standards-based teaching, 32,
    38, 46–47, 57, 94, 151–152, 166
State of flow, 55–56, 55 (figure)
Sternberg, R. J., 8, 10, 172, 227
Stiggins, R. J., 45
Stoddard, K., 268
Stoehr, J., 39, 53
Stress, 33, 62
Stroud, Y., 233, 235, 238
Student achievement, 2
    achievement gap, 6, 256
    behavior management and,
        14, 16–17, 25
    communication skill
        deficiencies and, 7
    differentiated learning and, 6
    life experiences and, 7
    marshmallow study and, 54–55
    positive feedback and, 37
    poverty and, 6, 7
    See also Contemporary youth;
        Cooperative learning; Educational
        challenges; Engaged learning;
        Instruction; Learning;
        Responsibility development;
        Teaching/learning theories
Suicidal ideation/tendencies, 26, 93
Summer programs, 7
Supportive relationships. *See* Cooperative
        learning; Positive classroom
        climate; Trust
Swick, A. M., 62, 69

Tateyama-Sniezek, K., 262
Taunting. *See* Bullying
T-chart device, 95, 95 (figure),
    107–108 (figures)
Teacher behavior continuum (TBC),
    214–216, 215 (figure)
Teacher-student conferences,
    210, 213, 222–223,
    224–225 (figures)
    closed questions and,
        222, 222 (figure)
    open questions and,
        222–223, 223 (figure)
    recognition reflex and, 223
Teacher talk, 35

Teachers:
    attention deficit disorders and,
        17–18, 18 (figure)
    behavior management strategies,
        14, 16–17
    co-teaching, 9, 36
    facilitator role of, 3
    negative teacher behaviors, 27, 83,
        85–86, 86–88 (figures)
    power sharing and, 64–65, 64 (figure)
    proactive approach of, 86–87, 89,
        144 (figure), 145, 205
    See also Educational challenges;
        Instruction; Teaching/learning
        theories
Teaching/learning theories,
    31–32, 31 (figure)
    behaviorist theories and, 32
    brain-based learning, 32–38
    cooperative learning, 57–59
    differentiated learning, 44, 45 (figure)
    emotional intelligence, 53–57
    multiple intelligences, 38–44, 40
        (figure), 42–43 (figures)
    performance assessment, 44–53,
        46 (figure), 48–50 (figures),
        52 (figure)
    standardized curriculum and, 32
    See also Social skills instruction
Team-building skills,
    57, 91 (figure), 111, 114
    base groupings and, 116
    behavior checklists for, 119, 121–123
        (figures)
    bonding activities, 124–128, 125–127
        (figures), 129–130 (figures)
    K-W-L matrix and, 114, 115 (figure)
    problems/solutions brainstorming,
        118–119, 118–120 (figures)
    role assignment, 116, 117 (figures)
    social skills for cooperation,
        116, 116 (figure)
    See also Cooperative learning;
        Social skills instruction
Technological age, 21, 26
Teenage population. *See* Contemporary
        youth
Television viewing, 14, 23–24, 26
Testing. *See* Assessment; High-stakes
        testing; Standardized tests
Theoretical foundation. *See*
        Teaching/learning theories
Thinking-at-right-angles journal, 262,
        263–264 (figures)
Thompson, A. M., 13, 15

Thousand, J. S., 9
Tileston, D. W., 195
Title I schools, 6
Tomlinson, C. A., 44
Townsend, B., 268
Toxic schools, 277
Trent, S. C., 149, 197
Tri-assessment model, 46
True-false quiz activity, 124–125
Trust, 262, 263–264 (figures), 265

Urban classrooms, 205, 208

Vaughn, R. S., 9, 227, 249, 261
Venn/triple Venn diagrams activity,
    125, 125–156 (figures)
Viadero, D., 249
Victimization. *See* Aggressive behaviors;
    Bullying; Violence in schools
Viegut, D., 37
Villa, R. A., 9
Violence in schools, 23
    academic achievement and, 25
    brain development and, 28
    criminal activity rates and, 23
    discipline procedures/practices,
        improvements in, 24–25
    legislation against, 23
    public response to, 23–24
    revenge-seeking behaviors and, 210
    statistics on, 24–25
    toxic schools and, 277
    violence-prone youth, 25, 27–28
    See also Aggressive behaviors;
        Contemporary youth; Disruptive
        behavior; Educational challenges;
        Social skills instruction
Virginia Tech, 27

Vocational Rehabilitation
    Act of 1973, 261
Vygotsky, L. S., 36

Wagner, T., 27
Walberg, H. J., 8, 23
Walker, H. M., 171
Wang, M. C., 8
Watson, J., 32
Weapons. *See* Violence in schools
Web graphic organizers, 108, 109
    (figure), 118 (figure), 120 (figure)
Weiner, L., 205
Wenglinksy, H., 25
Wenner, J., 48, 50
White students, 8, 21
Whole-child focus, 1, 57, 172
Williams, M. M., 14, 92, 172, 227
Wingert, P., 26
With-it-ness, 172–173, 229
Wolfe, P., 33
Wolfgang, C. H., 92,
    149, 150, 214, 215
Wong, H. K., 94
Wong, R. T., 94
Working memory, 35, 57
Worsham, M. E., 67, 68, 103
Wright, W. E., 19

Year-round schools, 7
You/I-messages,
    149–151, 149–150 (figures)
Youth. *See* Contemporary youth;
    Student achievement

Zero tolerance, 27
Zigmond, N., 9
Zins, J. E., 23

CORWIN PRESS

The Corwin Press logo—a raven striding across an open book—represents the union of courage and learning. Corwin Press is committed to improving education for all learners by publishing books and other professional development resources for those serving the field of PreK–12 education. By providing practical, hands-on materials, Corwin Press continues to carry out the promise of its motto: **"Helping Educators Do Their Work Better."**